M000205884

# The Exile of Adam in Romans

# The Exile of Adam in Romans

## The Reversal of the Curse against Adam and Israel in the Substructure of Romans 5 and 8

David P. Barry

LEXINGTON BOOKS/FORTRESS ACADEMIC
*Lanham • Boulder • New York • London*

Published by Lexington Books/Fortress Academic
Lexington Books is an imprint of The Rowman & Littlefield Publishing Group, Inc.
4501 Forbes Boulevard, Suite 200, Lanham, Maryland 20706
www.rowman.com

86-90 Paul Street, London EC2A 4NE, United Kingdom



British Library Cataloguing in Publication Information Available

**Library of Congress Cataloging-in-Publication Data**

Names: Barry, David P, 1987- author.
Title: The Exile of Adam in Romans : the reversal of the curse against Adam and Israel in the substructure of Romans 5 and 8 / David P. Barry.
Description: Lanham, Maryland : Lexington Books/Fortress Academic , [2021] | Includes bibliographical references and index. | Summary: "In this book, David P. Barry examines the 'divine son' motif in Romans 5 and 8 through the lens of exile and restoration, arguing that Paul deliberately employs both themes to show their fulfillment in Christ"— Provided by publisher.
Identifiers: LCCN 2021032985 (print) | LCCN 2021032986 (ebook) | ISBN 9781978712270 (cloth) | ISBN 9781978712287 (epub)
Subjects: LCSH: Bible. Romans, V-VIII—Criticism, interpretation, etc. | Adam (Biblical figure) | Exile (Punishment)—Biblical teaching. | Jews—Restoration—Biblical teaching.
Classification: LCC BS2665.52 .B37 2021 (print) | LCC BS2665.52 (ebook) | DDC 227/.106—dc23
LC record available at https://lccn.loc.gov/2021032985
LC ebook record available at https://lccn.loc.gov/2021032986

∞™ The paper used in this publication meets the minimum requirements of American National Standard for Information Sciences—Permanence of Paper for Printed Library Materials, ANSI/NISO Z39.48-1992.

*To Katie*

*πάροικος ἐγώ εἰμι ἐν τῇ γῇ μὴ ἀποκρύψῃς ἀπ' ἐμοῦ τὰς ἐντολάς σου Psalm 118:19, LXX.*

# Contents

# Abbreviations

| | |
|---|---|
| ABG | Arbeiten zur Bibel und ihrer Geschichte |
| *ABR* | *Australian Biblical Review* |
| ACCS | Ancient Christian Commentary on Scripture |
| AGJU | Arbeiten zur Geschichte des antiken Judentums und des Urchristentums |
| *BA* | *Biblical Archaeology* |
| *BBR* | *Bulletin for Biblical Research* |
| BDAG | Walter Baur, Danker, Frederick W., William F. Arndt, and F. Wilbur Gingrich. *Greek-English Lexicon of the New Testament and Other Early Christian Literature.* 3rd ed. Chicago: University of Chicago Press, 2000 (Danker-Bauer-Arndt-Gingrich) |
| BECNT | Baker Exegetical Commentary on the New Testament |
| BEvT | Beiträge zur evangelischen Theologie |
| BHT | Beiträge zur historischen Theologie |
| *Bib* | *Biblica* |
| BibInt | Biblical Interpretation Series |
| BibTS | Biblisch-theologische Studien |
| *BR* | *Biblical Research* |
| *BTB* | *Biblical Theology Bulletin* |
| BTCP | Biblical Theology for Christian Proclamation |
| BZAW | Behefte zur Zeitschrift für die alttestamentliche Wissenschaft |
| BZNW | Behefte zur Zeitschrift für die neutestamentliche Wissenschaft |
| *CBQ* | *Catholic Bible Quarterly* |
| CBR | Currents in Biblical Research |
| CCWJCW | Cambridge Commentaries on Writings of the Jewish and Christian World 200 BC to AD 200 |

| | |
|---|---|
| ConBNT | Coniectanea Biblica: New Testament series |
| ConBOT | Coniectanea Biblica: Old Testament Series |
| *CTJ* | *Calvin Theological Journal* |
| *CTQ* | *Concordia Theological Quarterly* |
| *CTR* | *Criswell Theological Review* |
| *CurBS* | *Currents in Research: Biblical Studies* |
| *CV* | *Communio viatorum* |
| *DBI* | *Dictionary of Biblical Imagery* |
| *DELG* | *Dictionnaire étymologique de la langue Grecque* |
| *DPL* | *Dictionary of Paul and His Letters.* Edited by Gerald F. Hawthorne, Ralph P. Martin and Daniel G. Reid. Downers Grove, IL: InterVarsity, 1993. |
| *dtrGB* | *deuteronomische Geschichtsbild* |
| EDB | Edizioni Dehoniane Bologna |
| *EDEJ* | *The Eerdmans Dictionary of Early Judaism.* Edited by John J. Collins and Daniel C. Harlow. Grand Rapids: Eerdmans, 2010. |
| EFN | Estudios de Filología Neotestamentaria |
| EGGNT | Exegetical Guide to the Greek New Testament |
| EH | Europäische Hochschulschriften |
| EJL | Early Judaism and its Literature |
| *ETL* | *Ephemerides theologicae Lovanienses* |
| ETSStud | Evangelical Theological Society Studies |
| *ExAud* | *Ex Audito* |
| *ExpTim* | *Expository Times* |
| *EvT* | *Evangelische Theologie* |
| FRLANT | Forschungen zur Religion und Literatur des Alten und Neuen Testaments |
| FZB | Forschung zur Bibel |
| HB | Hebrew Bible |
| *HBC* | *Harper's Bible Commentary* |
| HBAI | Hebrew Bible and Ancient Israel |
| *HBT* | *Horizons in Biblical Theology* |
| *HeyJ* | *Heythrop Journal* |
| HNT | Handbuch zum Neuen Testament |
| HSM | Harvard Semitic Monographs |
| *Int* | *Interpretation* |
| JAL | Jewish Apocryphal Literature Series |
| *JBL* | *Journal of Biblical Literature* |
| JCTCRS | Jewish and Christian texts in Contexts and Related Studies |
| *JETS* | *Journal of the Evangelical Theological Society* |
| *JJS* | *Journal of Jewish Studies* |

| | |
|---|---|
| *JPT* | *Journal of Pentecostal Theology* |
| *JSJ* | *Journal for the Study of Judaism in the Persian, Hellenistic, and Roman Periods* |
| JSJSup | *Journal for the Study of Judaism Supplement Series* |
| *JSNT* | *Journal for the Study of the New Testament* |
| JSNTSup | *Journal for the Study of the New Testament Supplement Series* |
| *JSOT* | *Journal for the Study of the Old Testament* |
| JSOTSup | *Journal for the Study of the Old Testament Supplement Series* |
| *JSPL* | *Journal for the Study of Paul and His Letters* |
| *JSPsup* | *Journal for the study of the pseudepigrapha. Supplement Series* |
| *KD* | *Kerygma und Dogma* |
| KEKNT | Kritisch-exegetischer Kommentar über das Neue Testament |
| LBI | Library of Biblical Interpretation |
| LCL | Loeb Classical Library |
| LHBOTS | Library of Hebrew Bible/Old Testament studies |
| LNTS | The Library of New Testament Studies |
| MNTC | The Moffatt New Testament commentary |
| NCCS | New Covenant Commentary Series |
| *Neot* | *Neotestamentica* |
| NICNT | The New International Commentary on the New Testament |
| NIGTC | The New International Greek Testament Commentary |
| NFTL | New Foundations Theological Library |
| *NIB* | *The New Interpreter's Bible.* Edited by Leander E. Keck. 12 vols. Nashville: Abingdon, 1994–2004. |
| *NIDOTTE* | *New International Dictionary of Old Testament Theology and Exegesis.* Edited by Willem A. VanGemeren. 5 vols. Grand Rapids, Zondervan: 1997 |
| *NJBC* | *The New Jerome Biblical Commentary* |
| *NovT* | *Novum Testamentum* |
| NovTSup | Supplements to Novum Testamentum |
| NSBT | New Studies in Biblical Theology |
| *NTBT* | Beale, G. K. *A New Testament Biblical Theology* |
| *NTPG* | Wright, N. T. *The New Testament and the People of God*. COQG 1. Minneapolis: Fortress Press, 1992 |
| *NTS* | *New Testament Studies* |
| NTSI | The New Testament and the Scriptures of Israel |
| *OTP* | *Old Testament Pseudepigrapha.* Edited by James H. Charlesworth. 2 vols. New York: Doubleday, 1983, 1985. |
| *PFG* | Wright, N.T. *Paul and the Faithfulness of God.* COQG 4. Minneapolis: Fortress, 2013. |
| *PRst* | *Perspectives in Religious Studies* |
| *PSTJ* | *Perkins (School of Theology) Journal* |

| | |
|---|---|
| PTMS | Pittsburgh Theological Monograph Series |
| *OALD* | *Oxford Advanced Learner's Dictionary* |
| OTL | Old Testament Library |
| OtSt | Oudtestamentische studiën |
| *RB* | *Revue biblique* |
| RBS | Resources for Bible Study |
| RNT | Regensburger Neuen Testaments |
| *RTR* | *Reformed Theological Review* |
| SBLDS | Society of Biblical Literature Dissertation Series |
| SBLSP | Society of Biblical Literature Seminar Papers |
| *SBTJ* | *Southern Baptist Journal of Theology* |
| SCS | Septuagint and Cognate Studies |
| SD | Studies and Documents |
| SFSHJ | South Florida Studies in the History of Judaism |
| SHR | Studies in the History of Religions |
| *SJT* | *Scottish Journal of Theology* |
| SNTW | Studies of the New Testament and its World |
| *ST* | *Studia Theologica* |
| StBib | Studi biblici |
| StBibLit | Studies in Biblical Literature (Lang) |
| STJD | Studies on the Texts of the Desert of Judah |
| StDSSRL | Studies in the Dead Sea Scrolls and Related Literature |
| StPB | Studia Post-Biblica |
| Str-B | Strack, Hermann Leberecht, and Paul Billerbeck. *Kommentar zum Neuen Testament aus Talmud und Midrasch.* 6 vols. München: Beck, 1922. |
| SVTP | Studia in Veteris Testamenti Pseudepigrapha |
| *TEG* | Traditio exegetica Graeca |
| *TDDSSE* | Florentino García Martínez and Eibert J. C. Tigchelaar, eds., *The Dead Sea Scrolls Study Edition*, 2 vols. (Leiden: Brill, 1997). |
| *TDNT* | Kittel, Gerhard, ed. *Theological Dictionary of the New Testament.* Translated by G. W. Bromiley. 10 vols. Grand Rapids: Eerdmans, 1964. |
| *TDOT* | Botterweck, G. Johannes, and Helmer Ringgren, eds. *Theological Dictionary of the Old Testament.* Translated by John T. Willis, G. W. Bromiley, and David E. Green. 15 vols. Grand Rapids: Eerdmans, 1978. |
| *TJ* | *Trinity Journal* |
| TPINTC | Trinity Press International New Testament Commentaries |
| TOTC | Tyndale Old Testament Commentaries |

| | |
|---|---|
| *TRE* | *Theologische Realenzklopädie*. Edited by Gerhard Krause and Gerhard Müller. Berlin: de Gruyter, 1977– |
| *TS* | *Theological Studies* |
| *TynBul* | *Tyndale Bulletin* |
| TynHS | Tyndale House Studies |
| *TZ* | *Theologische Zeitschrift* |
| *VT* | *Vetus Testamentum* |
| VTSup | Supplements to Vetus Testamentum |
| WBC | Word Biblical Commentary |
| WMANT | Wissenschaftliche Monographien zum Alten und Neuen Testament |
| *WTJ* | *Westminster Theological Journal* |
| WUNT | Wissenschaftliche Untersuchungen zum Neuen Testament |
| *ZAW* | *Zeitschrift für die alttestamentliche Wissenschaft* |
| *ZNW* | *Zeitschrift für die neutestamentliche Wissenschaft und die Kunde der älteren Kirche* |
| *ZTK* | *Zeitschrift für Theologie und Kirche* |

# Acknowledgments

This project has not been an individual effort. It reflects the influences of a lifetime of relationships, which have inspired and directed me toward a greater admiration for the word of God and, particularly, to the Pauline literature.

I would first like to express my gratitude to my parents. My late father, Dr. Carey Barry, modeled reverence for the Lord and disciplined study of the Scriptures. I regret that I will not have the opportunity to share with him any of the insights this research project has uncovered. Yet, I trust that insofar as what I have learned and written reflects the teaching of Scripture, it would no longer be news to him. Likewise, were it not for my mother, Susan Barry, it is unlikely I would have pursued education so far. Her great contribution is a lifetime of investing in her sons. I suspect that this has been her plan all along.

It is an honor to work with Fortress Academic. So many of the resources upon which I depended in this project are available because of their valuable publishing work. It is a great privilege to have this project included in that number. Special thanks to Dr. Neil Elliott for his work as editor.

I would also like to thank my doctoral advisor, Brandon Crowe. His capable and prompt guidance was indispensable. He consistently challenged and aided my thinking and gently corrected when I went afield. This project is better for the investment he made. I would also like to thank Drs. Greg Beale and Vern Poythress whose contribution has not only been in the classroom, but in the hallways of the Library. My interest in the notion of exile in Romans began in a doctoral seminar with Dr. Beale. I trust his influence will be apparent in the body of this study.

I am grateful for the excellent services of the staff of Montgomery Library. Director Alexander Finlayson has made every effort to enable and further my research. Thanks also to Karla Grafton, Marsha Blake, and Donna Roof. I expect the number of inter-library loans Mrs. Roof will need to request may decrease in my absence.

I would like to thank my patient colleagues and friends who have listened to hours upon hours of my ideas, read manuscripts and papers, or scanned resources that became unavailable after I accepted a position out of state. Thanks to Danillo Santos, Peter Moore, Will Wood, Laura Leon, Charles Williams, Warren Campbell, and to Michael Lynch, Ryan Biese, and David Irving. I am eager to return the favor.

Thanks are also due to the session of Midway Presbyterian Church. Not only did the church support me throughout my doctoral studies, but it extended a pastoral call to me knowing that I would need to continue to write for a season. I am particularly grateful to Dr. David Hall, Midway's Senior Pastor. If I was not able to tell my dad about my studies, I did tell Dr. Hall. He has been a constant friend and advisor, who consistently made the effort to call, encourage, read papers, and be available to a younger man. If I am striving to be a Timothy, he has been my Paul.

Finally—and most importantly—I am thankful to my wife, Katie. She was brave enough to marry a doctoral student and share her husband for the first three years of our marriage. She supported me by working difficult jobs, allowing me the time to study, and gently reminding me when it was time to stop working. She is a blessing. But, I am grateful to say that I am continually realizing that she is a greater blessing than I had previously thought.

# Introduction

Renewed interest in the first-century theology of exile and restoration has fueled study of the NT use of the Jewish scriptures, inner-biblical allusion and has juxtaposed the related topics of exile and NT eschatology. An intriguing question in this area that has so far received little attention is how Paul's use of the Hebrew Bible and inner-biblical allusion in Romans can illuminate his view of exile. The citation of Ps 44:22[1] in Rom 8:36 invites such an investigation.

At the conclusion of his discussion of life in the Spirit in Rom 5:1–8:39, Paul asserts that nothing can separate believers from the love of Christ (8:35). He then lists a series of seven hardships that might potentially divide them: tribulation, distress, persecution, famine, nakedness, danger, and sword. He then quotes Psalm 44:22 to name death as the eighth and final thing that might separate Christ and the Christian: καθὼς γέγραπται ὅτι *ἕνεκεν σοῦ θανατούμεθα ὅλην τὴν ἡμέραν, ἐλογίσθημεν ὡς πρόβατα σφαγῆς* ("As it is written, 'On your account we are being killed all they day, we are regarded as sheep for slaughter'"). On the surface, his point is that even afflictions like these cannot undo reconciliation to God accomplished in justification (cf. Rom 5:1, 10–11; 8:33–4). Beneath the surface, however, Paul is drawing upon the context of the psalm, employing a theology of exile.

Psalm 44 is a lament prayed by the suffering, righteous community in exile. Unlike some passages in the Hebrew Bible where the people admit that they deserve God's discipline (e.g., Jer 14:7; Dan 9:11, 13), the community of Psalm 44 opines that it has *not* broken God's covenant but, nevertheless, it undergoes exile despite its covenant faithfulness (v. 17). Paul applies that circumstance to the suffering that NT believers undergo before glory. His use of Psalm 44 suggests that they too will experience all kinds of trouble not only despite their righteousness but, in some cases, because of it. Like the community of Ps 44, before glory Christians are in exile notwithstanding their righteousness.

Despite the quotation from Psalm 44 being the only explicit citation in Rom 5 or 8, the reference to exile in Rom 8:36 is no anomaly. Paul depends upon, alludes to, and develops various passages from the Jewish scriptures throughout these chapters. Although he does not use the term "exile," he regularly applies prophetic restoration promises, that were seemingly intended for Israel, to NT believers. Reconciliation in Rom 5, for instance, is framed as the beginning of Israel's restoration.[2] Intriguingly, however, this return is not exclusively set against the historical background of Israel's exiles, but with mankind's original loss of peace with God in Adam (cf. Rom 5:14). G. K. Beale observes that "in Rom. 5 reconciliation is seen to be restoration from the hostile state of exile introduced by the first Adam and overcome by the last Adam."[3] Thus, Paul's theology of exile incorporates the backgrounds of both Adam and Israel. This book will explore how that is the case.

The structure of this book necessarily begins with literary backgrounds before moving to Romans itself. The first chapter introduces the thesis and its place in scholarship regarding exile and restoration. The second chapter surveys texts that witness to the duration and characterization of exile in the Hebrew Bible and Second Temple Jewish literature. The third chapter examines the relationship of Adam and covenant to exile and restoration in the Hebrew Bible and other Jewish literature. With the thought-world demonstrated, the fourth chapter begins the exegetical investigation of Romans with an analysis of Rom 5 with respect to Adam, separation from God as exile, and the mechanism of exile's reversal. The study then turns to Romans 8 in the fifth and sixth chapters to investigate similar motifs of exile, peace with God, the end of creation's futility, and the eschatological trajectory of humankind. Finally, I offer some overall findings and reflections in the conclusion.

## NOTES

1. Scripture references will refer to English versification throughout this study unless otherwise specified.

2. I argue this point in chapter 4.

3. G. K. Beale, *A New Testament Biblical Theology: The Unfolding of the Old Testament in the New* (Grand Rapids: Baker Academic, 2011), 542.

## *Chapter 1*

# Exile and Romans

Exile is an important and multifaceted concept in New Testament studies. Despite a relatively small number of lexical instances,[1] scholars have long recognized that exile is "quietly rampant" across the NT.[2] Likewise, restoration to God is a component of the broader theme of gospel hope.[3] Since it was a common belief among first-century Jews that Yahweh *had* promised an end to the historical exiles,[4] questions regarding the "end of the exile" and when such an end occurred are naturally pursued by investigating Israel's scriptures, Second Temple Jewish literature, the NT, and more narrowly, the NT use of Israel's scriptures.

While much of the NT addresses the theme of exile with reference to Israel,[5] Romans relates the theme to both Israel *and* Adam. The body of the letter is divided into four major sections: 1:18–4:25, 5:1–8:39, 9:1–11:36, and 12:1–15:13.[6] Generally speaking, the opening section presents the unrighteousness of man as the object of God's wrath and the possibility of righteousness apart from the law through faith in Jesus Christ. The second section (5:1–8:39) is Paul's presentation of the consequent life for believers. It answers the question, What does justification bring? It brings reconciliation to God, life in his Spirit, and an irreversible hope of glory. This study seeks to demonstrate that Paul presents these results of justification as humankind's restoration to God, the reversal of exile in Adam.

## RECENT STUDY OF EXILE

The debate in modern scholarship regarding first-century Jewish views on the extent of the exile and the timing of restoration is well known. N. T. Wright's reconstruction of the first-century Jewish worldview as centering upon the continuing narrative of exile and restoration has been a catalyst.[7] One general characteristic of the conversation has been a focus upon ethnic Israel. How would the *event* of exile influence the religion of this now-scattered people? What developments would the national catastrophe have produced in Israel's belief structure? How did subsequent leaders and religious thinkers develop the consequent *idea* of exile? Would the suffering, deportation, homelessness, and minority status result in a state of mind? Did "exile" become an existential descriptor that has nothing at all to do with geography?

One formative assumption in the conversation has been that the *event* of exile produced theological development or the *idea* of exile.[8] Accordingly, study of exile and the Jewish hope of restoration tends to begin with the historical event(s). Canonically earlier references to exile, such as Deut 4:25–31; 28:15–68; 30:1–10; 32:1–43, are categorized as *ex eventu* redactions.[9] For example, Peter R. Ackroyd writes, "after the passage of years which both dull the memory of the immediate disaster and also serve to impress the uncertainty of any possible restoration . . . the Deuteronomic History as we now have it [was] offered [as] a presentation of what Israel had experienced and what she was to learn from that experience."[10] Thus, the background of the exile debate is oriented toward Israel's (or *some* of Israel's)[11] experience and influenced by efforts to reconstruct the history behind the redaction layers.[12]

In my view, the conversation has been overly influenced by historical interests to the exclusion of canonical context. The suggestion that the theological idea of exile was produced by the historical events would have seemed quite alien to Paul. The final form of Israel's scriptures portrays the relationship between the idea of exile and the historical events somewhat differently. This study will approach the question of exile in the first century from the perspective of canonical-contextual exegesis. Rather than the event producing the idea, the idea of exile was used to caution God's people against covenant breaking long before the historical event(s) brought the warning to reality. From a canonical perspective, the *idea* of exile (to borrow Ackroyd's term) is a component of the covenant between Yahweh and his people. It is the climax of the curses threatened for disobedience (cf. Deut 28:58–68; par. Lev 26:14–45). In other words, exile, in its theological character, is fundamentally a facet of covenant theology and logically prior to the events it produces.

A second contribution gleaned by approaching the study of exile canonically is the theme of sonship in connection to exile. Just as Adam was called the son of God (Gen 5:1–3; Luke 3:38), in an analogous way, so too is Israel Yahweh's child (Exod 4:22; Hos 11:1–5; cf. Deut 14:1–2; Ps 80:15, 16, 17, 19;[13] Jer 3:19–20; Hos 1:10; cf. Sir 4:10; Wis 2:18; *Pss. Sol.* 13:9; 18:4). In an abbreviated sense, Israel inherited the position of Adam.[14] For all the discussions of exile as "curse" in secondary literature, the canonical context of curse is often neglected. From a canonical perspective, all humanity was cursed and separated from a land of rest in Adam. For the Apostle Paul, that curse remains in effect (Rom 5:12–21). Indeed, Jesus's primary mission was to reverse *that* curse (Gen 3:15; Gal 3:16; cf. Rom 16:20). For this reason, he is called ὁ ἔσχατος Ἀδὰμ (cf. Rom 5:12–13; 1 Cor 15:22, 45). Yet, it is commonly claimed that Jesus's work initiated restoration from exile, which is a category more often associated with Israel. This study asks how these two functions of Christ's ministry are related (i.e., Christ as last Adam and Christ as restorer). The Gospels are full of allusions to Christ's role as second Adam.[15] They are also full of references to restoration (e.g., Isa 61:1–2 in Luke 4:16–4:21).[16] I contend that Paul incorporates both of these perspectives into his articulation of reconciliation to God and life in the Spirit in Rom 5–8. Although Paul nowhere uses the word *exile*, a theology of exile and restoration undergirds the argument.

I will argue that Paul views the historical exiles to Assyria and Babylon inclusively with the expulsion of Adam from Eden. Although distinct events, they belong to a redemptive-historical type. Each is an example of God's covenant discipline. While restoration promises in the prophets unquestionably include the exiles to Assyria and Babylon, they have a broader scope. Israel and Judah's historical exiles are recapitulations of Adam's removal from God's presence in Eden, and humanity with him. Thus, in its fullest sense, the theological identity of Paul's exile refers to humanity's separation from God in Adam. Subsequent instances of exile echo that archetype. The Adamic theology Paul sets forth in Romans presumes humanity was separated from God in the fall in what should be understood as the paradigmatic exile. The resulting curse was cosmic in scope and involved both spiritual and physical separation from God's presence. In Romans, Paul employs restoration prophecies given with immediate reference to Israel, but the scope of fulfillment goes beyond the ethnic boundary of Israel to include the spiritual children of Abraham: Jew and Gentile. Together, this new covenant people is spiritually restored to God's presence by faith and will be bodily brought into his presence in glory. Thus, Pauline restoration from exile is inaugurated but not yet fully realized. As restoration it constitutes a return to God's presence, but it is not merely the renewal of the Edenic condition, which humanity was able to forfeit. Rather, the Pauline conception of restoration is the consummation of Edenic hope. Once restored, nothing will be able to separate the believer from God again (cf. Rom 8:35–7).[17]

In the recent academic focus upon Paul's Jewish milieu, the nature and extent of restoration is often presumed to arise only from the Assyrian or Babylonian captivities. That position considerably reduces the canonical context and fails to connect themes that, I argue, Paul puts together. If the full background is not merely the historical exiles of Israel, or even the Deuteronomic theology that interprets them, but includes the prototypical exile of Adam and the rupture of the first God-people-land covenant triangle, then Paul's cosmic language[18] comes into focus and the hope of restoration to God includes all the promises of Paradise.[19]

## Paul's Use of the Exile and the Original Recipients

But, could Paul's original Roman audience have recognized or appreciated such a subtle use of the Jewish scriptures? The first recipients were most likely a Gentile majority.[20] Such seems to be the clear reading of Rom 1:5–6, 13–15; 15:15–16 where Paul addresses his audience as Gentiles. As such, their cultural identity would not be so shaped by the effects of Israel's historical exiles. Certainly, some Gentile Christians would not have the familiarity with Jewish scripture to recognize the theological identity of the exile or the full significance of its reversal. Neither would some have detected Paul's use of the Hebrew Bible connecting the whole Christian community to the promised restoration. Nevertheless, each of these questions has an answer which is compatible with or even supports the present thesis.

To begin with, accepting that some or even all the original recipients of Romans may not have identified Paul's use of the Hebrew Bible or understood his hermeneutic does not at all prove what Paul did or did not say. Stanley Porter has helpfully argued that studies of the NT use of Jewish scriptures must adopt an author-centered rather than an audience-centered approach.[21] To reconstruct the "ideal" audience and speculate as to what it may or may not recognize misses the author who actually composes the message.[22] Richard B. Hays writes, "it must be affirmed that Paul was a hermeneutical theologian whose reflection on God's action in the world was shaped in decisive ways by his reading of Israel's sacred texts."[23] Paul's purpose in Rom 5, 8 is to articulate the new covenant reality of reconciled life in the Spirit through Christ. Romans is the declaration of something "promised beforehand" (1:2) and "kept secret for long ages" that has now been revealed "through the Scriptures of the prophets" (16:26). There will, therefore, be a fundamental continuity from earlier scripture and what Paul himself writes. We should expect that an author so influenced by these texts would repeat them, not only with marked citations, but more subtly as well. It would be "highly artificial" to suggest that only direct quotations reflects that influence.[24] Rather, marked citations are the proverbial tip of the iceberg. A balanced approach must deal with those instances of textual influence or development that may lack quotation formulas.

Furthermore, to recognize a Gentile majority is not to diminish the respect with which the Hebrew Bible was received. While Jewish converts most likely brought Christianity to Rome (cf. Acts 2:10), Claudius's expulsion of the Jews in AD 49 would have diminished Jewish influence and left the

Gentiles believers behind.[25] By the time Paul wrote Romans, the Jews would have been allowed home but would have returned to a more established Gentile community.[26] Yet, Paul's original audience still viewed the Hebrew Bible as authoritative.[27] Paul regularly grounds his argument in marked citation of the Jewish scriptures. For example, Paul cites Hos 2:23—ostensibly prophesying the restoration of Israel—in Rom 9:25–26 applying the restoration to Gentile believers.[28]

Indeed, the Gentile makeup of the Christian community in Rome renders the use of a theology of exile and restoration more likely not less. The inclusion of the Gentiles in Israel's second exodus is a theme in several restoration prophecies (e.g., Jer 3:17; Isa 49:6; Hag 2:7).[29] If Paul is indeed writing to a Gentile majority audience, such an expectation would likely have been at the forefront of his thought. Moreover, it would allow Paul to apply texts that refer to restoration more generally to his Roman audience, which in fact, he does. For example, Rom 5 describes gospel hope as secured through the outpouring of the Holy Spirit. That precise event is promised in various prophetic writings (e.g., Isa 32:15; 44:3; Ezek 36:27; 39:29; Joel 2:28; Zech 12:10). In those texts, the Spirit's outpouring was a sign of restoration from exile *for Israel.* But Paul invokes it in Rom 5:5 as evidence of secured hope for *all* believers. He does so in the same context where he shows that Christ reverses the curse of Adam, not just the exile of Israel. What's more, Paul regularly alludes to Israel's exodus tradition, portraying the Christian life for every believer as a second exodus bound toward a future inheritance (Rom 8:14–17).[30] Hence, Paul characterizes life in Christ as analogous to Israel's wilderness wandering as well as to its promised restoration. Hence, a Gentile audience would benefit from the promise of restoration to God just as much as a Jewish one. A Gentile audience would especially appreciate the focus upon inclusion and ingrafting into the people of God as Paul goes on to argue in Rom 9–11.

## The Focus on Romans 5 and 8

The choice to focus upon Rom 5 and 8 requires some justification. While the whole NT witnesses to the theme of exile,[31] Romans relates the theme of exile, which typically corresponds to Israel's history, to the figures of *both* Israel and Adam. The body of the letter is divided into four major sections: 1:18–4:25, 5:1–8:39, 9:1–11:36, and 12:1–15:13.[32] Generally speaking, the first section presents the unrighteousness of man as the object of God's wrath, but the possibility of righteousness apart from the law through faith in Jesus Christ. The second section (5:1–8:39) is Paul's presentation of the consequent life for believers. It answers the question, What does justification bring? Paul answers that it brings reconciliation to God, life in and through his Spirit, and an irreversible hope of glory. The primary object of the present study is to demonstrate that Paul viewed these results of justification as mankind's restoration to God from its exile in Adam.

Romans 5 and 8 are peculiarly suited to evaluate the place of exile and restoration in Pauline eschatology. They bookend the section about eschatological life in the Spirit. The majority of scholars recognize clear thematic connections between Rom 5 and 8. Although there was once some dispute as to whether Rom 5 belonged to the first section of Romans or the second,[33] increasingly scholars are placing the break in Paul's argument between Rom 4:25 and 5:1, where 5:1–11 functions as a literary bridge concluding Paul's previous argument, but simultaneously beginning the next.[34]

It has been often noted that Paul introduces themes in Rom 5 to which he later returns in Rom 8.[35] The theme of boasting in the hope of the glory of God in Rom 5:2 is dramatically expanded in Rom 8:31–39 in Paul's celebration of the certainty of glory. The tribulation believers will endure is mentioned in Rom 5:3–4 but expanded in Rom 8:15–27, 32–36. The eschatological outpouring of the Spirit is introduced in Rom 5:5, but nearly all of Rom 8 develops the significance of the Spirit as the source of life (8:1–11), the power to obey (8:12–13), the guide toward glory (8:14–17), and the comforter in struggle (8:15–16, 23–27). N. T. Wright calls all of chapter 8 the "long outworking" of 5:12–21.[36] Indeed, the dichotomies of death/life, flesh/Spirit, and slavery/freedom are built upon the foundation of the Adam/Christ typology which Paul develops in those verses. Thus, the main development from Rom 5 to Rom 8 may be viewed as a sort of "ring composition" or "chiasm."[37] Therefore, because of the significant thematic and literary parallels, I have selected Rom 5 and 8 for the present study. The bookends of Paul's exposition of life in the Spirit will enable a degree of clarification and corroboration which would not be possible apart from the chiastic framework. What is hinted in Rom 5 can be clarified by Rom 8 and vice versa.

Furthermore, the thesis that Paul employs a theology of exile and restoration in Rom 5–8 introduces a new angle from which to consider the transition to Rom 9–11. Many scholars, particularly in the first half of the twentieth century, have considered Rom 9–11 as out of place in the argument. C. H. Dodd even suggested "the epistle could be read without any gap, if these chapters were omitted."[38] More recently, commentators have recognized its contribution to the argument as a whole.[39] However, the present thesis serves to further clarify the movement from Rom 8 to Rom 9. If Paul is indeed building upon specific restoration promises from the Hebrew Bible in Rom 5–8 and applying them to believers who are not identified by ethnicity but by faith (Rom 4:16; 5:1–5), then his shift to address God's faithfulness to Israel and the future of ethnic Jews is not nearly so rough a transition as some have thought.

I will argue that Paul identifies NT believers as eschatological Israel.[40] For that reason, he describes them as "God's elect" (ἐκλεκτοὶ θεοῦ) in Rom 8:32, a term which the Hebrew Bible reserves for Israel.[41] The Israel *of faith* is being restored from exile. That identification naturally leads to the questions Paul takes up in Rom 9–11. If the NT people of God is marked out by faith and the object of the prophets' restoration promises, what about *ethnic* Israel? Has God's word to them failed (Rom 9:6)? Has God rejected his inheritance (Rom 11:1)? Does this mean they will continue in their exile forever? To the contrary, Paul concludes his discussion in Rom 9–11 declaring the salvation of πᾶς Ἰσραὴλ (11:26a). Furthermore, he defines that salvation by quoting Isaiah 59:20–21 (11:26b), which promises an end to Israel's exile. I suggest that the notion of restoration did not arise simply because Paul began addressing God's faithfulness to ethnic Israel in 9–11; it has been a component of the argument from the start. Paul's discussion of restoring the remnant of Israel (cf. Isa 10:22–23 in Rom 9:27; Rom 11:5) continues the already established subject of restoration. Hence, the substructural themes of exile and restoration in Rom 5–8 elucidate the tie to Rom 9–11.

## NOTES

1. For example, πάροικος ("strange" or "sojourn") occurs four time: Acts 7:6, 29; Eph 2:19; 1 Pet 2:11; παρεπίδημος ("exile," "strange," or "stranger") occurs three times: Heb 11:13; 1 Pet 1:1; 2:11.

2. Nicholas Perrin, "Exile," in *The World of the New Testament: Cultural, Social, and Historical Contexts*, ed. Joel B. Green and Lee Martin McDonald (Grand Rapids: Baker Academic, 2013), 26.

3. For instance, 1 Peter opens by addressing the "elect *exiles* of the dispersion" (ἐκλεκτοῖς παρεπιδήμοις διασπορᾶς, 1:1) then points to future glory (vv. 8–9). This study will use the text and apparatus of the NA[28]. All translations of Biblical Greek are my own unless otherwise specified.

4. See Nicholas G. Piotrowski's survey of exile in Second Temple literature and modern interpretations, "The Concept of Exile in Late Second Temple Judaism: A Review of Recent Scholarship," *CBR* 15 (2017): 214–47.

5. See Perrin, "Exile," 25–37.

6. Most modern commentators recognize these sub-units. See, for example, Richard Longenecker,

*The Epistle to the Romans,* NIGTC, ed. Marshall, I. Howard and Donald Hagner (Grand Rapids: Eerdmans, 2016), vi–viii; C. E. B. Cranfield, *A Critical and Exegetical Commentary on the Epistle to the Romans,* 2 vols., ICC (Edinburgh: T&T Clark, 1975), 1:xi, 2:443. For a helpful discussion of the structure of Romans, see Longenecker, *Introducing Romans: Critical Issues in Paul's Most Famous Letter* (Grand Rapids: Eerdmans, 2011), 388–458.

7. Initially, *The New Testament and the People of God.* COQG 1 (Minneapolis: Fortress, 1992), for worldview see, 244–338; for exile, see 268–72, 299–301. Cf. idem., *Jesus and the Victory of God,* COQG 2 (Minneapolis, Fortress, 1996), xvii–xviii, 126–7, 203–6, 246–51, 576–7; idem., *Paul and the Faithfulness of God,* COQG 4 (Minneapolis: Fortress, 2013), 139–63.

8. Peter R. Ackroyd is generally credited with the distinction between the event of the exile and the idea of the exile (developed in the Cambridge Hulsean Lectures of 1960–1962, later published as *Exile and Restoration,* [Philadelphia, Westminster Press, 1968], see especially 237–47). Particularly in light of the Babylonian exile, Ackroyd argues that Israel was forced to reexamine what deportation meant sociologically, for its national identity, and theologically, in its relationship to the covenant God.

9. E.g. Jacob Neusner, *Self-Fulfilling Prophecy: Exile and Return in the History of Judaism*, SFSHJ 2 (Atlanta: Scholars Press, 1990), 27–30. Cf. also Martin Noth, *A History of Pentateuchal Traditions*, trans. Bernard W. Anderson (Chico, CA: Scholars Press, 1981), 42–197; Hans Walter Wolff, "Das Kerygma des deuteronomistischen Geschichtswerks," *ZAW* 73 (1961): 171–86.

10. Ackroyd, *Exile and Restoration,* 72–3.

11. See Neusner, *Self-Fulfilling Prophecy*, 32–4.

12. Another scholar who significantly influenced to the historical background of the conversation regarding the role of exile in Israel's history and theology is Odil H. Steck, who argued that two antithetical strands of restoration expectation coexisted during the Second Temple period ("Das Problem theologischer Strömungen in nachexilischer Zeit," *EvT* 28 [1968]: 445–58). Whereas the "theocratic" strand expected the political restoration of the kingdom of Israel and the reestablishment of the temple cult, the "eschatological" strand believed that Israel's exile would continue until Yahweh atoned for Israel's sin and himself returned to Zion. In addition, Steck meticulously investigated the Deuteronomic pattern of sin-exile-redemption (S-E-R) in the theology of later prophets and Second Temple Jewish writings (see especially, *Israel und das gewaltsame Geschick der Propheten,* 110–95). In Steck's view, the dominant Jewish framework in the Second Temple period, beginning with the Assyrian captivity, was a self-conception of being in a protracted period of exile, grounded in the covenantal framework of Deuteronomy (Ibid., 184–92). According to Steck, the influence of this so-called *deuteronomische Geschichtsbild* (*dtrGB*), defined as a "Konzeption der Metahistorie ganz Israels" (idem, *Das apocrypha Baruchbuch: Studien zu Reception und Konzentration "kononischer" Überlieferung,* FRLANT 160 [Göttingen, Vandenhoeck & Ruprecht, 1993], 81n44), is evident in the exilic and post-exilic Hebrew Bible (1 Kgs 8:46–53; Ezra 9:11; Neh 9:26; 2 Chr 30:6–9) and in later apocryphal (Sir, Tob, Bar 3:9–5:9) and pseudepigraphal (*T. 12 Patr.; 1 En.* 93:1–10; 91:12–17; 85–90; *Jub.; Pss. Sol.; As. Mos.; LAB*) writings as well as in the DSS (idem, *Israel und das gewaltsame Geschick der Propheten*, for prophets see 110–28; for later Jewish literature, see 146–84).

13. Ps 80 uses vine imagery for Israel, calls Israel a son, and prays for restoration from exile. Restoration is depicted as the turning back of God's face.

14. Israel's role was Adam-like, but did not have the same scope or influence. For a helpful discussion on Adam's commission recurring in Scripture, see Beale, *NTBT,* 30–3, 46–57.

15. See Brandon D. Crowe, *The Last Adam: A Theology of the Obedient Life of Jesus in the Gospels* (Grand Rapids: Baker Academic, 2017).

16. For example, Max Turner describes Luke 4:16–31 as the place where Christological and missiological foci converge in the new exodus motif (*Power from on High: The Spirit in Israel's Restoration and Witness in Luke-Acts* [Sheffield: Sheffield Academic, 1996], 249–50).

17. See chapter 6 for the full discussion on exile in Rom 8:31–39.

18. For example, "*all creation* groans," Rom 8:22.

19. Timo Eskola also notes the theological relationship of exile with several other longitudinal themes in redemption in his recent narrative theology: "the story of exile and restoration provides a metanarrative where issues such as Davidic messianism, the return of the Holy Spirit, renewed adoption as God's children, the congregation as the temple of salvation, and even resurrection eschatology can be consistently explained" (*A Narrative Theology of the New Testament: Exploring the Metanarrative of Exile and Restoration*, WUNT 350 [Tübingen: Mohr Siebeck, 2015] and James M. Scott's edited volume *Exile: A Conversation with N. T. Wright* [Downers Grove: IVP Academic, 2017], 247).

20. Longenecker, *Introducing Romans*, 75–8; Thomas H. Tobin, *Paul's Rhetoric in Its Contexts: The Argument of Romans* (Peabody, MA: Hendrickson, 2004), 37.

21. Stanley Porter, "The Use of the Old Testament in the New Testament: A Brief Comment on Method and Terminology," in *Early Christian Interpretation of the Scriptures of Israel: Investigations and Proposals* (Sheffield: Sheffield Academic, 1997), 93, 95–6.

22. J. Ross Wagner cautions that "a reader-focused approach to Paul's use of scripture in Romans that depends heavily on a reconstructed historical audience is clearly inadequate by itself for interpreting the letter on historical, let alone literary or theological, grounds" (*Heralds of the Good News: Isaiah and Paul "in Concert" in the Letter to the Romans*, NovTsup 101 [Leiden: Brill, 2002], 34).

23. Richard B. Hays, "'Who Has Believed Our Message?' Paul's Reading of Isaiah," *Society of Biblical Literature 1998 Seminar Papers*, 2 vols., SBLSP 37 (Atlanta: Society of Biblical Literature, 1998), 1:207–8.

24. Ibid., 208.

25. Tobin, *Paul's Rhetoric in Its Contexts*, 37–8.

26. Longenecker, *Introducing Romans,* 48–50; Tobin, *Paul's Rhetoric in Its Contexts,* 44–5.

27. Tobin, *Paul's Rhetoric in Its Contexts*, 7.

28. On this and similar texts, see David Starling, *Not My People: Gentiles as Exiles in Pauline Hermeneutics*, BZNW 184 (Berlin: De Gruyter, 2011). For Hos 2:23 in Rom 9, see pp. 107–66.

29. Eskola, *Narrative Theology*, 29–30.

30. See Sylvia Keesmaat, *Paul and his Story: (Re)-Interpreting the Exodus Tradition,* JSNTSup 181 (Sheffield: Sheffield Academic, 1999), 54–135; and idem, "Exodus and the Intertextual Transformation of Tradition in Romans 8:14–30," *JSNT* 54 (1994): 29–56. Keesmaat makes a powerful case for the presence of the exodus tradition in Rom 8.

31. See Perrin, "Exile," 25–37.

32. Most modern commentators recognize these sub-units. See for example Longenecker, *Romans,* vi–viii; Cranfield, *Romans,* 1:xi, 2:443.

33. Especially in the previous generation of scholars, many placed the transition from Paul's first argument to his second after Romans 5, viewing Rom 6–8 as self-contained, for example, John Murray, *The Epistle to the Romans: The English Text with Introduction, Exposition, and Notes*, NICNT (Grand Rapids: Eerdmans, 1959), 211; James D. G. Dunn, *Romans 1–8*, WBC 38A (Dallas, TX: Word Books, 1988), 242–3; W. Sanday and Arthur C. Headlam, *A Critical and Exegetical Commentary on the Epistle to the Romans,* ICC (Edinburgh: T&T Clark, 1902), xlvii–xlix. Others place the transition between Rom 5:11 and 5:12, e.g., J. Christiaan Beker, *Paul the Apostle: The Triumph of God in Life and Thought* (Philadelphia: Fortress, 1980), 85; Martinus de Boer, *The Defeat of Death: Apocalyptic Eschatology in 1 Corinthians 15 and Romans 5*, JSNTSup 22 (Sheffield: JSOT Press, 1988), 148–9.

34. Ulrich Luz, "Zum Aufbau von Röm 1–8," *TZ* 25 (1969): 178; Neil Elliott, *The Rhetoric of Romans: Argumentative Constraint and Strategy and Paul's Dialogue with Judaism*, JSNTSup 45 (Sheffield, England: JSOT Press, 1990), 223, 227; Longenecker, *Romans*, 553; Christopher Bryan, *A Preface to Romans: Notes on the Epistle in Its Literary and Cultural Setting* (Oxford: Oxford University Press, 2000), 120–1; Thomas R. Schreiner, *Romans,* BECNT (Grand Rapids: Baker Books, 1998), 246. Similarly, see Patricia M. McDonald, "Romans 5:1–11 as a Rhetorical Bridge," *JSNT* 40 (1990): 81–96.

35. See, for example, Nihls A. Dahl, "Two Notes on Romans 5," *ST* 5 (1952): 37–48.

36 N.T. Wright, *PFG*, 762.

37. Douglas J. Moo, *The Epistle to the Romans,* NICNT (Grand Rapids: Eerdmans, 1996), 294.

38. C. H. Dodd, *The Epistle of Paul to the Romans*, Rev. ed., MNTC 6 (London: Collins, 1959), 149.

39. e.g., Krister Stendahl, *Paul among Jews and Gentiles: And Other Essays* (Philadelphia: Fortress, 1976), 28, 85; Joseph A. Fitzmyer, *Romans,* 539–43.

40. See chapters 4, 5, 6.

41. Longenecker, *Romans,* 769.

## *Chapter 2*

# The Duration and Characterization of Exile in the First Century AD

This chapter will review diverse views in the continuity of exile leading up to the first century AD. While the portrayal of exile varies among texts and time periods, I will show a general expectation for some form of restoration. Even texts which suggest exile has ended *in some sense* (e.g., Ezra-Nehemiah) also hope for a greater restoration than what has already occurred. As Brunson puts it, "Restoration would be unnecessary had the exile *actually* ended."[1]

I argue that the core concept of continuity naturally arises from the Hebrew Bible's characterization of exile, particularly in Deuteronomy. Thus, it is highly probable that Paul would have been familiar with various views of Israel's continuing exile. Notwithstanding this likelihood, I will not attempt to show any dependence upon specific Second Temple writings. Rather, these will be used to demonstrate variegated Jewish beliefs in ongoing exile leading up to the first century. Instead, I argue that the NT exhibits a multifaceted, but consistent theology of ongoing exile arising from Israel's scriptures. Moreover, I will lay preliminary groundwork to show that Paul would not have viewed "the exile" as limited to the sixth and eighth century deportations, but would have considered these events to be instances of a broader, recurring type[2] which would include Adam's expulsion from the garden of Eden.

In this chapter I will discuss two central issues in recent scholarship regarding the exile, viz., the questions of the *duration* of the exile (i.e., is it over?) and the *theological characterization* of the exile (i.e., what is the exile and why did it happen?).

## DURATION AND CHARACTERIZATION

At a basic level, the term "exile" in biblical studies may refer to either the Assyrian deportation of the northern kingdom in 722 BC (2 Kgs 15–17) or, more commonly, to the subsequent defeat and captivity of the southern kingdom by the Babylonians in 597 and 587 BC (2 Kgs 24–25; 2 Chr 36:17–20) or to both. From a literary standpoint, "exile" may also refer to a literary trope—a culturally significant sign, whose meaning is dependent on literary context and the author's background—and may or may not refer to an underlying historical event.[3]

The question of the continuity of exile was catapulted from relative obscurity to the forefront of biblical studies when N. T. Wright proposed that Israel's exile was both ongoing and a central factor in the self-conception and belief structure of Second Temple Judaism.[4] The discussion surrounding exile in the first century has been hotly debated since.[5] Some have questioned whether there even *was* a historical exile underlying the literary witness.[6] Others hold that "exile" is inherently geographical in meaning and could not have continued for Israelites who returned to Palestine.[7] Still others contend that "exile" transcended its historical background becoming a state of mind or ideology in the Second Temple period.[8] In sum, there is considerable disagreement regarding the nature of "the exile" and, hence, its cause. Likewise, the circumstances by which the exile will end are disputed, and, hence, its duration. It is noteworthy that the debate has predominantly focused upon questions of *duration* (i.e., is the exile ongoing?). The logically prior question of the *theological character* of the exile is typically discussed in the service of answering the duration question. I will begin by examining the question of the exile's duration; however, this book's primary interest is to determine how Paul would have defined exile.

First century Jews living in Palestine were either in a state of exile or they were not. A straightforward approach would conclude that no citizen living in his own land could be in exile.[9] A Jewish household in Jerusalem would not be labeled as remaining in exile, but others living in Alexandria or Syria would be. But, that approach risks over-individualizing the notion. Not every single Jewish person was carried to Assyria or Babylon, but we do not see discussions about numerous distinct exiles. Rather exile is viewed corporately. The foregoing discussion illustrates the basic challenge: to delimit the duration of exile is to define it.

Wright defines exile as a non-geographical, unified condition for God's people where only a specific set of circumstances can bring it to a close. Exile is a catch-all descriptor of "the dominant state of affairs" of the Second Temple era.[10] It is a "period of history characterized by the suffering and oppression, which, according to the prophets, had resulted from national sin."[11] In Wright's reconstruction, the majority of first-century Jews would have self-identified as "still in exile" because (1) the promises of Isaiah 40–66, Ezekiel, Zechariah, and other prophets remained unfulfilled, (2) the power of paganism remained unbroken, (3) Yahweh had not yet returned to Zion to reinhabit the temple as he had in the past (Exod 40:34–35; 1 Kgs 8:10–11//2 Chr 7:1), (4) the covenant had not been renewed, (5) Israel's sins had not been forgiven, (6) the "new exodus" had not happened, (7) and the second temple was *not* the true and final temple.[12] Until all of these requirements were met, the exile would continue. But, Wright's definition faces a basic problem: it evacuates exile of its basic geographical meaning. Why not speak in terms of "curse" instead of "exile"?

Another strategy for viewing first-century Jews as continuing to live in an estate of exile defines restoration comprehensively. Brant Pitre argues that the exile would last as long as *all* Israel remained dispersed.[13] The ten northern tribes received no equivalent to Cyrus's decree. For Pitre, Israel's hope of restoration was for a complete undoing of the curse. After all, there is an incongruity to the notion that Jews who had returned from Babylon would have considered themselves to remain in the *Babylonian* exile. To the contrary, "Wright has the *right insight* but the *wrong exile*."[14] Many of the restoration promises recorded in the prophets speak of the restoration of all Israel (e.g., Isa 11:10–16; 14:1–2; 27:2–13; 43:4–6, 49:5–6; 66:18–21; Jer 23:5–8; Ezek 36:24; 37:11–14, 15–28), which would certainly include the ten tribes which had not been restored. Thus, exile *can* be ongoing well beyond the return of the Babylonian captives if the Assyrian exile is taken into account. To redefine exile as non-geographical is unnecessary. The exile continues because *some* Jews are still in exile. Similarly, Michael E. Fuller has noted a sense of corporate solidarity in early Jewish literature between those Jews in the land and those who remain scattered: "Until the return of those outside the homeland, all of Israel, *even those already within the Land,* remains (theologically) in exile."[15]

Overall, there seems to be a growing academic consensus that Israel's exile continues beyond the sixth century and that such is attested in the Jewish scripture and Second Temple writings.[16] However, the interest of this study is specifically to determine the theological characterization of the exile *as Paul would have seen it*. In other words, what theology does Paul employ or develop when he writes πᾶς Ἰσραὴλ σωθήσεται? ("All Israel will be saved," Rom 11:26a)? Surely it is related to the promise of restoration from exile in Isa 59:20–21 (and Isa 27:9), quoted in the same sentence: καθὼς γέγραπται· ἥξει ἐκ Σιὼν ὁ ῥυόμενος, ἀποστρέψει ἀσεβείας ἀπὸ Ἰακώβ (as it is written, "The Deliverer will come from Zion, he will turn away impiety from Jacob," Rom 11:26b).[17] In Romans, Paul frames restoration from exile as a component of salvation. In chapters 4–6, I will argue for the relationship between these ideas. I will go on to argue that Paul's view is shaped by Israel's scriptures, the final form of which spoke of Israel's exile in the Pentateuch (Lev 26; Deut 28) and foreshadowed it in Adam's expulsion from Eden.[18] For the remainder of this chapter, however, I will discuss the notion of the exile's duration and its theological characterization the Hebrew Bible, Second Temple literature,[19] and, briefly, the NT.

## THE DURATION AND CHARACTERIZATION OF EXILE IN THE HEBREW BIBLE

The theme of exile and restoration is expressed in various modes in the Hebrew Bible. Whereas the Prophets speak of restoration in sweeping eschatological terms, Ezra-Nehemiah is historically oriented and restoration is muted. Both Prophets and historical works are informed by the pentateuchal warnings of various curses which culminate in and may be summed up with the term "exile." I will begin with Deuteronomy, before moving to the Prophets.[20] Finally, as a point of contrast with the Prophets, I will conclude with Ezra-Nehemiah's characterization of exile and restoration. But, the contrast is not absolute. Each book has its own unique voice, but there is a consistent theme in the Hebrew Bible. Exile and restoration are part of the unfolding story of redemption. That story stretches back to the Garden of Eden and forward to eternity. Even the restored Jewish people in Ezra-Nehemiah look for a fuller, eschatological restoration.

### Deuteronomy

Much of early Jewish characterization of exile has directly arisen from Deuteronomy, specifically its covenant theology. Kenneth Turner explains, "The notion of exile arises in covenantal contexts as a threat to Israel if she persists in idolatrous worship (Deut 4:25–28), and serves as the climax of the covenant curses (28:15–68)."[21] Warnings about the consequences of failing to love Yahweh and follow him are explicit across the book (e.g., 4:25–27; 28:15–68; 32:5–6, 15–25). The land was a conditional blessing held between God and people, constituting a covenant triad, symbolizing rest.[22] That triad is ruptured in exile.[23] However, the fundamental loss is not land, but solidarity with Yahweh. Once the relationship is ruptured, the land cannot be retained. Deuteronomy describes exile as a "redemptive reversal," the undoing of Israel's deliverance from Egypt.[24] While covenant obedience would lead to life and land, disobedience would involve the loss of both. Turner sums it up in this way: "Exile constitutes the death of Israel as a nation in covenant—a covenant comprised of a dynamic relationship between Yahweh, the nation, and the land. Whatever existence continues, it is discontinuous from the past."[25] He continues, "The people will continue to exist physically in exile; yet, as a single entity, Israel is said to 'perish' and 'be destroyed'. So, it is not Israel as an historical or socio-religious people, but Israel as Yahweh's elect son and servant (Deut 1:31, 7:6, 14:1) that is [metaphorically] put to death."[26] Therefore, since Israel "dies" in the exile (cf. Deut 28:48, 63-64), restoration is only possible through resurrection. Thus, the characterization of the exile of Deuteronomy is grounded in the covenant between Yahweh and Israel, his corporate son.

Deuteronomy promises that exile will result from idolatry, but that Yahweh will ultimately restore his people (Sin-Exile-Restoration; or S-E-R). Nevertheless, Deuteronomy does not give a specific duration nor does it communicate that restoration will be merely the outworking of a fixed time period. Rather, restoration requires the removal of sin. Deuteronomy 4:27–28 threatens exile; 4:29 claims restoration will be preceded by repentance. Likewise, Deut 30:1 prescribes the order of exile, and then restoration. Even the Song of Moses in Deut 32, which denied Israel's sonship, promises that Yahweh will "vindicate" (יָדִין; LXX: κρινεῖ) his people and have compassion on his servants (32:36). Similarly, the Song closes in Deut 32:43 repeating the promise that Yahweh will restore. There is a call for rejoicing both because Yahweh will avenge the blood of his "servants" (MT: עֲבָדָיו) or "sons" (LXX: τῶν υἱῶν αὐτοῦ; 4QDeut$^{q}$: בניו)[27] and will "cleanse" or "atone for" the land (אַדְמָתוֹ וְכִפֶּר; LXX: καὶ ἐκκαθαριεῖ κύριος τὴν γῆν 32:43).[28] It is noteworthy that the Song has focused upon Israel's sin and exile, but God promises to avenge and restore. Nevertheless, there is no clear indication of timing. Sin and Israel's "death" are the obstacles to restoration. These must be remedied for restoration to be possible.

These filial themes in Deuteronomy are part of a larger whole in the Pentateuch. They reflect a pattern of Yahweh caring for his "sons." Brandon D. Crowe has argued that the father–son characterization "deepens and adds an emotive element" to the covenantal obedience Yahweh expects.[29] The filial relationship is not original to Deuteronomy, but may be traced to Exodus 4:22, where Israel is called Yahweh's "firstborn son" (בְּנִי יִשְׂרָאֵל בְּכֹרִי; LXX: υἱὸς πρωτότοκός μου Ισραήλ).[30] The deliverance from Egypt is meant to enable filial obedience. Moses's message to Pharaoh from Yahweh is to let his son go "that he may serve me" (וְיַעַבְדֵנִי; LXX: ἵνα μοι λατρεύσῃ). But, after Israel's disobedience is foretold in Deut 32:5, Yahweh pronounces the verdict that Israel is no longer his child (לֹא בָּנָיו; LXX: οὐκ αὐτῷ τέκνα).

The failure of a son of God, the "death" of that son, and his removal from a land of rest is not a new scriptural pattern. It corresponds to the story of Adam in Gen 1–3. Seth D. Postell observes that this correspondence between Adam and Israel functions as bookends for the Pentateuch.[31] Deuteronomy ends where Genesis begins, focusing upon the land God prepares for his covenant people to inhabit. From this perspective, the Pentateuch highlights the themes of the gift of land and exile as the corresponding blessing and curse of his covenant. It opens and closes with a focus upon un-possessed land. From a lexical perspective alone, the relationship between Gen 1–3 and Deut 32 is clear. Seth Postell writes:

> Only in Genesis 1:1–2:4 and Deuteronomy 32 do the following cluster of terms all appear together in the Hebrew Bible: ארץ and שמים ("heaven" and "earth"),[32] תהו ("waste," Gen 1:2; Deut 32:10), רחף ("hover," Gen 1:2; Deut 32:11), עשב and דשא ("herbage" and "grass," Gen 1:11, 12; Deut 32:2), and תנין ("sea monster," Gen 1:21; Deut 32:33). The theme of God as creator in Deuteronomy 32:6 is also a likely reference to Genesis 1, and the use of אחרית ("end," Deut 32:20, 29) may be intentionally employed here for its semantic resonance with the first word of the Torah. (ראשית, "beginning")[33]

While the correspondence is noteworthy, the more compelling correlation is in Adam's role with Israel's. Israel is early fruition of God's promise to bless the world through Abraham (cf. Exod 1:7). Scholars have noted that what Abraham receives in promise-form closely corresponds to Adam's failed commission.[34] While not identical, it can be concluded that Israel did inherit a form of Adam's role through the Abrahamic promise.[35] Thus, a biblical pattern emerges from Adam to Israel where both were sons of God, but both failed to be the blessing for the world which the position of "son" intended. Hence, Deuteronomy characterizes exile as a function of God's covenant. It is the result of covenant breaking and will endure until sin is atoned.

## Isaiah[36]

From Isaiah's perspective, exile continues. A second and greater exodus was the perfect image for the people's need for restoration.[37] But, what is the exile from which the new exodus is the restoration?[38] How does Isaiah characterize it? Undoubtedly, exile was a historical reality. Isaiah the son of Amoz saw the deportation of the northern kingdom. It was he who told Hezekiah that the southern kingdom would soon follow suit (2 Kgs 20:14–17). He experienced Assyrian armies occupying territory within ten miles of Jerusalem.[39] Yahweh had said that the land must lie desolate for a time (Isa 6:11–12). The tree (i.e., the Jewish people) would be removed leaving desolation (6:13a). Equally inevitable, however, is that a holy seed would grow from the stump (6:13b).[40] The prophet even named his son "a remnant will return" (καταλειφθεὶς Ιασουβ/יָשׁוּב שְׁאָר) (Isa 7:3).

Because of the historical context, it would be natural to conclude that these geopolitical events led to Isaiah's characterization of exilic theology. However, from a canonical perspective, and based upon Isaiah's use of Deuteronomy, it the opposite.[41] The holiness of Yahweh, the sinfulness of his people, and their unwillingness to repent led to the historical events. The underlying cause of exile precedes the historical outworking and is grounded in Yahweh's covenant. Particularly Isaiah 40–66 evinces the influence of the Deuteronomic tradition.[42] Instances of verbal similarity range from the correspondence of individual words to larger phrases and concepts. It is especially noteworthy to my overall argument that Isaiah demonstrates a particularly focused dependence upon Deut 32, which contains the Deuteronomic theology *in nuce*.[43] The correspondence, as well as Paul's frequent use of both Isaiah and Deuteronomy,[44] renders it probable that the exile of Isaiah is understood in light of Deuteronomy. Differences may be understood as developments within the covenantal framework of Yahweh's dealings with his people.

If covenant breaking is the cause of exile for Isaiah, what will enable restoration? Isaiah expects restoration through a singular figure: the servant.[45] This second Moses figure is humiliated.[46] He has no beauty (53:2b); his face is marred (52:14); he is cut off from the land of the living (53:8b–9). But, Yahweh will exalt him and reward him (53:12). The servant's suffering is not due to his own rebellion, but Israel's.[47] Moreover, Anthony Ceresko has shown that the terminology for the servant's suffering is drawn from the particular curses in Deuteronomy by which God assured Israel he would send them into exile.[48] The singular servant experienced *their* infirmities (Isa 53:4a, cf. Deut. 28:59b, 61a) and afflictions (Isa 53:4b; cf. Deut. 28.59a, 61a).[49] Not only does the servant's experience parallel the Deuteronomic curses, but it also echoes the travails of Israel in Egyptian servitude.[50] Ceresko adduces numerous parallels: the servant being "taken away" (לֻקָּח, Isa 53:8a) echoes a description of Israel's being "taken away (כִּי־לֻקַּח) without cause" in their Egyptian servitude in the previous chapter (Isa 52:4–5); the servant's affliction (ענה, Isa 53:4, 7) also echoes Israel's oppression in Egypt by their taskmasters who "afflicted" (ענה) them with heavy burdens (Exod 1:11–12). The "heavy burdens" (סְבָלוֹת) which Israelites were forced to carry are also echoed in the servant carrying (סְבָלָם) [the burdens of] our sorrows (Isa 53:4). Thus, there are clear inner-biblical links between Israel's bondage in Egypt and its redemption in the first exodus, and Isaiah's second exodus. Egypt becomes a symbol of slavery and curse; the promised land represents freedom and blessing. Covenant breaking brings curse and a return to "Egypt"; righteousness brings blessing and inheritance.

The servant's individual experience leads to his individual exaltation as well as the corporate restoration of Israel, as the servant embodies Israel.[51]

Whereas Isaiah saw Yahweh "high and lifted up" (MT: רוּם וְנִשָּׂא) the servant also will achieve a status of being "high and lifted up" (MT: רָם וְנִשָּׂא).[52] Thus, the restoration of Israel through the singular work of the servant will far surpass prior conditions. The restored remnant will include worshiping Gentiles (Isa 2:3; 11:10; 14:1; 18:7; 24:14–16; 25:6–8; 40:3–5; 49:6; 55:5; 56:7–8; 60:3, 10; 66:19–21), a newly created cosmos (Isa 43:18–21; 55:12–13),[53] and the exaltation of the people to the glory of God (Isa 46:13; 55:5; 60:1–2, 19). Richard J. Clifford summarizes the servant's work as follows: "Due to the servant's exemplary bearing of the guilt of all Israel, the whole people is now free to enjoy the great gift—the land."[54] In sum, Isaiah anticipates a singular figure who will atone for Israel's sin and enable restoration.

Hugenberger notes multiple parallels between Isaiah 40–55's descriptions of the servant and that of Cyrus in 44:28–45:13.[55] The Spirit of Yahweh rests upon the servant; Cyrus is anointed (Isa 42:1//45:1). Both are called by Yahweh (42:6//45:4). Both are chosen by Yahweh (42:1//45:4). Yahweh has "taken [each] by the hand" (42:6//45:1). Israel is delivered from exile by both Cyrus and the servant (42:7; 49:5–13//45:4, 13). These parallels indicate that Cyrus's decree is characterized as "restoration," but that Isaiah anticipates more to come.[56] The expansive, eschatological expectations of full restoration were not realized under Cyrus, though he did return Israel to their land. The element Cyrus could not provide, of course, was atonement. His decree enables a restoration of land, without resolving the lingering dilemma of the harm to covenant relationship. The servant, however, will repair that relationship. I will discuss Cyrus's restoration below in the section on Ezra-Nehemiah.

How does Isaiah describe restoration? In the Book of Consolation, Yahweh informs his servant that exile will give way to an eternal restoration:

> With a little wrath I turned my face away from you, but with eternal mercy (ἐλέει αἰωνίῳ) I will have mercy on you said the Lord who delivered you. (Isa 54:8)

Isaiah 65:17–25 also describes the promised restoration as a life free from pain or care.[57] It is worthy of note that there is no stage in Israel's history in which such a description could be true. So, in what sense could this be a *restoration,* which would typically be understood as a return to how things were?

Isaiah's new exodus is a restoration in the sense that God's people are restored to his presence. However, it transcends recent historical circumstance in virtually every way. The new exodus will be greater than the first; it cannot be reversed; and it will be led by the servant who will incorporate the Gentiles into the restored people along with the tribes of Jacob and the diaspora of Israel.[58] The new condition Isaiah describes is escalated in comparison to the eras of David or Solomon and encompasses the idea of a completely new creation.[59] To put it poetically, restoration is the doorway to paradise.[60] Thus, Isaianic restoration retains its basic geographical meaning, but is expanded in scope to include the whole world.

The cosmic scale of the restoration envisioned in Isaiah 40—66 makes any historical event or figure apart from Christ incapable of bringing it about. However, restoration should not be equated with eschatological salvation itself. Rather, it is the transition. It is a relational movement back into God's presence which is tethered to a geographical movement to the place where that fellowship can thrive. Isaianic restoration is the restoration of Israel to God's presence through the redeemer who came from Zion. But, the people Christ restores will come from every nation, tribe, and tongue. And, the curse he reverses was not brought through Israel's disobedience alone, but Adam's.

## Ezekiel

Ezekiel's message of restoration is similar to Isaiah's, but more direct: God will restore Israel for his name's sake.[61] Like Isaiah, Ezekiel characterizes exile as covenant curse by regularly alluding to Deuteronomy, as well as Leviticus).[62] At times these traditions will be used distinctly.[63] For instance, the scattering (διασπείρω) and sword (μάχαιρα) of Lev 26:33 appear to be echoed in Ezek 5:2, 5:12 and 12:14.[64] At other times Ezekiel will fuse the traditions.[65] One good example for the present study is the use of Lev 26 and Deut 32 in Ezek 5:16–17, which describes Ezekiel's prophetic sign-actions of the siege of Israel and upcoming exile.

> 16 When I send out my arrows of famine (βολίδας μου τοῦ λιμοῦ) upon them, they will be utterly forsaken, and I will break into pieces your support of bread. 17 And I will send a famine (λιμὸν) against you and wild animals and I will punish you, and pestilence (θάνατος; MT: דֶּבֶר) and blood will come upon you, and I will bring a sword (ῥομφαίαν) all around you. I, the Lord, have spoken. (Ezekiel 5:16–17)[66]

Ezekiel draws the word grouping "sword," "famine," "wild animals," and "plague" used in Ezek 5:16 (cf. 14:13, 15, 19, 21) from Lev 26:22, 25, 26.[67] Deuteronomy 32 also describes exilic tribulations involving famine (32:42) and arrows (32:23–25).[68] Not only does the Song of Moses share these descriptions of exile, but the depiction of Yahweh casting arrows of exilic punishments upon his own people is unique to these texts in the Hebrew Bible.[69] As a final piece of evidence that Ezekiel draws upon Deut 32 in addition to Lev 26, the בהם ("against them") of Ezek 5:16, which is often emended to the smoother בכם ("against you"), may be a literary remnant of the third person voice used in Deut 32:23 where בהם appears.[70] I will argue in chapter 6 that Paul employs precisely this pattern of drawing terminology from the pentateuchal covenant curses to describe the woes of God's people.

How long does Ezekiel indicate the exile will last? In Ezekiel 4:4–8 the exile(s) is clearly described as protracted. The prophet symbolically undergoes the exile of Israel by lying on his left side for 390 days then lies on his left side for 40 days for the exile of Judah. Each day represents a year of exile. The sum of both totals 430 years of exile. The number resonates with biblical-theological symmetry as Israel was in bondage in Egypt for 430 years before Yahweh delivered them in the exodus (Exod 12:40; cf. Gen 15:13). Scott observes that this symmetry is "in accordance with much of the Old Testament/Jewish tradition (e.g., Dan. 9:15–19) which views the deliverance from exile as a 'redemption' of Israel from bondage and a new exodus." Rather than defining an explicit time period, the significance of the number seems to rest more in its representative value in linking the exile with Egyptian bondage.[71]

## Ezra-Nehemiah

Ezra-Nehemiah is sometimes categorized as belonging to a theocratic strand of early Judaism, which believed the exile ended with Cyrus's decree and the rebuilding of the Second Temple.[72] Michael E. Fuller refers to the "remarkably positive manner" in which Ezra-Nehemiah portrays restoration which is "*prima facie* incompatible" with the prophets.[73] To be sure, significant elements of the Babylonian exile ended with Cyrus's decree ca. 538 BC (Ezra 1:1–8; 2 Chr 36:22–23). After their return, the temple was rebuilt, and a semblance of worship was restored. Jerusalem's walls were being reconstructed (cf. 2 Macc 1:23–9). For some, the geographical displacement was over. But was "exile" over? From the perspective of Ezra-Nehemiah, the answer is both yes and no.

How does Ezra-Nehemiah characterize exile and restoration? Did the return of some captives bring exile to an end? Would a new king? Would a new temple? Despite the suggested categorization of these texts as "theocratic" and hence "purely historical" in their outlook,[74] it is clear that Ezra-Nehemiah characterizes the historical exile as the covenant discipline of which Moses spoke. It can be concluded from the corporate prayer in Neh 9 that the exile was understood in Deuteronomic terms. After the people celebrate the Feast of Booths (Neh 8:18), their leaders pray a corporate penitential prayer (9:6–37), including a recital of Israel's history (9:6–31) and a petition for deliverance from their current "tribulation" (θλίψει μεγάλῃ; cf. 1 Macc 1:27) in which the community found itself (9:32–37). These sorrows are framed as the result of their own sin (9:33–34). The prayer even borrows language from the

Song of Moses to characterize Israel's failings (cf. Neh 9:25; Deut 32:15).[75] The prayer indicates that the exile has certainly not ended. The petition opens by describing God's righteousness and their trouble:

> And now our God, the strong, the great, the powerful and the fearful one who keeps covenant and steadfast love. Do not let all the tribulation (תְּלָאָה; LXX: μόχθος) be little before you, which has come upon us and our kings and our princes and our priests and our prophets and our fathers among all your people from the days of the Kings of Assyria *until this day.* (Neh 9:32, my emphasis)[76]

The tribulation in which the people *within the land* find themselves began at the time of the Assyrian conquest. They go on to describe themselves in Neh 9:36 as "slaves" (עֲבָדִים; LXX: δοῦλοι; see also, Ezra 9:11) in the land, concluding with an allusion to Deut 28:51 in Neh 9:37, in which God promises the curse will "consume the descendants of your cattle (בְּהֶמְתְּךָ; LXX: τῶν κτηνῶν σου) and the fruit of your land":[77]

> The land . . . its rich produce belongs to the kings who you set over us because of our sins. They rule over our bodies and our cattle (וּבִבְהֶמְתֵּנוּ; LXX: κτήνεσιν ἡμῶν) as they please and we are in great tribulation (וּבְצָרָה גְדוֹלָה; LXX: θλίψει μεγάλῃ). (Neh 9:36–37; cf. Deut 28:53, 55, 57).[78]

The hardship (תְּלָאָה; LXX: μόχθος) in which the people currently find themselves *in the land* alludes to those their fathers had experienced in Egypt and the wilderness (Exod 18:8; Num 20:14).[79] Thus, mere entrance to the land did not constitute full restoration, for even within the land the Yehudites were experiencing "wilderness." What was needed was a salvation analogous to the Red Sea deliverance (Exod 14) or the parting of the Jordan (Josh 3), which ended Egyptian bondage and wilderness hardships.

Yet there is some sense in which Israel's exile can be said to have ended. J. G. McConville has convincingly shown allusions to restoration prophecies in Ezra-Nehemiah drawn from Isaiah and Jeremiah.[80] A series of parallels indicates that Ezra-Nehemiah interprets the return to Palestine as prophetic fulfillment—if only the beginning of it. Terminology from Jeremiah 31 (38 LXX), which contains both the promise of the new covenant (31:31–34) and of restoration from captivity (31:7–8), is echoed throughout a relatively brief section of Ezra (8:15–9:15). Overlaps include the "remnant of Israel" (Jer 31:7/Ezra 9:14); "gathering" (Jer 31:8, 10/Ezra 8:15); God's giving of "good things" (Jer 31:12, 14/Ezra 8:22); and being led on a "straight path" (Jer 31:9/Ezra 8:21).[81] McConville further observes that beyond the shared vocabulary, there are conceptual parallels. Jeremiah predicts the return of a remnant (31:7–8); Ezra leads a returned remnant (8:15).[82] Jeremiah predicts the need for repentance (Jer 31:31–34); Ezra leads the people in repentance (Ezra 9:3–4, 6). Further, Ezra's reference to the remnant of Israel echoes restoration language from Isaiah (Isa 37:1–2/Ezra 9:14).[83] The beginning of Ezra's return from Babylon "on the first of the first month" also echoes Isaianic restoration (Isa 2:3/Ezra 7:9).[84] Blenkinsopp corroborates this point noting that the specific timing evokes the timing of the exodus from Egypt on the first, just before the Passover (cf. Exod 12:2; Num 33:3).[85] It can be concluded from such parallels that the writer of Ezra considered the return to the land to be partial fulfillment. However, the earlier references to continuing Deuteronomic hardships equally point to the continuity of covenant discipline.

I conclude that the provisional nature of restoration is due to a continuing exile.[86] Of course, geographically speaking, those Yehudites who had returned were not physically "in exile," but that misses the theological point being made. God's full presence and blessing were not present in the way they had been. Some had indeed returned, but many more Jews remained in Babylon. The ten tribes exiled by Assyria remained dispersed. The temple was far from its former glory and the Spirit of God had not filled it (Ezra 3:12). The people were free, but the non-Jewish inhabitants of the land were persecuting the returned people (Ezra 4:1–5) and leading them away from Yahweh (Ezra 9:1–2; 10:1–17). The people's suffering in the land was such that Ezra could characterize their condition as Egypt-like, saying, δοῦλοί ἐσμεν . . . ἐν τῇ δουλείᾳ ἡμῶν ("We are slaves . . . in our bondage," Ezra 9:9). In this sense the captives were restored, but they were still "slaves." The restoration was incomplete with an abiding sense of loss. Rather than presenting a purely historical, "theocratic" restoration, Ezra-Nehemiah describes a real—if provisional—restoration that longs for something more.

## THE DURATION AND CHARACTERIZATION OF EXILE IN SECOND TEMPLE JUDAISM

Second Temple writings portray exile in complementary and, sometimes, contradictory ways. They reflect the influence of the historical exiles, but from different perspectives. The term "exile" may refer to a period of captivity that ended with Cyrus (Josephus). Or it may refer to an ongoing period of estrangement from God that will end before the end of the present age (Tob; CD). Finally, it may refer to one that will conclude only at the end of the age (Sir; *Jub.*). Thus, there are various perspectives on the duration of the exile. Not only is the duration of exile in question, so is its theological characterization. Some texts clearly portray the exile as Deuteronomic curse (e.g., Bar, Tob), others clearly do not (e.g., Josephus; Philo).

## The Duration of the Exile in Second Temple Judaism

There is scant support in Second Temple literature for the view that Cyrus's decree resulted in full restoration. The exceptions are Philo and Josephus, though even they require qualifications. To be sure, Philo has a sharply negative attitude toward exile itself. In his commentary on Abraham, Philo describes exile (φυγή)[87] as worse than death (*Abraham* 64). Only great wickedness earns φυγή. When Philo speaks of Adam's removal from Eden it was an "eternal banishment" (ἀίδιον φυγήν, *Cherubim 1:2*). Likewise, Cain goes forth in banishment (φυγή) "from the face of God" (ἀπὸ προσώπου τοῦ θεοῦ, *Posterity* 1:1; 2:9). But, Philo does not consider the Jewish diaspora to be exile at all.[88] Even when Philo speaks eschatologically of a return, he describes a regathering of exiles (ἀπῳκισμένους) from "spiritual dispersion which vice has wrought" (ἐκ διασπορᾶς ψυχικῆς) living across the earth (*Rewards* 116–7).[89] Philo is apparently alluding to Deut 30:4, but spiritualizing the context.[90] For him, vice did not lead to Israel's *physical* dispersal, but to a *spiritual* lack of wisdom. He considers the fruitfulness of the nation as a blessing and pentateuchal promises of restoration to the "land of wisdom" are understood as the gaining of wisdom and virtue (*Rewards* 115). For Philo, the growth of the Jewish people is a product of the Abrahamic promise (*Spec. Laws* 1.7; *Moses* 2.232; *Prelim. Studies* 3). The Jewish diaspora is a blessing not a curse (*Flaccus* 45–46); it is certainly not φυγή.

Similarly, Josephus shies away from speaking of Israel's dispersion or concrete expectations of restoration. Louis H. Feldman remarks upon the total absence in Josephus of any mention of sorrow or grief at his own exile from Palestine.[91] A compelling study by Betsy Halpern-Amaru demonstrates that in the retelling of biblical narratives, Josephus often omits details of covenant, the land promise, or vocabulary of the exile.[92] Instead, Josephus regularly focuses on dispersion and colonizing as a positive.[93] It takes little imagination to see why. Josephus walked a political tightrope between his identity as a Jew and as a beneficiary of Roman support.[94] Josephus is a politically savvy writer who knows that de-emphasizing Israel's land-expectations will keep the peace.

A more common view is that exile is ongoing. The majority of Second Temple texts look for a future end of exile either within the present age (Tob; CD) or at the last day (Sir; *Jub.*). For instance, Tobit frames hardships in the Jewish diaspora as exilic curse. As Fuller puts it, for Tobit "Diaspora *is* exile."[95] Tobit is also marked by a hope for restoration (13:3–6, 13; 14:5), for a renewed temple (13:7, 10, 16–18; 14:5), and for the conversion and gathering of the Gentiles into the rebuilt temple (13:11; 14:6).[96] Restoration hopes are presented in the Deuteronomic pattern of sin, exile (repentance), and restoration (14:5).[97] Tobit 13 alludes to Deut 32 to describe the tribulations of the Jewish minority. Tobit 13:6, "[he] will no longer hide his face," recalls Deut 32:20, "[He] said, 'I will hide my face from them.'"[98] Tobit 13:2, "there is no one who can escape his hand," recalls Deut 32:29, "there is none that can deliver from my hand."[99]

Tobit's farewell discourse (14:1–11) provides more detail as to the manner of restoration. Particularly 14:5–7 demonstrate an eschatological perspective:

> 5 But God will again have mercy on them: God will bring them back to the land of Israel. They will rebuild the Temple, although not like the first one, until the era when the appointed times shall be completed. Afterward all of them will return from their exile and will rebuild Jerusalem in her splendor. And the Temple will be rebuilt within her, just as the prophets of Israel spoke concerning her. 6 then all the nations in the entire world will all be converted and will worship God in sincerity. They will abandon their idols, which have deceitfully led them into error, 7 and in righteousness they will bless the eternal God. All the Israelites who are spared in those days and are truly loyal to God will be brought together and will come to Jerusalem. Thereafter they will live securely in the land of Abraham, which will be given to them. (Tob 14:5–7)

The exile continues but will end with the return of a remnant of Israel to the land (14:5a, 7), the reconstruction of the temple (14:5b), and the conversion of all the nations (14:6). Of particular note is 14:5, regarding the restoration of the temple, which seems to occur both at the first regathering (14:5a) *as well as* when the remainder of exiles return (14:5b).[100] Restoration hopes are thus portrayed as both imminent *and* distant.

Qumran is similar. Among the various perspectives of the DSS, there is a fairly consistent self-conception of being in exile or in the process of returning from it.[101] The community[102] assimilated the history of Israel as its own and forecasted its eschatological expectations in those terms. Although the DSS exhibit an awareness of Israel's sojourn in Egypt[103] and the Assyrian captivity[104] of the northern tribes, the Babylonian exile receives the most attention.[105] The *Damascus Document* (CD),[106] for example, retells Israel's exilic history, but very differently than the account in Ezra-Neh. Although the opening verses refer to Babylonian exile, they ignore any hint of previous restoration, indicating instead that God's wrath against the forefathers (lines 1–3) had given way to the salvation of the remnant (viz., Qumran).[107] Shemaryahu Talmon argues that the group represented in CD "intended to obliterate it [i.e., the 6th century restoration] entirely from their conception of Israel's history, and to claim for themselves the distinction of being the first returnees after the destruction."[108] Instead of Ezra and Nehemiah's generation, the imminent hope of restoration belonged to the community of the *Damascus Document*. The author of CD continues to claim that God "visited them and caused to sprout from Israel and from Aaron a shoot of the planting, in order to possess (8) his land and to become fat with the good things of his soil" (CD-A I, 7–8). Thus, they were saved (lines 4–5), but the community considered it its task to complete the God-given work of restoration.[109] They were the remnant that God would preserve and plant.[110]

Although the eschatology of the DSS is somewhat inconsistent,[111] restoration uniformly involves a physical return to the land of Israel and to Jerusalem.[112] Within those parameters, restoration hopes include the return of the faithful, repentant Jewish remnant (4Q171 III, 11; 4Q385 2; 4Q386 1; 4Q509 1 I, 3), restored worship (CD III, 21–IV, 4), the temple (11QT XXIX, 9; 4Q174 1 I, 2–9), the victory of the righteous over the wicked (1QM I, 2–3; CD XX, 20–21, 32–33), and "all the glory of Adam" (1QS IV, 23). In sum, the DSS fully attest to a belief in continuing exile from which restoration can come within the present age.

Sirach also views the Jewish people as continuing in exile. A good example is the prayer of lament in Sirach 36. The prayer is divided into four stanzas beginning with an appeal that God glorify himself by delivering Israel from the nations (36:1–5). The second stanza details ways to humble Israel's enemies: "pour out wrath, humble the enemy, scatter the foe" (36:8–9); "smash the heads of hostile rulers" (36:12). The third prays for Israel, beginning with a petition for restoration from exile:

> 13 Gather all the tribes of Jacob (πάσας φυλὰς Ιακωβ) . . . 16 that they may inherit the land as in the days of old. 17 Show mercy to the people called by your name: Israel, whom you named your firstborn. 18 Take pity on your holy city, Jerusalem, the foundation of your throne. 19 Fill Zion with your majesty, your temple with your glory. (Sir 36:13, 16–19)[113]

The request is for all of Jacob (i.e., the full twelve tribes of a re-constituted Israel). In whatever sense the release of the Babylonian captives had been a restoration, for Ben Sira in Jerusalem, restoration remained incomplete. The enduring dispersion could only be resolved by placing a reunified Israel in the land of promise "as in the days of old" (36:16). Moreover, the appeal is made on the basis of Israel's role as God's firstborn (36:18) and restoration is described as the return of God's glory to the temple (36:19; cf. Exod 4:22–23; Hos 11:1; Hag 2:7; Wis 18:13).

This is near to Paul's theology of restoration. I will argue in subsequent chapters that Paul views restoration to be inaugurated by the Spirit being poured upon the NT people of God who hope in glory (Rom 5:2, 5) and are the temple of God (1 Cor 3:16–17; cf. Rom 8:1–11). Several similarities to Romans stand out. The eschatological hope is for an inheritance of sons (Sir 36:17; Rom 8:14–17); the hope is for returned glory (36:19; Rom 5:2; 8:18,

21); and, the manner of restoration will be "as in the days of old" (36:17) most likely referring to an exodus. Even the manner in which the enemies of God's people will be defeated is the same (36:12, "Smash the heads of the hostile rulers"; Rom 16:20). Thus, as with Paul, Ben Sira hopes in a future restoration, a second exodus, which will lead God's sons to an inheritance and glory.

*Jubilees* also portrays exile as a continuing condition with an eschatological hope for return. According to James M. Scott, "the implicit expectation of the book is that there will be another jubilee of jubilees in the future, that is, another liberation from slavery (exile) and restoration to the Land."[114] It retells the first exodus when Israel was enduring the difficulties of the wilderness. By extension, *Jubilees* characterizes Palestinian Jews as once again in wilderness conditions looking to (re)gain their inheritance. The opening scene involves Moses ascending Mt. Sinai and receiving the law (*Jub.* 1:1–4a). God goes on to list all Israel's sins they will commit within the land (1:7–12) culminating in the consequence: "And I shall hide my face from them, and I shall give them over to the power of the nations to be captive, and for plunder, and to be devoured. And I shall remove them from the midst of the land, and I shall scatter them among the nations" (1:13).[115] It is noteworthy that exile is more than physical, including the sundering God's relationship by turning his face away. Thus, *Jubilees* is written to encourage the still-exiled people of God that they are not abandoned. If the exile has ended, a primary purpose of the rewriting in the second century fades away.

The text continues with Moses pleading with God not to exile Israel (1:19–25) because they are his inheritance (1:19). However, God responds that Israel's relationship to him will not prevent justice. Rather, God will restore when Israel repents (1:22–25).[116] As the narrative continues, it describes a new creation that will marks the end of the present age (1:23–25).[117] It should be noted further that *Jubilee's* depiction of new creation (cf. 1:29; 4:26) is analogous to the renewal of Zion depicted in Isa 65:17–25.[118] On the basis of this comparison, Scott concludes that restoration/new creation in *Jubilees* is cosmic in scope.[119] In other words, the *Jubilees* restoration is not merely a restoration to what Israel was under David or Solomon, but the realization of a perfect world, the only Jewish analogue of which is the garden of Eden.

## The Characterization of Exile as Deuteronomic Curse

As I have already indicated, several texts characterize exile in Deuteronomic terms. I have already shown Tobit's dependence upon Deuteronomy. Another clear example of that relationship is Baruch. Although it is best dated to the second century BC, well after Cyrus granted return to the Babylonian captives, Baruch assumes the shame and trauma of the Babylonian exile as its own.[120] The hardships of the community are framed as exilic curse.

Baruch opens with a corporate penitential prayer, appealing for God to withdraw his wrath and restore Israel from exile (1:15–3:8). This prayer was a regular component of synagogue liturgy, suggesting that its contents are especially representative of the religious expectations of that time.[121] The prayer's structure reflects the Deuteronomic S-E-R pattern: sin (1:15–21), exile (2:1–10), and restoration (2:11–35).[122] The concluding petition (3:1–8) contains all three elements of sin (3:2, 4a, 5), exile (3:3, 4b)—repentance (3:7)—and hope of restoration (3:5, 7). The prayer closes with the people acknowledging:

> Behold, *we* (ἡμεῖς) are today in our exile (ἀποικία) where you scattered us for disgrace and for curse (ἀρά) and for punishment according to all the iniquities of our fathers, who fell away from the Lord our God." (Baruch 3:8)[123]

The writer affirms that exile is ongoing for the community. The Deuteronomic shape of the prayer and the reference to the ancestors' sins indicates that this prayer characterizes the community's affliction as Deuteronomic curse. It is the consequence Moses promised for covenant breaking. Restoration will not come because the allotted time expires, but through corporate repentance (2:30–34; 3:7). Furthermore, it will involve the permanent restoration of Israel's land ("I will never move my people Israel from the land which I have given to them," 2:35). Thus, the continuing hardships of the Jewish community are often framed in terms of an ongoing exile. At times, it is characterized in Deuteronomic terms, indicating that repentance must precede restoration. N. T. Wright's claim that the self-conception of Palestinian Jews was shaped by ongoing exile finds considerable support in this corpus.

## THE DURATION AND CHARACTERIZATION OF EXILE IN THE NEW TESTAMENT

Although it can be missed through familiarity or overshadowed by other emphases, Nicholas Perrin's observation is surely correct: the theme of exile is "quietly rampant" across the NT.[124] Every corpus of NT writing evinces a theology of exile: Gospels, Pauline Epistles, and General Epistles.

The Gospels display a theology of exile and restoration in numerous ways.[125] For example, Jesus claimed to be the fulfillment of Isaianic restoration prophecies (e.g., Isa 61:1–2 in Lk 4:18–21). When he claimed to have a ministry of proclaiming "liberty to captives" he did not divorce Isa 61 from its original meaning of restoration from Israel's exile. Rather, Jesus quotes a portion of Isaiah, which has been argued to summarize all of the restoration expectations of Isa 40–55.[126] John D. W. Watts notes that Isa 61:1–2 itself closely resembles Isa 40:1–11, but depicts the comfort and restoration of God's people as having come to pass.[127] Jesus claims to fulfill this text in himself. In the same vein, Rikki Watts has argued that Jesus's physical healing in the course of his earthly ministry (specifically in Matt 4:23–5; 8:16) fulfills the prophecy of Isaiah's servant bearing sorrows in Isa 53:4 and launching Israel's restoration.[128] Finally, Simeon's famous dictum, the *Nunc Dimittis* (named for the first two words in Latin), in Lk 2:29–32, when he sees the infant Jesus, is likely an affirmation of the end of Israel's exile. David W. Pao and Eckhard J. Schnabel note numerous references to Isaiah 40–55 in this short section concluding that Simeon recognized the fulfillment of prophecy and the inclusion of the Gentiles into an eschatological people of God.[129] There would be no need for restoration if the exile was not still in effect. The Gospels presume continuing exile.

The General Epistles also demonstrate an exilic theology. First Peter's emphasis upon exile has long been recognized. From the opening appellation of its recipients as ἐκλεκτοῖς παρεπιδήμοις διασπορᾶς ("chosen exiles of the dispersion," 1 Pet 1:1) to the mention of "Babylon" as the letter closes (1 Pet 5:13), the motif is prevalent throughout the letter. V. F. Furnish argues that the phrase ἐκλεκτοῖς παρεπιδήμοις "introduces a major and pervasive conception in 1 Peter: Christians are the elect of God and thus only temporarily resident in this present world."[130] Their description as exiles reflects the marginalization they were experiencing and the focus of the letter itself upon that problem.[131] It is evocative of the previous exiles of God's people who were themselves "chosen" and "exiled" (cf. Isa 14:1; 41:8; 44:1–2, 45:1). The opening verses of 1 Peter not only introduce the motif of exile, but they explain its cause. The recipients are exiles ἐν ἁγιασμῷ πνεύματος.[132] The exiles of the dispersion are sanctified by the Spirit.[133] However, whereas the cause of Israel's exile was covenant breaking, in 1 Peter it is faith and the obedience of faith which leads to the temporary period of suffering which gives way to glory. Thus, 1 Peter understands his readers' hardships as belonging to the same class as Israel's exilic travails. But, the solution to those hardships is not living in Jerusalem as opposed to the Diaspora, but to conduct themselves with fear during their time of exile and to hope in the resurrection (1 Peter 1:17–25; cf. 4:12–14).

The Epistle to the Hebrews also points to the fulfillment of the land promise for God's eschatological people.[134] The already-not yet framework I will argue that Paul employs in Romans is clearly at play for the writer of Hebrews as well. He describes previous generations of believers as "strangers and exile" on the earth (ξένοι καὶ παρεπίδημοί, Heb 11:13) and points to the *future* rest for God's people (Heb 4:1–3) which is not a physical return to

Canaan, but heavenly rest.[135] Thus, the experience of sojourning is shared by the patriarchs (Heb 11:4–13) but continues until God brings a truly unshakable home (Heb 12:26–28). Hebrews 10:32–34 gives some insight into the wilderness estate of God's people. They will endure hard struggles (10:32), the reproach of the world (10:33), and all kinds of loss (10:34). But, the writer reminds them that that any earthly loss is as nothing because of a better and abiding (heavenly) possession.

In sum, Perrin's assertion that the theme of exile and the hope for restoration was "quietly rampant" is true. The NT has a variety of voices, but they harmonize on this theme: believers in Christ will continue for a time in an ongoing exile. Restoration will bring them to heavenly rest. As for the specific characterization, each book and author have their own emphasis. I will argue for the remainder of this book that Paul's characterization in Romans is that the exile began with Adam and has been reversed, but not fully ended, by the last Adam. God has been restored to his people in Spirit, but they still hope for the restoration of their bodies to a blessed land.

## CONCLUSION

I have shown that exile is a regular and variegated theme in both the Hebrew Bible and Second Temple Jewish literature. Although hardly uniform, there is a general expectation for restoration. Even many texts which suggest exile has ended *in some sense,* also hope for a greater restoration than what has already occurred. Even Ezra-Nehemiah looked for the greater future restoration upon which the Prophets focus. I have also argued that any conclusion of the duration of the exile must be given with respect to its theological character.

I argue that Paul also employs a Deuteronomic theology of exile and restoration. Furthermore, along with many of his contemporaries, Paul did not consider the return granted by Cyrus to be the full promised restoration. It could not be. Israel's underlying sin had not yet been removed. I will argue in subsequent chapters that did not Paul view the exile as a solitary event or exclusive to the history of Israel and Judah, but inclusively as Israel recapitulated the sin of Adam. As Adam broke covenant with God and was exiled from Eden, so Israel broke covenant and was exiled from the promised land. For Paul, Jesus resolves not only Israel's separation, but Adam's curse as well. The gospel involves the work of ὁ ἔσχατος Ἀδὰμ and the launch of a new exodus.

However, before this study can turn its full attention to Paul and Romans, it must turn to Adam. Having now introduced the overlap between Adam and Israel, in the next chapter I will explore the use of the Adam tradition in Second Temple Judaism and elsewhere in the NT.

## NOTES

1. Andrew C. Brunson, *Psalm 118 in the Gospel of John: An Intertextual Study on the New Exodus Pattern in the Theology of John*, WUNT 2/158 (Tübingen: Mohr Siebeck, 2003), 68. My emphasis.

2. Defined as analogical correspondence among persons, events, or institutions in scripture which foreshadow future recapitulations (G. K. Beale, *Handbook on the New Testament Use of the Old Testament: Exegesis and Interpretation* [Grand Rapids: Baker Academic, 2012], 14).

3. See Carolyn J. Sharp, "The Trope of 'Exile' and the Displacement of Old Testament Theology," *PRSt* 31 (2004): 153.

4. N.T. Wright, *The New Testament and the People of God*, COQG 1 (Minneapolis: Fortress, 1992), 268–72, 299–301. Later followed by: idem, *Jesus and the Victory of God*, COQG 2 (Minneapolis: Fortress, 1996), xvii–xviii, 126–7, 203–6, 246–51, 576–7; idem., "In Grateful Dialogue: A Response," in *Jesus & the Restoration of Israel: A Critical Assessment of N.T. Wright's Jesus and the Victory of God,* ed. Carey Newman and Craig A. Evans (Downers Grove, IL: InterVarsity Press, 1999), 244–77; and idem, *Paul and the Faithfulness of God*, 2 vols., COQG 4 (Minneapolis: Fortress, 2013), 1:139–63.

5. See, for example, the various essays in Carey C. Newman, ed., *Jesus and the Restoration of Israel: A Critical Assessment of N.T. Wright's Jesus and the Victory of God* (Downers Grove, IL: InterVarsity Press, 1999).

6. For example, Robert P. Carroll, "Exile? What Exile? Deportation and the Discourses of Diaspora," in *Leading Captivity Captive: The "Exile" as History and Ideology*, ed. Lester L. Grabbe, JSOTSup 278 (Sheffield: Sheffield Academic, 1998), 62–79; Charles C. Torrey, *The Composition and Historical Value of Ezra-Nehemiah*, BZAW 2 (Giessen: J. Ricker, 1896), 51–65.

7. For example, Maurice Casey, "Where Wright is Wrong: A Critical Review of N.T. Wright's Jesus and the Victory of God," *JSNT* 69 (1998): 95–103; Clive Marsh, "Theological History? N. T. Wright's Jesus and the Victory of God," *JSNT* 69 (1998): 77–94; Brant Pitre, *Jesus, the Tribulation, and the End of the Exile: Restoration Eschatology and the Origin of the Atonement,* WUNT 2/204 (Tübingen: Mohr Siebeck, 2005), 35–8; Steven M. Bryan, *Jesus and Israel's Traditions of Judgement and Restoration,* SNTSMS 117 (Cambridge: Cambridge University Press, 2002), 12–20.

8. See, for example, Ackroyd, *Exile and Restoration*, 237–47 (esp. 243). More recently, see Martien A. Halvorson-Taylor, *Enduring Exile: The Metaphorization of Exile in the Hebrew Bible*, VTSup 141 (Leiden: Brill, 2011), who argues that the metaphorical use of "exile" was not a later development, but developed in pre-exilic Israel in response to the *threat* of exile.

9. Maurice Casey asserts that exile is inextricably linked to geography and no one living in his homeland could be in exile ("Where Wright is Wrong," 99–100).

10. Wright, *JVG*, xviii.

11. Idem, "In Grateful Dialogue," 259.

12. Idem, *NTPG*, 269–70.

13. *Jesus, the Tribulation, and the End of the Exile: Restoration Eschatology and the Origin of the Atonement*, WUNT 2/204 (Tübingen: Mohr Siebeck, 2005), 35.

14. Ibid., 35. Referring to Wright's definition in *NTPG*, 268–9.

15. *The Restoration of Israel: Israel's Re-Gathering and the Fate of the Nations in Early Jewish Literature and Luke-Acts*. BZNW 138 (Berlin: De Gruyter, 2006), 26. Emphasis his.

16. See, James M. Scott, "'For as Many as Are of Works of the Law Are under a Curse' (Galatians 3:10)," in *Paul and the Scriptures of Israel*, ed. James A. Sanders and Craig A. Evans, JSNTSup 83 (Sheffield: Sheffield Academic, 1993), 213. Notwithstanding Wright's chastened skepticism (*PFG*, 139n63).

17. On Paul's textual, hermeneutical, and theological use here, see Mark Seifrid, "Romans," in *Commentary on the New Testament Use of the Old Testament*, ed. G. K. Beale and D. A. Carson (Grand Rapids: Baker Academic, 2007), 672–9.

18. See chapter 3.

19. Only consider texts which were likely written before the writing of Romans will be considered.

20. The brevity of this survey ought not be taken as an attempt to smooth out the unique voice or contribution of any individual book. Despite my argument below that Isaiah reflects the influence of Deuteronomy, my conclusion is *not* that Isaiah says nothing more than Deuteronomy, but that the two voices complement one another in a unified foundation in the Hebrew Bible upon which Paul's thought is grounded.

21. Kenneth J. Turner, "Deuteronomy's Theology of Exile," in *For Our Good Always: Studies on the Message and Influence of Deuteronomy in Honor of Daniel I. Block*, ed. Jason S. DeRouchie, Jason Gile, and Kenneth J. Turner (Winona Lake, IN: Eisenbrauns, 2013), 190.

22. On the so-called triangle of ancient Near-Eastern relationships among god-people-land, see Daniel I. Block, *The Gods of the Nations: Studies in Ancient Near Eastern National Theology*, ETSStud 2 (Grand Rapids: Baker Academic, 2000), ch. 3.

23. Turner, "Deuteronomy's Theology of Exile," 195.

24. Peter M. Head, "The Curse of Covenant Reversal: Deuteronomy 28:58-68 and Israel's Exile," *Churchman* 111 (1997): 224–5. Cf. Joseph Blenkinsopp, "Deuteronomy," *NJBC*, 106.

25. Kenneth J. Turner, *The Death of Deaths in the Death of Israel: Deuteronomy's Theology of Exile* (Eugene, OR: Wipf & Stock, 2011), 75.

26. Ibid., 225.

27. For further discussion regarding the variant reading of "sons," see Brandon D. Crowe, *The Obedient Son: Deuteronomy and Christology in the Gospel of Matthew*, BZNW 188 (Berlin: De Gruyter, 2012), 109–10.

28. In light of the possible connection to Gen 1-3, the choice of MT אֲדָמָה in place of אֶרֶץ is noteworthy.

29. Crowe, *The Obedient Son*, 94.

30. Ibid., 94. Cf. John J. Schmitt, "Israel as Son of God in Torah," *BTB* 34 (2004): 69–79.

31. Seth D. Postell, *Adam as Israel: Genesis 1–3 as the Introduction to the Torah and Tanakh* (Eugene, OR: Pickwick, 2011), 136–48.

32. He cites: Gen 1:1, 15, 17, 20, 26, 28, 30; 2:1, 4; Deut 32:1; see also 33:13.

33. Postell, *Adam as Israel,* 136. He lists numerous lexical correspondences (not all of which are equally convincing) in pp. 136–8.

34. For example, N. T. Wright, *The Climax of the Covenant: Christ and the Law in Pauline Theology* (Edinburgh: T&T Clark, 1991), 21–2.

35. See chapter 3.

36. For the purposes of this study, "Isaiah" is intended to refer to the canonical form of the prophetic book or, less frequently, to the individual.

37. G. P. Hugenberger, "The Servant of the Lord in the 'Servant Songs' of Isaiah: A Second Moses Figure," in *The Lord's Anointed: Interpretation of Old Testament Messianic Texts*, ed. P. E. Satterthwaite, R. S. Hess, and G. J. Wenham, TynHS (Grand Rapids: Baker, 1995), 124.

38. Despite disagreement, scholars have increasingly recognized the thematic unity of the whole of Isaiah, often apart from the question of authorship. See Marvin A. Sweeney, "The Book of Isaiah in Recent Research," *CurBS* 1 (1993): 141–62; Ronald E. Clements, "The Unity of the Book of Isaiah," *Int* 36 (1982): 117–29; Christopher R. Seitz, "Isaiah 1–66: Making Sense of the Whole," in *Reading and Preaching the Book of Isaiah* (Philadelphia: Fortress, 1988), 105–26; O. Palmer Robertson, *The Christ of the Prophets* (Phillipsburg, NJ: P&R, 2004), 212–40.

39. Robertson, *Christ of the Prophets,* 229.

40. Ibid., 219–20. The majority of commentators hold this positive view of Isa 6:13b. G. K. Beale, however, has argued a negative interpretation of this passage that the "holy seed" is the unfaithful remnant of Israel and not a symbol of restoration at all, but of judgment (see G. K. Beale, *We Become What We Worship: A Biblical Theology of Idolatry* [Downers Grove, IL: IVP Academic, 2008], 51–64).

41. H. G. M. Williamson, "Deuteronomy and Isaiah," in *For Our Good Always: Studies on the Message and Influence of Deuteronomy in Honor of Daniel I. Block* (Winona Lake, IN: Eisenbrauns, 2013), 251–68.

42. See Benjamin D. Sommer, *A Prophet Reads Scripture: Allusion in Isaiah 40–66* (Stanford, CA: Stanford University Press, 1998), 132–4.

43. See Thomas A. Keiser, "The Song of Moses a Basis for Isaiah's Prophecy," *VT* 55 (2005): 486–500; Ronald Bergey, "The Song of Moses (Deuteronomy 32.1–43) and Isaianic Prophecies: A Case of Early Intertextuality?," *JSOT* 28 (2003): 33–54.

44. See, for example, James M. Scott, "Paul's Use of Deuteronomic Tradition," *JBL* 112 (1993): 645–65. The profound influence of Isaiah upon Paul is well recognized (See, e.g., Florian Wilk, *Die Bedeutung des Jesajabuches für Paulus*, FRLANT 179 [Göttingen: Vandenhoeck & Ruprecht, 1998]; J. Ross Wagner, *Heralds of the Good News: Isaiah and Paul "in Concert" in the Letter to the Romans*, NovTSup 101 [Leiden: Brill, 2002]). J. Ross Wagner lists no fewer than sixteen marked citations of Isaiah in Romans ("Moses and Isaiah in Concert: Paul's Reading of Isaiah and Deuteronomy in the Letter to the Romans," in *"As Those Who Are Taught": The Interpretation of Isaiah from the LXX to the SBL* [Atlanta: Society of Biblical

Literature, 2006], 87–105). The majority of these citations occur in Rom 9–11 which specifically addresses the question of Jewish restoration (e.g., Rom 9:27–28; 11:1–2). However, the previous section of Romans (5:1–8:39) sets the context for restoration by discussing reconciliation to God and its significance. Beginning with Rom 4:25, which functions as a transitional verse in Paul's argument, Shiu-Lun Shum has identified six possible allusions to Isaiah, several of which directly relate to Isaianic restoration prophecies (*Paul's Use of Isaiah in Romans: A Comparative Study of Paul's Letter to the Romans and the Sibylline and Qumran Sectarian Texts*, WUNT 2/156 [Tübingen: Mohr Siebeck, 2002], x, and throughout. Shum argues that Rom 4:25 alludes to Isa 53:6, 11, 12; Rom 5:1 alludes to Isa 32:17; Rom 5:6, 8b allude to Isa 53:8; Rom 5:19b alludes to Isa 53:11; Rom 8:32 alludes to Isa 53:6; and Rom 8:31b, 33–34 alludes to Isa 50:8–9).

45. Notwithstanding the ongoing debate regarding the specific identity or number of servants, I argue that the Apostle Paul identifies him singularly in Rom 4:25 as Jesus Christ (see ch. 4). Because of Paul's identification and the NT focus of this study, it will not be necessary to engage with such debates further. For a survey of interpretive options, see Hugenberger, "The Servant of the Lord," 106–19 and literature cited.

46. See ibid., 129–38.

47. See, for example, J. De Regt Lénart, "Language, Structure, and Strategy in Isaiah 53:1–6: אָכֵן, Word Order, and the Translator," in *Tradition and Innovation in Biblical Interpretation: Studies Presented to Professor Eep Talstra on the Occasion of His Sixty-Fifth Birthday*, ed. E. Talstra, W. Th van Peursen, and J. W. Dyk (Leiden: Brill, 2011), 419; Anthony R. Ceresko, "The Rhetorical Strategy of the Fourth Servant Song (Isaiah 52:13–53:12): Poetry and the Exodus-New Exodus," *CBQ* 56 (1994): 53.

48. Ceresko, "Rhetorical Strategy," 49–50.

49. Rikki E. Watts, "Messianic Servant or the End of Israel's Exilic Curses?: Isaiah 53.4 in Matthew 8.17," *JSNT* 38 (2015): 90; Ceresko, "Rhetorical Strategy," 49–50.

50. Ceresko, "Rhetorical Strategy," 47–9. See these pages for the remainder of the paragraph.

51. On the corporate solidarity of Israel and the servant, see Hugenberger, "The Servant of the Lord," 105–40.

52. Robertson, *Christ of the Prophets,* 225. Cf. Richard Bauckham, *God Crucified: Monotheism and Christology in the New Testament* (Grand Rapids: Eerdmans, 1998), 49–51.

53. See Rikki E. Watts, *Isaiah's New Exodus and Mark*, WUNT 2/88 (Tübingen: Mohr Siebeck, 1997), 53–90.

54. Richard J. Clifford, "Isaiah 40–66," in *HBC*, ed. James Luther Mays (San Francisco: Harper & Row, 1988), 584, quoted in Ceresko, "Rhetorical Strategy," 54.

55. Hugenberger, "The Servant of the Lord," 115–6. See these pages for the following parallels.

56. Hugenberger describes it as a "limited topological (material)" restoration (ibid., 125).

57. See Richard L. Schultz, "Intertextuality, Canon, and 'Undecidability': Understanding Isaiah's 'New Heavens and New Earth' (Isaiah 65:17–25)," *BBR* 20 (2010): 31–7.

58. Robertson, *Christ of the Prophets,* 222–3.

59. Ibid., 224.

60. Ben C. Ollenburger writes, "In II Isaiah's terms . . . the restoration of cosmic order [which is defined as 'the righteousness that belongs to the cosmic realm'] entails the restoration of Zion/Jerusalem" ("Isaiah's Creation Theology," 68).

61. Preston M. Sprinkle, *Paul and Judaism Revisited: A Study of Divine and Human Agency in Salvation* (Downers Grove, IL: IVP Academic, 2013), 60.

62. For a detailed analysis of Ezekiel's use of Deuteronomy, see Dalit Rom-Shiloni, "Deuteronomic Concepts of Exile Interpreted in Jeremiah and Ezekiel," in *Birkat Shalom*, vol. 1 (Winona Lake, IN: Eisenbrauns, 2008), 111–23. For Ezekiel's use of Leviticus, see Michael A. Lyons, *From Law to Prophecy: Ezekiel's Use of the Holiness Code*, LHBOTS 507 (New York: T&T Clark, 2009), 117–22, 183–4. Cf. also Jason Gile, "Deuteronomy and Ezekiel's Theology of Exile," in *For Our Good Always: Studies on the Message and Influence of Deuteronomy in Honor of Daniel I. Block* (Winona Lake, IN: Eisenbrauns, 2013), 287–306; Daniel Gile, "Ezekiel 16 and the Song of Moses: A Prophetic Transformation?," *JBL* 130 (2011): 87–108.

63. J. Gile, "Deuteronomy and Ezekiel's Theology of Exile," 288–9, 291–3.

64. Ibid., 288–9.

65. For example, Risa Levitt Kohn has demonstrated an intricate interweaving of Deuteronomy and Leviticus throughout Ezek 20:1–44 (*A New Heart and a New Soul: Ezekiel, the Exile and the Torah*, JSOTSup 358 [London: Sheffield Academic, 2002], 98–103), 96–104.

66. My translation of the Göttingen LXX with reference to the MT. The Greek θάνατος, can signify "sickness leading to death" (see my discussion in chapter 6). In light of the MT, דֶּבֶר ("pestilence"), I have translated θάνατος accordingly.

67. Lyons, *From Law to Prophecy,* 94. "Famine" (λιμός) does not explicitly occur but is conceptually present in the Lev 26:26 reference to an absence of food (ibid.).

68. Ibid.

69. J. Gile notes that Num 24:8 also refers to Yahweh using arrows against non-Israelites ("Deuteronomy and Ezekiel's Theology of Exile," 103n67).

70. J. Gile, "Deuteronomy and Ezekiel's Theology of Exile," 104 following Ka Leung Wong, *The Idea of Retribution in the Book of Ezekiel*, VTSup 87 (Leiden: Brill, 2001), 94.

71. Scott, "For as Many," 208.

72. This language reflects Odil H. Steck's division of Second Temple Judaism into two antithetical strands of restoration expectation. He argued for the presence of two antithetical strands of restoration expectation during the Second Temple period. Whereas the "theocratic" strand expected the political restoration of the kingdom of Israel and the reestablishment of the temple cult, the "eschatological" strand believed that Israel's exile would continue until Yahweh atoned for Israel's sin and himself

returned to Zion (Odil H. Steck, "Das Problem theologischer Strömungen in nachexilischer Zeit," *EvT* 28 [1968]: 445–58).

73. Fuller, *The Restoration of Israel,* 23.

74. Otto Plöger, *Theocracy and Eschatology*, trans. S. Rudman (Richmond: John Knox Press, 1968), 42.

75. Joseph Blenkinsopp, *Ezra-Nehemiah: A Commentary,* OTL (Philadelphia: Westminster Press, 1988), 305.

76. My translation of the MT.

77. Blenkinsopp, *Ezra-Nehemiah,* 307.

78. My translation of the MT.

79. Ibid.

80. J. G. McConville, "Ezra-Nehemiah and the Fulfillment of Prophecy," *VT* 36 (1986): 206–7, 18–9 (213–24). The remainder of this paragraph will draw from these pages.

81. See McConville's chart of eight allusions to Jeremiah, ibid., 215. Cf. idem, *Grace in the End: A Study of Deuteronomic Theology* (Grand Rapids: Zondervan, 1993), 123–44.

82. Ibid.

83. Ibid., 220.

84. Ibid., 219.

85. Blenkinsopp, *Ezra-Nehemiah*, 139.

86. Michael A. Knibb, "Exile in the Literature of the Intertestamental Period," *HeyJ* 17 (1976): 268.

87. φυγή is a standard word for exile in the first century. See Louis H. Feldman, "The Concept of Exile in Josephus," in *Exile: Old Testament, Jewish, and Christian Conceptions*, ed. James M. Scott, JSJsup 56 (Leiden: Brill, 1997), 145–6.

88. Fuller, *The Restoration of Israel,* 91 (86–101).

89. Feldman, "The Concept of Exile in Josephus," 146.

90. See, Colson (Philo, On *Rewards and Punishments,* trans. F. H. Colson, LCL, 115 note c).

91. Feldman, "The Concept of Exile in Josephus," 149.

92. Betsy Halpern-Amaru, *Rewriting the Bible: Land and Covenant in Post-Biblical Jewish Literature* (Valley Forge, PA: Trinity Press International, 1994), 96–115 (esp. 95).

93. Feldman, "Exile in Josephus," 152.

94. John M. G. Barclay, *Jews in the Mediterranean Diaspora: From Alexander to Trajan (323 BCE - 117 CE)* (Edinburgh: T&T Clark, 1996), 347.

95. Fuller, *The Restoration of Israel,* 28. My emphasis.

96. Ibid., 28–9.

97. Tobit 12–14's dependence upon Deuteronomy is well recognized. See Alexander A. Di Lella, "The Deuteronomic Background of the Farewell Discourse in Tob 14:3–11," *CBQ* 41 (1979): 380–9; Carey A. Moore, *Tobit: A New Translation with Introduction and Commentary*, AB 40A (New York: Doubleday, 1996), 284–5; Steven Weitzman, "Allusion, Artifice, and Exile in the Hymn of Tobit," *JBL* 115 (1996): 49–61.

98. This and subsequent translations by Moore, *Tobit.*

99. This and the previous allusion are noted by Steven Weitzman, who argues that the content is "clearly" drawn from Deut 32 ("Allusion, Artifice, and Exile," 53–4).

100. The RSV makes the two part construction clearer: "and they will rebuild the house of God, though it will not be like the former one until the times of the age are completed. After this they will return from the places of their captivity, and will rebuild Jerusalem in splendor. And the house of God will be rebuilt there with a glorious building for all generations for ever, just as the prophets said of it" (Tob 14:5).

101. Martin G. Abegg, "Exile in the Dead Sea Scrolls," in *Exile: Old Testament, Jewish, and Christian Conceptions*, ed. James M. Scott, JSJsup 56 (Leiden: Brill, 1997), 111–25 (115).

102. Or communities. Whether there were multiple groups represented by the DSS is beyond the present focus. The singular, "community," will be used as a convention and is not intended to assert unity which may not have existed. In addition, this study will refrain from identifying the sectarians as "the Essenes" following Philip R. Davies, "The Birthplace of the Essenes: Where Is 'Damascus'?," *RevQ* 14 (1990): 503–19 (esp. 506–8).

103. See 4Q158 XIV, 5–8; 4Q383 I, 1–2, 5; 4Q365 XXV, 2; 4Q379 XII, 3–5; 11QT LIV, 16 (Deut 13:6); LXI, 14 (Deut 20:1).

104. See 4Q372 I, 2–5; 4Q371 I, 8–9.

105. Abegg, "Exile in the Dead Sea Scroll," 125.

106. The text and translation of CD and all DSS are drawn from Florentino García Martínez and Eibert J. C. Tigchelaar, eds., *The Dead Sea Scrolls Study Edition*, 2 vols. (Leiden: Brill, 1997).

107. The community's identification as the remnant is a recurring theme. Cf. CD II, 4–5; III, 19–IV, 3; VI, 2–7.

108. Shemaryahu Talmon, "Waiting for the Messiah: The Spiritual Universe of the Qumran Covenanters," in *Judaisms and Their Messiahs at the Turn of the Christian Era*, ed. Jacob Neusner, William Scott Green, and Ernest S. Frerichs (Cambridge: Cambridge University Press, 1988), 116–7. Similarly, J. G. Campbell writes, "CD does not mention the sixth century BCE return directly, because the writer considered the exile to have ceased only with the foundation of his own community" ("Essene-Qumran Origins in the Exile: A Scriptural Basis?," *JJS* 46 [1995]: 148).

109. Ibid., 117.

110. Cf. similar plant imagery in Jer 24:6; 31:28 (38:28 LXX); 32:41 (39:41 LXX); 42:10 (49:10 LXX); *1 En.* 93.10.

111. Mark Adam Elliott, *The Survivors of Israel: A Reconsideration of the Theology of Pre-Christian Judaism* (Grand Rapids: Eerdmans, 2000), 541.

112. Lawrence H. Schiffman, "The Concept of Restoration in the Dead Sea Scrolls," in *Restoration: Old Testament, Jewish, and Christian Perspectives*, ed. James M. Scott, JSJsup 72 (Leiden: Brill, 2001), 205.

113. The Greek versification makes it appear as if vv. 14–15 are omitted when no text at all is missing. The verse numbers 14 and 15 are not used in Sir 36 LXX.

114. *On Earth as in Heaven: The Restoration of Sacred Time and Sacred Space in the Book of Jubilees* (Leiden: Brill, 2005), 165.

115. Translations of *Jubilees* by Wintermute, OTP 2.

116. Davenport, *Eschatology*, 27.

117. See Brunson, *Psalm 118 in the Gospel of John*, 66–8.

118. Scott, *On Earth as in Heaven,* 165.

119. Ibid.

120. George W. E. Nickelsburg, *Jewish Literature between the Bible and the Mishnah: A Historical and Literary Introduction* (Minneapolis: Fortress, 1981), 109.

121. Hans-Peter Rüger, "Apokryphen I," *TRE* 3:307.

122. Odil H. Steck, *Das Apokryphe Baruchbuch: Studien Zu Rezeption Und Konzentration "Kanonischer" Überlieferung*, FRLANT 160 (Göttingen: Vandenhoeck & Ruprecht, 1993), 80.

123. All references to Baruch are my own translation of the Göttingen LXX.

124. Nicholas Perrin, "Exile," in *The World of the New Testament: Cultural, Social, and Historical Contexts*, ed. Joel B. Green and Lee Martin McDonald (Grand Rapids: Baker Academic, 2013), 26.

125. There are numerous studies on exile or restoration in the Gospels. See, for example, Nicholas G. Piotrowski, *Matthew's New David at the End of Exile: A Socio-Rhetorical Study of Scriptural Quotations*, NovTsup 117 (Leiden: Brill, 2016); Fuller, *The Restoration of Israel*, 197–253; John A. Dennis, *Jesus' Death and the Gathering of True Israel: The Johannine Appropriation of Restoration Theology in the Light of John 11:47-52*, WUNT 2/217 (Tübingen: Mohr Siebeck, 2006), 213–318; Douglas S. Mccomiskey, "Exile and the Purpose of Jesus' Parables (Mark 4:10–12; Matt 13:10–17; Luke 8:9–10)," *JETS* 51 (2008): 59–85.

126. See W. M. Beuken, "Servant and Herald of Good Tidings: Isaiah 61 as an Interpretation of Isaiah 40–55," in *Book of Isaiah-Le Livre d'Isaïe. les oracles et leurs relectures. unité et complexité de l'ouvrage*, ed. J. Vermeylen, BETL 81 (Leuven: Leuven University Press, 1989), 411–42. Cf. Bernard Gosse, "L'année de grâce du Seigneur selon Is 61,1-2a et sa citation en Lc 4,18-19," *Science et Esprit* 69 (2017): 91–106.

127. John D. W. Watts, *Isaiah 34–66*, WBC 25 (Waco, TX: Thomas Nelson, 2000), 873.

128. Watts, "Messianic Servant," 81–95. Cf. idem, *Isaiah's New Exodus*.

129. David W. Pao and Eckhard J. Schnabel, "Luke," in *Commentary on the New Testament Use of the Old Testament*, ed. G. K. Beale and D. A. Carson (Grand Rapids: Baker Academic, 2007), 271–3. Cf. Larry R. Helyer, "Luke and the Restoration of Israel," *JETS* 36 (1993): 317–29; David W. Pao *Acts and the Isaianic New Exodus*. WUNT 2/130 (Tübingen: Mohr Siebeck, 2000), ch. 7.

130. Victor Paul Furnish, "Elect Sojourners in Christ: An Approach to the Theology of 1 Peter," *PSTJ* 28 (1975): 3.

131. Charles Bigg, *A Critical and Exegetical Commentary on The Epistles of St. Peter and St. Jude*, ICC (Edinburgh: T&T Clark, 1978), 88.

132. Peter H. Davids, *The First Epistle of Peter,* NICNT (Grand Rapids: Eerdmans, 1990), 48.

133. Mark Dubis, *1 Peter: A Handbook on the Greek Text* (Waco, TX: Baylor University Press, 2010), 3; J. Ramsey Michaels, *1 Peter,* WBC 49 (Waco, TX: Word Books, 1988), 11.

134. See Oren R. Martin, *Bound for the Promised Land: The Land Promise in God's Redemptive Plan*, NSBT 34 (Downers Grove, IL: InterVarsity Press, 2015), 140–8.

135. The classic study of the theme of an eschatological journey towards rest in Hebrews is Ernst Käsemann, *The Wandering People of God: An Investigation of the Letter to the Hebrews*, trans. R. A. Harrisville and I. L. Sundberg (Minneapolis: Augsburg, 1984). For more recent studies, see David M. Allen, *Deuteronomy and Exhortation in Hebrews: A Study in Narrative Re-Presentation,* WUNT 2/238 (Tübingen: Mohr Siebeck, 2008); Benjamin Dunning, "The Intersection of Alien Status and Cultic Discourse in the Epistle to the Hebrews," in *Hebrews: Contemporary Methods—New Insights,* ed. G. Gelardini (Leiden: Brill, 2005), 179–98; Thomas R. Schreiner, *Commentary on Hebrews*, BTCP (Nashville, TN: Holman Reference, 2015), 32–3, 491–3; Matthew Thiessen, "Hebrews 12.5–13, the Wilderness Period, and Israel's Discipline," *NTS* 55 (2009): 366–79.

## *Chapter 3*

# Adam's Curse as Exile in the Hebrew Bible and Jewish Literature

The previous chapter outlined a variety of views of ongoing exile which existed during the Second Temple period. I argued that a basis for those beliefs naturally arose from the Hebrew Bible. The idea of ongoing exile is present in Ezra-Nehemiah, is prominent in the Prophets, and finds its canonical foundation in the books of Moses. This chapter will show that Israel's exile was also prefigured in Gen 1–3 where Adam forfeits the blessings of the Edenic land and the relationship with God he enjoyed in it. Adam's dignity and loss becomes a pattern in the history of redemption. Israel is also called God's son and receives the Adamic commission to be a blessing. But, Israel fails and falls just as Adam did. From the perspective of the storyline of the Hebrew Bible, Israel's covenant breaking and exile is a recapitulation of Adam's transgression and its result. I will demonstrate the literary and redemptive-historical connection between Israel's exile and Adam's expulsion from Eden.

I will first sketch the general relationship between Israel and Adam, before proceeding to Adam's removal from Eden as the paradigm for Israel's exile. From there, I will survey the Adam tradition in Second Temple Judaism, giving particular attention to the categories of Adam's protological role and its frustration. Finally, I will move to give an overview of Adam's presence in the NT before narrowing my focus to Paul and Romans.

### ISRAEL AS ADAM

The beginning of the Hebrew Bible ascribes enormous dignity to Adam (and to humanity in him).[1] God forms Adam (אָדָם; LXX: ἄνθρωπον) in his image (צֶלֶם; LXX: εἰκόνα) and likeness (דְמוּת; LXX: ὁμοίωσιν) and commissions him to have dominion over the rest of creation (Gen 1:26–28). Adam is like the creator but is not to be identified with him—as a son is analogous to his father (Luke 3:38; cf. Gen 5:1–3).[2] By explicit reference, Adam plays a relatively minor role beyond the early chapters of Genesis.[3] But, in many ways, Israel recapitulates the story of Adam in its own history.[4] The nation corporately assumes Adam's role. Like Adam, Yahweh draws Israel from the disordered waters (Deut 32:10–11; cf. Gen 1:2) and promises the people a paradisiacal land (Gen 2:8). The descriptions of Eden in Gen 2:9–14 closely resemble those of Canaan in Deut 8:8–10 and 11:10–11. Like Adam, Israel is given a commission involving blessing for obedience and cursing for disobedience. Indeed, scholars have observed that elements of Adam's commission recur in the Abrahamic blessing.[5] No longer as a command, but now as promise, God tells Abram, "I will bless you" and "in you all the families of the earth will be blessed" (Gen 12:2–3; cf. 17:2, 6, 8; 22:17–18). He promises to multiply Abraham, make him "exceedingly fruitful," and give his descendants the land of his sojourning (Gen 17:2, 6, 8).[6] This land is described in Gen 13:10 as "like the paradise of God" (ὡς ὁ παράδεισος τοῦ θεου).[7] Abraham (and the people who come from him) is a "second Adam."[8] The rest of Genesis regularly reiterates what Beale calls the "promissory application" of the Adamic commission.[9]

As Genesis closes and Exodus begins, promise begins to turn to early fulfillment. Israel becomes fruitful (Exod 1:7, 12, 20; cf. Gen 48:3–4). They begin to fill the world as Adam was originally tasked to do. In the early chapters of Exodus, Israel begins to be treated as a unit, a corporate figure. When Moses arrives in Egypt to deliver Yahweh's demand, the rationale is that "Israel is my [Yahweh's] firstborn son" (υἱὸς πρωτότοκός μου Ισραηλ, Exod 4:22).[10] The nation of Israel, which has received the Adamic commission through Abraham, is now called Yahweh's *son*, following Adam's role as image-bearer.[11] From this point forward, all imperatives directed toward Israel from God in the Pentateuch are in the masculine singular.[12] The motif of Israel as son continues through Leviticus and Numbers and is especially emphasized in Deuteronomy.[13] Moses describes Yahweh's care for Israel in the wilderness as "a man carrying his son" (ὡς εἴ τις τροφοφορήσει ἄνθρωπος τὸν υἱὸν αὐτοῦ, Deut 1:31). In Deut 8:5 Moses warns Israel, "as a man disciplines his son, in this manner the Lord your God disciplines you" (ὡς εἴ τις παιδεύσαι ἄνθρωπος τὸν υἱὸν αὐτοῦ οὕτως κύριος ὁ θεός σου παιδεύσει σε, Deut 8:5). Israel's sonship is again affirmed in Deut 14:1 in order to provide a basis for obedience to the holiness laws being given.[14] The sonship of Israel is also a key theme of the Song of Moses in Deut 32.[15]

Yahweh informs Moses of Israel's future infidelity and exile (Deut 31:16–18) and instructs Moses to give the Song of Moses as both a warning and a prophecy (31:19–21). The Song (32:143) reiterates Yahweh's faithfulness as a father, in contrast to Israel's adolescent waywardness.[16] For instance, Deut 32:5 claims that the people have sinned and are no longer his sons (οὐκ αὐτῷ τέκνα; MT: לֹא בָּנָיו). In 32:10–11, the Song describes the formation of Israel in terms allusive (in Hebrew) of Gen 1. Referring to the exodus deliverance from Egypt but alluding to creation in Gen 1:2a, 32:10 describes Yahweh caring for Israel in the "empty wilderness" (MT: מִדְבָּר וּבְתֹהוּ). The rare word "emptiness" (תֹּהוּ) corresponds to the emptiness (תֹּהוּ) of creation before God spoke (Gen 1:2). Deuteronomy 32:11 describes Yahweh's *Shekinah* presence as "hovering" over its young in the wilderness (MT: רָחַף; cf. Gen 1:2b where the Spirit hovers [רָחַף] over the waters). In this manner, God's redemption of Israel, his son, is compared to his creation of the world, including Adam.[17] Thus, beginning the Pentateuch and ending it, Moses focuses upon God's son who was blessed, commissioned for faithfulness, but who would fail and forfeit the land of inheritance. As a corporate figure, Israel conforms to an Adamic pattern.

This conclusion is supported in later Judaism, where Israel's story is seen as a recapitulation of Adam's.[18] God's promise to Abraham and his seed reflects the progress of the story of redemption. Although there are clear differences,[19] there is sufficient exegetical evidence to recognize the role of divine son is bestowed upon both figures. Adam is, thus, a paradigm for future figures who, through a special relationship with Yahweh, would be asked to reveal him to the world (cf. Isa 42:6; 49:6; Rev 21:23–24).

## ADAM'S LOSS IN THE HEBREW BIBLE

The comparison of Adam and Israel as God's sons who each, *mutatis mutandis,* received the commission to be a blessing to the world also invites a comparison of the consequences of their failure to do so. Whereas much of the Jewish Scripture predicts or describes Israel's covenant breaking and exile, the Adam narrative anticipates the same story. Just as Israel violated God's covenant and received the consequent curse, there is good reason to conclude that Gen 1–3 describe a covenantal relationship which involved blessing for obedience and cursing for disobedience. Thus, in order to grasp fully the significance of Adam's loss, it is necessary to consider both what he already possessed in Eden and what he could have gained, both for himself and for the world.

First, contingent upon continued obedience, Adam enjoyed the land of Eden as its king and priest.[20] He knew the blessing of the earth's fruitfulness apart from curse and fellowship with God unhindered by sin. Adam and Eve were intended to image the invisible God in the garden and, by virtue of the command to multiply, they were likely expected to expand the holy realm to cover the world with God's presence.[21] This image-bearing function is related to the concept of glory in the Hebrew Bible. The כְּבוֹד יְהוָה regularly functions in a technical sense referring to visible manifestations of God's presence within creation.[22] In a general sense, all of creation demonstrates the glory of God (Ps 19:1). But, by virtue of the divine image, Adam surpassed the rest of creation. Robin Scroggs writes, "In Gen. 1 man, as εἰκὼν τοῦ θεοῦ, is that being who is most like God and who exercises God's vice-regency on earth. Jewish theology understood this when it claimed that before his fall Adam manifested glory, a glory originating, however, not with him but with God."[23] Indeed, reflecting God's likeness was Adam's filial duty as God's son (Gen 5:1, 3; Luke 3:38).[24] Meredith G. Kline writes, "the biblical exposition of the image of God is consistently in terms of a glory like the glory of God. The apostle Paul brings it all into focus when he describes man as 'the image and glory of God' (1 Cor 11:7)."[25]

Second, there was potential for still greater blessing. Adam's commission (Gen 1:26–28) is related to enjoying or more fully realizing the blessing before him. The commands to "be fruitful and multiply" (αὐξάνεσθε καὶ πληθύνεσθε; Gen 1:28), "fill the earth" (πληρώσατε τὴν γῆν), and "have dominion over it and rule" (κατακυριεύσατε αὐτῆς καὶ ἄρχετε) reflected mankind's role. Had Adam completed these tasks, it follows that his vocation would have adjusted.[26] Thus, Adam's likeness to God and his vocation are linked. His likeness to God enables his work and his work images God's presence.

The serpent's temptation is related to Adam's filial responsibility as image-bearer. The cunning suggestion, which clearly hit on an area of human desire, was that Adam and Eve would be *like* God (ἔσεσθε ὡς θεοὶ; MT: כֵּאלֹהִים, Gen 3:5). The serpent prompted rebellion against the holy God by leading Adam and Eve to believe they would become more conformed to *God's* image.[27] But, the result is implied by the literary relationship between the serpent who was cunning (ערום) and the man and woman who were naked (עֲרוֹם) and are then cursed (אָרוּר).[28] In grasping for greater likeness to God (which itself suggests that some degree of advancement was possible), Adam and Eve's action reflected the serpent rather than God. They obscured the image they already possessed and forfeited God's presence and their land.

The curse narrative (Gen 3:14–24) sums up the consequences of Adam's loss in Gen 3:23–4 with Adam's exile: God drove him out (ἐξέβαλεν) of the "the paradise of delight" (παραδείσου τῆς τρυφῆς). The use of ἐκβάλλω (MT: גרשׁ) to describe Adam's removal from Eden is significant. Ἐκβάλλω describes covenant dissolution. For instance, it can be used to denote divorce.[29] It is also used in the LXX idiomatically together with ἀπὸ προσώπου (to cast away from [someone's] face) to imitate the Hebrew idiom (cf. Gen 4:14; Exod 10:11; Deut 33:27).[30] This is likely significant due to its similarity with

Deuteronomic terminology for exile, "I will hide my face from them . . . for it is a perverted generation, sons (υἱοί) in whom is no faithfulness" (Deut 32:20; cf. 31:17–18). Ἐκβάλλω is also used in Deut 29:27 LXX to describe Israel's exile: "And the Lord drove them away from their lord in anger and wrath and exceedingly great provocation, and he cast them into another land" (καὶ ἐξῆρεν αὐτοὺς κύριος ἀπὸ τῆς γῆς αὐτῶν ἐν θυμῷ καὶ ὀργῇ καὶ παροξυσμῷ μεγάλῳ σφόδρα καὶ ἐξέβαλεν[31] αὐτοὺς εἰς γῆν ἑτέραν).

In the first instance of ἐκβάλλω in the NT (assuming Markan priority), Jesus is driven by the Spirit into the wilderness in a typological recapitulation of Adam's being driven from Eden.[32] After his triumph, and for the remainder of Mark's Gospel, ἐκβάλλω is principally used describing demonic exorcisms.[33] Although seemingly unrelated, it is likely that Christ's effectively resisting temptation and ministering in the power of the Spirit reflects is framed as reversing the effect of Adam's sin. Christ was first cast into the wilderness, but from that point forward it is the powers of evil that are cast out.[34]

In sum, Adam's loss in Eden was the loss of life, land, and God's presence in that land. The effect of Adam's transgression extended to the entire world. Genesis 3:17 shows that the curse against Adam included a curse (ἐπικατάρατος) upon the ground (ἡ γῆ; MT: אֲדָמָה). By virtue of his representative role over the first creation, the curse that removed mankind from Eden also resulted in what Paul will call the futility (ματαιότης) of creation (Rom 8:20).[35] Paul will argue that this futility is "because of the one who subjected it" (διὰ τὸν ὑποτάξαντα, Rom 8:20).

Having considered Adam's blessing and curse in Genesis, I will now turn to survey early Judaism's views of Adam leading up to the first century.

## THE USE OF THE ADAM TRADITION IN SECOND TEMPLE JUDAISM

Although the presence of Adam is muted in the Hebrew Bible, Adamic theology was actively developing during the Second Temple period.[36] Jewish literature made use of the Adam tradition for a variety of purposes that were not chiefly historical, but apologetic and ideological. Two broad patterns are significant to my argument in this study. Texts would either (1) honor Adam as the first man or (2) develop the consequences of his sin.[37] For example, Philo invokes Adam's transgression to explain human estrangement from the divine. Before his expulsion from Eden, Adam was believed to occupy a place of close proximity to the Creator which entailed a dignity beyond any that have lived since. Along with Eve, he was "clothed" in glory. The sin of Eden not only cost mankind the "glorious land," but their removal from God's presence also cost them the holy investiture. With respect to Jewish tradition, Adam's loss is centrally the loss of glory.[38] But, that original glory also functions as a paradigm for eschatological hope. There is an expectation in Second Temple Judaism that *Endzeit* would correspond to *Urzeit*, that Adam's glorious existence in God's presence in the garden would one day be realized again and somehow advanced.

Both of these uses of the Adam tradition are significant backgrounds for Paul in Romans. Humankind's original dignity in Adam stands in the background its estrangement from God and need for reconciliation. The obvious example is the causal relationship between Adam's transgression and the reign of Sin and Death in Rom 5:12–21 as well as the subsequent Adam-Christ parallels that are grounded in it (e.g., life/death, flesh/spirit, slavery/freedom). However, the influence of the Adam in Romans is more widespread. The correspondence of *Urzeit* to *Endzeit* that is common to the Adam tradition in early Judaism is also part of the argument in Romans. For example, Paul's assertion in Rom 3:23 that all have fallen short of the δόξα τοῦ θεοῦ is a reference to the Adam tradition.[39] Likewise, the hope of δόξα (Rom 5:2) and restoration to it reflect Paul's similar use of the Adam tradition which we will see in early Jewish writings.

## Adam's Dignity and Decline

Before his expulsion from Eden, Adam was believed to occupy a place of close proximity to the Creator which entailed a dignity beyond any that have lived since. That dignity is often expressed in terms of Adam's "glory." He and Eve were "clothed" in glory. Hence, the sin of Eden not only cost mankind the land, but the glory investiture.

Sirach is an example of a text that employs Adam because of his honor. It regularly refers to the Adam tradition (e.g., 14:17; 17:1–4; 24:28; 49:16), but never raises it for bare historical reasons. Rather, Adam functions anthropologically, to extrapolate to humanity or to develop the relationship between Adam and Israel. The most prominent example is the often-cited "glory of Adam" passage in Sir 49:16:

> Σημ καὶ Σηθ ἐν ἀνθρώποις ἐδοξάσθησαν, καὶ ὑπὲρ πᾶν ζῷον ἐν τῇ κτίσει Αδαμ
>
> Shem and Seth among men were glorified, and beyond every living thing in creation was Adam (glorified).[40]

The aim is not to interpret Genesis, but to claim Adam among Israel's patriarchs and so promote Israel's importance with respect to the rest of creation.[41] Ben Sira is primarily discussing *honor*. The broader context of Sir 49:16 (44:1–50:24) honors a series of Israel's ancestors. Forms of the δόξα word group occur thirty times throughout this section[42] which ascribes δόξα to Israel's patriarchs from Enoch (44:16), forward to Nehemiah (49:13), and back to Adam (49:16).

However, the δόξα in question is more than sociocultural honor, but a participation in the divine honor mankind had once enjoyed.[43] The section begins by observing that the Lord πολλὴν δόξαν ἔκτισεν ὁ κύριος τὴν μεγαλωσύνην αὐτοῦ ἀπ' αἰῶνος ("created much glory, his majesty from eternity," 44:2). The δόξα which the patriarchs of Israel share is a participation in God's majesty (cf. 49:8). And none shared so much δόξα as Adam before his fall. Thus, "glory" in Sirach is closely related to God's presence.

The foregoing discussion illustrates Adam's dignity, but Sirach also speaks to its decline. One of Sirach's central themes is the problem of Israel's exile and ignominy. Beginning with Solomon who "blemished his glory" (ἔδωκας μῶμον ἐν τῇ δόξῃ σου, 47:20), Sirach describes Israel's deterioration. The summary in Sir 49:4–5 is that the kings of Judah gave their glory to a strange nation (ἔδωκαν . . . τὴν δόξαν αὐτῶν ἔθνει ἀλλοτρίῳ). Therefore, the redemption mentioned in the final verse of this section (Sir 50:24) should be understood as an appeal for Israel's sins to be forgiven, specifically the sins that cause the exile to persist. Yet Israel should be assured that God will not allow exile to last forever, but will restore Israel to a glory beyond even that of David (Sir 47:1–11) to glory like Adam's.

Philo offers a different perspective on the use of the Adam tradition. His chief interest in the figure of Adam is as an exemplar of philosophical dualism. Nevertheless, dignity and decline remain central themes. It should come as no surprise that Philo articulates a hierarchy of creation with humanity at the top (*Creation* 65–88). He reasons that nothing in creation more resembles the divine than the first man (*Creation* 69, 134–6). Yet with each passing generation, humanity loses a measure of created dignity. The analogy he uses is a chain of copies where the greatest sculpture would be based upon the original, but each copy of a copy would be a degree less accurate (*Creation* 140–41). Philo attributes humanity's decline to Adam's interest in Eve, who was similar in form to himself but dissimilar. Whereas he should have been attracted to virtue, he chose woman. This was the "disaster" (κακοπραγία) that led to decline.[44] On this point, Philo aligns himself with the portion of Judaism that points to concupiscence as the primal sin (cf. *Apoc. Mos.* 19:3; *Apoc. Abr.* 23:6–11; *4 Macc.* 18:8–9):[45]

> Pleasure does not venture to bring her wiles and deceptions to bear on the man, but on the woman, and by her means on him . . . [Man's] Reason is forthwith ensnared and becomes a subject instead of a ruler, a slave [δοῦλος] instead of a master, an alien [φυγάς] instead of a citizen, and a mortal instead of an immortal [θνητὸς ἀντ' ἀθανάτου]. (*Creation* 166; cf. *Virtues* 203–5)

I quote at length in order to note the vocabulary employed to describe the decline from the created state. The reversal of original intent is clear: man was meant to rule, but was enslaved (δοῦλος). He was meant to be a citizen, but became an exile (φυγή). He was intended for immortality, but became subject to death. A few sections before, Philo terms the choice of woman instead of virtue as an "exchange" (ὑπαλλάσσω) of his intended estate for something less:[46]

> And this desire caused likewise pleasure to their bodies, which is the beginning of iniquities and transgressions, and it is owing to this that men have exchanged [ὑπαλλάσσω] their previously immortal [ἀθανάτος] and happy existence for one which is mortal [θνητός] and full of misfortune. (*Creation* 152)[47]

This description of human decline is similar to Paul's in Rom 1:18–32 where man exchanges (ἀλλάσσω) the glory of God for images of created things (Rom 1:23). The correspondence between Philo Paul does not prove dependence, but it does invite comparison. Both interpreters, drawing upon the Adam tradition in the first century, describe a fall from glory in terms of exchange from dignity for shame.

## *The Correspondence of* Endzeit *to* Urzeit

The examples of Sirach and Philo present Adam's initial dignity and the subsequent decline of humankind. However, early Jewish writings also envision a reversal where the fortunes of humanity will be restored. The eschatological vision often includes elements of the Adam tradition, reflecting a general belief in early Judaism that the eschatological last days (*Endzeit*) would conform to the pattern established by the first days (*Urzeit*).[48] For instance, a series of episodes in *Vita Adae et Evae*[49] lays out the decline of mankind as well as the manner of restoration. In *Apoc. Mos.* 20:1–2, Eve narrates the result of eating the forbidden fruit:

> And at that very moment my eyes were opened and I knew that I was naked of the righteousness with which I had been clothed. 2 And I wept saying, "Why have you done this to me, that I have been estranged from my glory with which I was clothed?"[50]

By this account, Eve possessed a protological glory that functioned like clothing. Upon its forfeiture, she had to seek physical clothing (*Apoc. Mos.* 20:3–5). The loss of righteousness coincided with the loss of glory; these in turn are closely linked to the loss of immortality.[51] Eve then speaks to Adam "unlawful words of transgression such as brought us down from great glory" (21:2). When Adam eats the fruit, he too forfeits the splendor of his innocence, exclaiming: "O Evil woman! Why have you wrought destruction among us? You have estranged me from the glory of God" (21:6). Juxtaposing their statements, I conclude that they both possessed a righteous glory that was derived from God.

In another scene where Eve again is deceived by the devil, she reproaches him, "Woe to you, O devil. Why do you assault us for nothing? What have you to do with us? What have we done to you, that you should pursue us with deceit? Why does your malice fall on us? Have we stolen your glory and made *you* to be without honor" (*Vita* 11:2–3, my emphasis)? Eve's rebuke implies that the devil has robbed them of glory and honor.

Of course, the loss of glory-righteousness and the loss of paradise go hand-in-hand. Adam's loss included the land of paradise from which he was cast (ἐκβάλλω; *Apoc. Mos.* 27:1; 29:1). But, as *Ap. Mos.* closes with Adam's burial, God promises restoration:

> Yet now I tell you that their joy shall be turned to sorrow, but your sorrow shall be turned into joy; and when that happens, I will establish you in your dominion on the throne of your seducer. (*Apoc. Mos.* 39:2)

*Endzeit* is patterned after *Urzeit*. The *LAE* envisions a renewed humanity that is reestablished to dominion over the world with the conditions of Eden restored and the shame of its loss removed.[52]

Similarly, the Adam theology of Qumran includes the notion of protological glory which was lost in the fall, exile from Eden, and an eschatological hope of restoration of both Eden and glory. One significant text in which the Adam theme arises is the Damascus Document (CD) III, 20. The broader context in CD II, 4–IV, 12b[53] is an argument that the Qumran community is the true heir of God's promises to Israel.[54] There are interpretive difficulties to this text which go beyond our focus.[55] However, what is clear is that the passage acknowledges the sin of God's people, but divine mercy to forgive and bless:

> 12 But with those who remained steadfast in God's precepts, 13 with those who were left from among them, God established his covenant with Israel for ever, revealing to them 14 hidden matters in which all Israel had gone astray. (CD-A III, 12–14)

> 18 But God, in his wonderful mysteries, atoned for their iniquities and pardoned their sin. 19 And he built for them a safe home in Israel, such as there has not been since ancient times, not even till 20 now. Those who remained steadfast in it will acquire eternal life, and all the glory of Adam is for them. As 21 God

> swore to them by means of Ezekiel the prophet saying: Ez. 44:15 "The priests and the levites and the sons of IV, 1 Zadok who maintained the service of my temple when the children of Israel strayed 2 far away from me; they shall offer me the fat and the blood." (CD-A III, 8b–IV, 2a)

The focus is not historical, but future toward the Eschaton. The "safe house" is most likely a reference the Davidic covenant (cf. 1 Sam 2:35; 25:28; 1 Kgs 11:38).[56] The future rewards of the covenant are described as "the glory of Adam" and "eternal life." This inheritance would accompany Israel's restoration from exile and the construction of the world-temple.[57] Michael Wise writes:

> The CD community and its heirs believed that, though they were now disenfranchised, they would inherit the land in the End of Days . . . The land would regain its Edenic luxuriance, and they would offer to God, for the first time since the beginning a proper worship . . . that [the author] and others like him could, as it were, return to Eden whence Adam was banished.[58]

From one perspective, the Adamic content of the sectarians' eschatology is precisely what might be expected. The community's worldview is shaped by *pesher* interpretation.[59] "Eschatology is like Adam" would have been a natural way to express hope for the undoing of sin and renewed blessing. Even so, the projection of *Israel's* future in the form of *Adam's* created state is striking. For the sectarians, the community's restoration from exile would be the reclamation of what Adam had lost. I argue that Paul makes a similar point in Romans. But, rather than merely restoring what was lost through Adam, by virtue of Christ's superiority to him (Rom 5:13–17), Paul announces restoration and the consummation of God's purposes in humanity.

## Summary of Adam in Second Temple Judaism

The Adam tradition was employed in early Jewish literature for a variety of purposes that were not chiefly historical, but apologetic and ideological. The tradition is used to claim honor for Israel as the first patriarch (Sirach), as an explanation of human estrangement from the divine (Philo), and as a paradigm for eschatological hope. Before his removal from Eden, Adam was believed to occupy a place of close proximity to the Creator which entailed a dignity—a glory—beyond any that have lived since. However, Adam's transgression resulted in the loss of land, glory, and proximity to the divine. Restoration to Adam's original glory is employed as a paradigm for eschatological hope. I have shown a general Jewish expectation that *Endzeit* would correspond to *Urzeit*, that Adam's idyllic existence in God's presence in the garden would one day be realized again and even advanced. Early Jewish writings (e.g., Sirach, DSS), and hence communities, saw the Jewish condition as one of continuing exile well beyond the construction of the Second Temple. The identity of that exile was informed by both Adam and Israel traditions. The deliverance for which they hoped was from both Israel's exile *and* the Edenic curse. Protology undergirded eschatology. It follows from these uses of the Adam tradition in Second Temple literature, to ask how Adam is employed in the NT. To this question we now turn.

## THE USE OF THE ADAM TRADITION IN THE NEW TESTAMENT

The subject of Adam in the NT naturally trends toward considering Paul's use of Adam, as it is the most clearly developed and frequently discussed. Indeed, outside of Pauline references, Adam is mentioned by name only twice (Luke 3:38; Jude 14). However, renewed interest in the use of the Hebrew Bible in the NT has resulted in numerous studies which find allusions to Adam, particularly in the Gospels. The presence of the Adam tradition in the NT may be viewed narrowly by explicit occurrence of the proper noun, Ἀδάμ, or broadly by literary allusion or theological reference to the Primeval History.

In contrast to the significance ascribed to Adam by biblical scholars and theologians—including Paul—the proper noun, Ἀδάμ, occurs only nine times in the NT (Luke 3:38; Rom 5:14a and 14b; 1 Cor 15:22, 45a and 45b; 1 Tim 2:13, 14; Jude 14). Every instance carries a historical reference, but to a greater or lesser degree most have an added typological significance. Jude 14 is an apparent example of the bare historical use: ἕβδομος ἀπὸ Ἀδὰμ Ἑνὼχ ("Enoch, the seventh from Adam"). The name Ἀδάμ is used to situate Ἑνὼχ historically and without a clear typological function.[60] Similarly, Luke 3:38 lists Jesus's genealogy going back to Adam. This links Jesus, not only with the Jews, but to all humanity.[61] There seems to be a deliberate comparison of Jesus, the Son of God (υἱὸς . . . τοῦ θεοῦ, Luke 4:3) with Adam, the son of God (Ἀδὰμ τοῦ θεοῦ, Luke 3:38). The juxtaposition of the genealogy (Luke 3:23–38) with Luke's temptation account (Luke 4:1–13) is notable.[62] The genealogy is immediately followed by the temptation narrative where Christ is tempted on the basis of his sonship. Just as Adam was filled with the breath of life (πνοὴν ζωῆς, Gen 2:7), Jesus was filled with the Spirit of God (πλήρης πνεύματος ἁγίου, Luke 4:1).[63] Scholars are likely correct in asserting that an Adam–Jesus typology underlies the passage.[64] I will discuss explicit references to Adam in the Pauline corpus in a later section.

The impact of Adam upon the NT cannot be consigned to explicit references. More frequently, it lies just beneath the surface, both in the Pauline corpus and outside it. For example, it has long been recognized that the Adam motif underlies the Markan temptation narrative. Even Joachim Jeremias grants that Jesus's temptation by Satan among the wild animals in the Markan temptation narrative (1:12–13; cf. par. Matt 4:1–11; Luke 4:1–13) is an instance of Adamic typology.[65] Nevertheless, scholars have been doubtful of an Adamic Christology in the Gospels, believing that this was developed later.[66] But, that reticence is diminishing. Recent studies have increasingly uncovered allusions to Adam in the Gospels.[67]

As Jeremias's conclusion suggests, a clear implicit reference to Adam in the Gospels is the Markan temptation account. Jesus lives among the wild animals (cf. Gen 2:19).[68] A deceiver also comes to tempt him. The temptations are related to his divine sonship as were Adam's.[69] In key details, however, the parallels are not identical but reversed. Adam's temptation was in paradise and resulted in being "cast out" (ἐκβάλλω, Gen 3:24 LXX) into the wilderness, whereas Jesus was first cast (ἐκβάλλω, Mk 1:12) into the wilderness where his temptation took place. Adam failed in paradise leading to an advance in the kingdom of Satan, but Jesus succeeded in the wilderness leading to the weakening of Satan's earthly power.[70] That weakening is illustrated by the sequence of the Gospel. Following Jesus's being cast (ἐκβάλλω, Mk 1:12) into the wilderness and subsequent triumph, it is the demons who begin to be cast out (ἐκβάλλω; cf. Mk 3:22–23).[71] Crowe concludes that the Gospel of Mark deliberately portray Jesus as an obedient Son of God in contrast to the first Adam's disobedience.[72] Similarly, scholars have found allusions to Adam in Luke 13:10–17[73] when Jesus straightened the bent woman and in Pilate's unusual declaration about Jesus in John 19:5, ἰδοὺ ὁ ἄνθρωπος ("Behold, the man").[74]

Such instances are typically developed in isolation from one another and are not employed to argue for a broader theology. However, some scholars have recently suggested that Adam's presence in the Gospels goes beyond isolated instances to include an early Adamic Christology.[75] As Joel William Parkman argued, "The fact that Paul's Adam Christology shows signs of being not particularly Pauline but a part of a larger common tradition, plus the appearance of Adam Christology in Hebrews, suggests the widespread existence and importance of this biblical theme."[76] Yongbom Lee has argued that this early Adamic Christology is a potential source of Paul's more developed theology of Jesus as the glorious last Adam.[77] Similarly, Dan G. McCartney argues that the arrival of the Kingdom of God in the work of Jesus Christ is the "reinstatement of the originally intended divine order for earth" where mankind functions as God's regent.[78] He argues that this is Adamic in kind but more advanced in that the prelapsarian purpose is fulfilled in Christ.[79] Thus, while not widely held, a fuller recognition of Adamic Christology has been noted in the Gospels.

## ADAM IN THE PAULINE CORPUS

There is evidence for the influence of Adam traditions outside of the Pauline corpus, but there should be no doubt that Pauline thought represents its most developed NT form. In addition to Rom 5, the Pauline corpus explicitly references Adam in 1 Cor 15:22, 45a, 45b, and 1 Tim 2:13, 14.[80] Beyond these, there is further evidence of allusions to Gen 1–3 and a correspondence of *Endzeit* with *Urzeit*.[81] The origin, interpretation, and breadth of Paul's Adamic Christology is clearly beyond the scope of this study. However, a brief treatment of Paul's use of the Adam tradition outside of Romans demonstrates the influence of Gen 1–3 upon his thought and, in particular, demonstrates a precedent for Adam theology as a substructure.[82]

### Explicit References to Adam in Paul

Explicit references to the Adam tradition in the Pauline corpus are complex. Although they require the historical reference to retain their force,[83] Adam is not named merely to assert his historicity, but in order to demonstrate the theological basis of male–female relationships (1 Tim 2:13–14) or the typological contrast between Adam and Christ (Rom 5; 1 Cor 15).

First Timothy 2:13–14 employs the historical context of the Genesis narratives to ground the relationship of men and women in the church: "For Adam was fashioned first, then Eve. And Adam was not deceived, but the woman being deceived fell in transgression" (1 Tim 2:13–14). The order of creation is proffered as normative for male–female roles. Similarly, Paul's use of Adam in 1 Cor 15 is meant to highlight historical sequence. The first reference to Adam in 15:22 reviews the intrusion of death into the world and resurrection as its reversal:[84]

> For it is recognized that through a man, death, and through a man, resurrection from the dead. For just as in Adam all die, so also in Christ all will be made alive. (1 Cor 15:21–22)

The sequence, here, is not the sequence of creation but of redemption. Paul's reference is clearly to Adam in Gen 3.[85] The transgression in the garden resulted in death for him and death for all in him. This reversal and falling short from humanity's created purpose embodies what the apostle Paul will later call "futility" (Rom 8:20; 1 Cor 3:20; cf. Rom 1:21). It represented the undoing of divine purpose in man and introduced the created desire for consummation of a new creation and a remedial need for redemption.[86]

The next reference in the context of 1 Cor 15:35–58 focuses on the bodily nature of resurrection. Paul introduces the discourse with the rhetorical questions: πῶς ἐγείρονται οἱ νεκροί; ποίῳ δὲ σώματι ἔρχονται; ("How are the dead raised? And with what sort of body do they come?," 15:35). He then proceeds to answer in terms apparently drawn from Gen 1–3. He argues by analogy, pointing to the agricultural order of seed then plant (15:37; cf. Gen 1:11–12). He then argues with kinds of "bodies." There is a variety of fleshly bodies (15:39; cf. Gen 1:20–22) and astronomical bodies (15:40–41; cf. Gen 1:14–18).[87] Each type of body has its own degree of δόξα (15:41). Paul writes: Οὕτως καὶ ἡ ἀνάστασις τῶν νεκρῶν. σπείρεται ἐν φθορᾷ, ἐγείρεται ἐν ἀφθαρσίᾳ· σπείρεται ἐν ἀτιμίᾳ, ἐγείρεται ἐν δόξῃ· σπείρεται ἐν ἀσθενείᾳ, ἐγείρεται ἐν δυνάμει (1 Cor 15:42–43, "In this manner also is the resurrection from the dead. It is sown in corruption, it is raised in incorruption; it is sown in dishonor, it is raised in glory; it is sown in weakness, it is raised in power"). The substance of the argument is both that God designed the progression from natural to spiritual and that the spiritual stage has greater δόξα (15:44).

Paul depends upon the Genesis narratives to show the intended sequence. The body begins mutable (φθορά), but will pass beyond such an existence (ἀφθαρσία). If there was doubt about Paul's drawing upon the Genesis narratives for the order of creation, 15:45 provides further corroboration by quoting from and expanding upon Gen 2:7: οὕτως καὶ γέγραπται· ἐγένετο ὁ πρῶτος ἄνθρωπος Ἀδὰμ εἰς ψυχὴν ζῶσαν, ὁ ἔσχατος Ἀδὰμ[88] εἰς πνεῦμα ζῳοποιοῦν ("Thus it is written: The first man, Adam became a living being; the last Adam (became) a living-giving Spirit"). Benjamin L. Gladd has argued that, in addition to the quotation from Gen 2:7, Paul draws upon Gen 5:3 as a background for this phrase in that Adam passed his now-sinful image onto his son, Seth.[89] Similarly, the last Adam passes his righteous image to believers as God's adopted sons.

This theme of passing on one's image is consistent with Paul's hermeneutic. He continues, 15:49: καὶ καθὼς ἐφορέσαμεν τὴν εἰκόνα τοῦ χοϊκοῦ, φορέσομεν[90] καὶ τὴν εἰκόνα τοῦ ἐπουρανίου ("Just as we have worn the image of the man of dust, we will also wear the image of the man of heaven," 1 Cor 15:49). The language of "wearing" (φορέω) the image is investiture language.[91] Just as all mankind in Adam was compelled to "wear" his shame, so will those in Christ "wear" his heavenly image (i.e., be glorified). Thus, Paul's use of Ἀδάμ is meant to show the trajectory of God's plan. Man was made for ἀφθαρσία and to be clothed with δόξα, but that consummate, spiritual condition would be preceded by the natural. In Christ, ὁ ἔσχατος Ἀδὰμ, this is already realized in the Spirit and will be consummately realized for the new humanity.

## Implicit References to Adam in Paul

There is reason to see an underlying Adamic theology in Paul's letters beyond explicit references. Outside of Romans (to which I will return in the next section), there are a number of passages which allude to Adam (e.g., 2 Cor 3:18; 4:4–6; 5:1–10; Phil 2:5–11; 3:20–21).[92]

To begin, the reference in 1 Cor 15:49 to wearing the image of the heavenly man is closely related to statements about believers being conformed to the image of Christ in Rom 8:29, 2 Cor 3:18, and Col 3:10. It cannot be denied that Paul's description of Jesus as εἰκὼν τοῦ θεου (2 Cor 4:4; Col 1:15; cf. Rom 8:29; 1 Cor 15:49; 2 Cor 3:18; Col 3:10) is akin to Gen 1:27, Adam's creation κατ' εἰκόνα θεοῦ. Indeed, the connections between Gen 1–2 and Pauline εἰκών-Christology are numerous. The theme of glory, which I have already shown is closely connected to accounts of the image of God in early Judaism and the Hebrew Bible, is regularly repeated (2 Cor 3:18; 4:4, 6). Paul directly cites the Genesis narratives in 2 Cor 4:6 (Gen 1:3) and 1 Cor 15:45 (Gen 2:7). Obviously, the phrase "image of God" first appears in Gen 1:27. Naming Christ *the* image as opposed to describing him as κατ' εἰκόνα may be a distinction between the heavenly archetype-image (*Urbild*) and the earthly prototype (*Abbild*).[93] In other words, Adam is an image-bearer, but Christ is the image itself (or better, *him*self).

The Christ-hymn beginning in Col 1:15 is among the strongest declarations of Christ's deity in the NT. In Col 1:13, Jesus is called God's "beloved Son" into whose kingdom "we" have been transferred out of the kingdom of darkness (μετέστησεν εἰς τὴν βασιλείαν τοῦ υἱοῦ τῆς ἀγάπης αὐτου). Then Paul begins the hymn of praise: ὅς ἐστιν εἰκὼν τοῦ θεοῦ τοῦ ἀοράτου, πρωτότοκος πάσης κτίσεως ("Who is the image of the invisible God, the firstborn of all creation," 1:15). Christ is God's Son, God's image, and the firstborn of creation. Each of these elements also describes Adam, who was created in God's image, the king of Eden. He was intended to spread that image over the whole world (Gen 1:28–30). Adam was the firstborn son of God and the pinnacle of creation. Paul is describing the eschatological role of Christ in terms that parallel the protological role of Adam. In light of the above observations, Jacob Jervell summarizes his exegesis saying, "we have before us [in Col. 1], therefore, a christological interpretation of Gen. 1."[94]

It has also been suggested that Adam lies in the background of the Christ-hymn of Phil 2:5–11.[95] There is some question because, as Gordon Fee puts it, there is a "lack of actual *linguistic* ties between this passage and Gen 2–3."[96] Typical objections to finding an Adam-Christ typology in these verses rest on (a) the absence of linguistic connections, and (b) an asserted semantic difference between μορφὴ θεοῦ and εἰκὼν θεοῦ ruling out Gen 1:27 as a possible background.[97] But, while not completely synonymous, μορφὴ and εἰκὼν are both possible renderings for the Semitic word צלם ("image"; cf. Gen 1:27).[98] Seyoon Kim notes a "fine nuance" between μορφὴ and εἰκὼν, but concludes that "to the extent that the μορφὴ θεοῦ in Phil 2.6 retains the sense 'form of God' in some way, it is equivalent to the phrase εἰκὼν τοῦ θεοῦ, the image, likeness form, representation of God."[99] In other words, scholars who assert there is *no* literary link between them overstate the case.

Ridderbos concludes his discussion of εἰκών-Christology saying it is "inescapable" to avoid the "direct relationship between Genesis 1:27 and the Pauline pronouncements concerning Christ as the image of God."[100] In the same vein, Seyoon Kim argues that Christ as εἰκών is related to but *precedes* Christ as Adam in Paul's theological development.[101] He explains that Paul saw the resurrected, exalted Christ on the road to Damascus shining with heavenly light (φῶς ἐκ τοῦ οὐρανοῦ, Acts 9:3). The apostle would go on to describe Christ as εἰκὼν τοῦ θεοῦ ("image of God," 2 Cor 4:4; Col 1:15) and τὸν κύριον τῆς δόξης ("the Lord of glory," 1 Cor 2:8). It is difficult to imagine that his *actual* vision of the exalted Christ does not lie at the back of his description of Jesus as εἰκών.[102] It is a small step farther to compare the exalted Son of God in glory with the first son of God who was also considered to have possessed a righteous glory (cf. Sir 49:16; *Apoc. Mos.* 20:1–2; 21:6; 1QS IV, 23; 4Q504 8 I, 4).[103] Thus, there is good reason to see an underlying Adamic theology throughout the Pauline corpus. Paul's εἰκών-Christology cannot be wholly distinguished from his Adamic Christology.

N. T. Wright has argued on the basis of Paul's use of Adam in Rom 5 and 1 Cor 15, as well as Second Temple writings, that Paul viewed Jesus as the true Israel, which itself was the last Adam.[104] For Wright, the key difference between Adamic theology in the worldview of Second Temple Judaism and Paul's own theology is the pivot from viewing Israel as last Adam to viewing Jesus as true Israel. He writes,

> The use of 'Adam' themes in the Jewish literature which may without controversy be considered a part of the background to the New Testament—i.e., the Old Testament, the Scrolls, and the Apocrypha and Pseudepigrapha—consistently makes one large and important point: God's purposes for the human race in general have devolved on to, and will be fulfilled in, Israel in particular.[105]

Thus, "Paul's Adam-Christology is basically an Israel-Christology."[106] This goes a measure too far. While there are certainly parallel between Adam and Israel for which I have argued over the past several chapters, Wright's proposal puts the figure of Israel should-to-shoulder with Adam and Christ. It is doubtful Paul would have made such a move. Paul calls Jesus the last Adam, but never ascribes such a title to Israel.[107] Richard B. Gaffin Jr. observes, "The order of Paul's outlook [in 1 Cor 15] is such that Adam is 'the first' (ὁ πρῶτος); there is no one *before* him. Christ is 'the last' (ὁ ἔσχατος); there is no one *after* him, he is literally the *eschatological man*."[108] Moreover,

> Christ is not only "the last," he is also, as such, "the second" (ὁ δεύτερος, [1 Cor 15:]47); there is no one between Adam and him. In other words . . . the sweep of Paul's covenant historical outlook, the overarching hierarchy of his concerns here, is such that no one comes into consideration but Adam and Christ—not David, not Moses and the law given at Sinai, not even Abraham as the promise holder, not Noah, nor anyone else.[109]

Despite being Adam-*ic,* Israel is not a "second Adam" but exists under his influence, as Paul will argue in Rom 5. Adam and Christ bookend humanity in the history of redemption.

In sum, the Adam tradition is an integral component of numerous texts ranging from praise for Christ (Phil 2:6–11; Col 1:15f.) to describing the sanctification and glorification of believers in him (2 Cor 4:4–6). Moreover, the themes surrounding the Adam tradition in the NT and, particularly, in Paul are closely related to those in the Hebrew Bible and early Judaism.

Having now seen the existence of an underlying Adam theology, or substructure, outside of Romans, I now turn to examine the Adam tradition in Paul's most famous letter.

## Adam across Romans

It has already been noted that Paul's Adamic Christology depends upon the explicit references in Rom 5:14. There should be no doubt that Paul typologically contrasts Adam as the representative of the first creation with Christ as the head of the new. The redemptive-historical progression from first Adam to last is central to the portrayal of life in the Spirit in Rom 5–8. In addition to the explicit typology, however, Adamic theology also informs the background of much of Paul's argument throughout the epistle. From beginning to end, there are regular allusions to the Adam tradition. It is my contention that these allusions are an important component of the context within which Paul describes redemption. I will present a series of allusions to Adam in Romans, particularly in 1:18–32, 3:23 and 16:20.[110]

The first allusion to Adam is in Paul's opening paragraph of the letter body (1:18–32), which begins a lengthy indictment of humankind (1:18–3:20). Scholars have chiefly noted an allusion to Ps 106:20 (Ps 105:20 LXX).[111] However, there are also parallels to the early chapters of Genesis. Paul's complaint is cosmic. *All* fail to honor God as Creator. That failure is termed an *exchange of* the glory of God. I argue that Romans 1:23 alludes to both Adam, who paradigmatically chose to obey the serpent instead of God, and to Israel who recapitulated the sin of Adam with the golden calf.[112] A comparison of Rom 1:23 with Ps 106:20 (105:20 LXX)[113] and Gen 1:26 demonstrates various levels of Paul's use of the Hebrew Bible.

**Table 3.1 Psalm 105:20 LXX and Genesis 1:26 in Romans 1:23**

| *Romans 1:23* | *Ps 105:20 LXX* | *Genesis 1:26 LXX* |
|---|---|---|
| καὶ ἤλλαξαν τὴν δόξαν τοῦ ἀφθάρτου θεοῦ ἐν ὁμοιώματι[a] εἰκόνος φθαρτοῦ ἀνθρώπου καὶ πετεινῶν καὶ τετραπόδων καὶ ἑρπετῶν | καὶ ἠλλάξαντο τὴν δόξαν αὐτῶν ἐν ὁμοιώματι μόσχου ἔσθοντος χόρτον | καὶ εἶπεν ὁ θεός ποιήσωμεν ἄνθρωπον κατ' εἰκόνα ἡμετέραν καὶ καθ' ὁμοίωσιν καὶ ἀρχέτωσαν τῶν ἰχθύων τῆς θαλάσσης καὶ τῶν πετεινῶν τοῦ οὐρανοῦ καὶ τῶν κτηνῶν καὶ πάσης τῆς γῆς καὶ πάντων τῶν ἑρπετῶν τῶν ἑρπόντων ἐπὶ τῆς γῆς |
| And they exchanged the glory of the incorruptible God for an image in the likeness of corruptible man and birds and four footed animals and reptiles. | And they exchanged their glory for the likeness of an ox which eats grass (Ps 106:20 EVV). | And God said, let us make man according to our image and likeness and let him rule the fish of the sea, the birds of the heaven, and the cattle and all the earth and every creeping thing that creeps upon the earth. |

*Note*: Solid underlines indicate direct parallels. Dashed underlines show thematic connections.
[a] Cranfield notes that the use of ἐν with the dative reflects the underlying Hebrew, בְּ, indicating the object acquired by exchange (*Romans*, 1:120n1).

The correspondence between Romans 1:23 and Ps 106 is nearly word-for-word.[114] Paul substitutes τὴν δόξαν αὐτῶν for τὴν δόξαν τοῦ ἀφθάρτου θεοῦ. He most likely makes the change because of the exegetical tradition that God was Israel's glory,[115] as well as replacing the singular image of the ox (μόσχου ἔσθοντος χόρτον) for the broader spectrum of created things (φθαρτοῦ ἀνθρώπου καὶ πετεινῶν καὶ τετραπόδων καὶ ἑρπετῶν).

The allusion to Ps 106 is conspicuous because the psalm is a deliberate rehearsal of the sins of Israel from the Red Sea to mixing with the remnant of the Canaanite people in the promised land. It does so, finishing Book 4 of the Psalter, in order to prepare the way for the theme of restoration from exile which arises in Book 5.[116] After identifying Israel's idolatry with the calf, the psalm goes on to explain that such sin would result in exile (Ps 106:26–7, 41a). In other words, Paul compares *Israel's* rebellion with that of *all* humanity (Rom 1:18).

There is a consensus that Paul draws upon Ps 106 (and perhaps Wis 13–15)[117]; however, a cohort of scholars has observed a conceptual and literary connection to Gen 1–3.[118] With the exception of φθαρτός, every word of Rom 1:23 also occurs in Gen 1:20–6 LXX.[119] Although this view does not command widespread support,[120] I argue that there are a number of valid reasons to conclude that Paul does indeed allude to Adam. The first reason is a series of references in Rom 1:18–32 which appear to allude to Gen 1–3. These references are as follows:

(1) All must admit that Paul refers to the events of Gen 1–2 in Rom 1:20 when he claims that God's unseen attributes have been perceived by the things that are made ἀπὸ κτίσεως κόσμου ("from the creation of the world"). This initial reference provides a frame of reference.
(2) The phrase "ὁμοιώματι εἰκόνος" in Rom 1:23 echoes Gen 1:26 LXX where God creates ἄνθρωπος κατ' εἰκόνα and καθ' ὁμοίωσιν. The second term, εἰκόνος, does not arise from the psalm nor is it necessary to communicate the notion of "likeness."[121] Instead, the doubled concept of "likeness" recalls the first place in Scripture such a pattern appeared, the creation of humanity in Gen 1:26.
(3) Although Ps 106 references the exchange of God's glory for an ox, Paul instead says that the exchange was for four categories of created things which correspond to the order given in Gen 1:26: human beings, birds, cattle, reptiles (cf. Gen 1:20, 24).[122]

The grammatical number of the listed creatures also corresponds to Gen 1. Animals are plural; man is singular. Indeed, Paul began discussing the sin of *human beings,* ἀνθρώπων (Rom 1:18) but changes to that of *man,* ἀνθρώπου (1:23). An allusion to Genesis explains the shift to singular.[123]

(4) Paul's description of men exchanging God's truth τῷ ψεύδει (for *the* lie) in Rom 1:25 uses the article. An anarthrous noun would point to

**Table 3.2 Genesis 1:26 in Romans 1:23**

| *Genesis 1:26 LXX* | *Romans 1:23* |
|---|---|
| καὶ εἶπεν ὁ θεός ποιήσωμεν ἄνθρωπον κατ' εἰκόνα ἡμετέραν καὶ καθ' ὁμοίωσιν καὶ ἀρχέτωσαν τῶν ἰχθύων τῆς θαλάσσης καὶ τῶν πετεινῶν τοῦ οὐρανοῦ καὶ τῶν κτηνῶν[a] καὶ πάσης τῆς γῆς καὶ πάντων τῶν ἑρπετῶν τῶν ἑρπόντων ἐπὶ τῆς γῆς | καὶ ἤλλαξαν τὴν δόξαν τοῦ ἀφθάρτου θεοῦ ἐν ὁμοιώματι εἰκόνος φθαρτοῦ ἀνθρώπου καὶ πετεινῶν καὶ τετραπόδων καὶ ἑρπετῶν |
| And God said, let us make man according to our image and likeness and let him rule the fish of the sea, and the birds of the heaven, and the cattle and all the earth and all the reptiles that creeps upon the earth (Gen 1:26 LXX). | And they exchanged the glory of the incorruptible God for an image in the likeness of corruptible man and birds and four footed animals and reptiles (Rom 1:23). |

*Note*: Solid underlines indicate direct parallels. Dashed underlines show thematic connections.
[a]Genesis 1:24 LXX uses τετράπους not κτῆνος.

the generic concept of falsehood. This is likely an anaphoric use of the article to indicate a particular, prominent lie. In that both Gen 3 and Rom 1 speak specifically of the rejection of God's authority *as Creator,* the lie in question is likely the serpent's lie "you will be like God."[124]

(5) Paul gives reference to Gen 1:27 when he refers to God making human beings "male and female" (Rom 1:26–7).[125]

(6) In Rom 1:32 when Paul points to the prohibition against evil practice as worthy of "death" (cf. Gen 2:17).[126]

(7) There may be a connection to Gen 3. While Paul omits some of the creatures listed in Gen 1:20–6, he includes a reference to the serpent (ἑρπετόν) in close proximity to humankind having rejected the truth for *the* lie and served *the* creature rather than the creator (Rom 1:25).[127]

Some of these possible allusions are fully convincing in isolation from the rest. However, the two criteria of volume and recurrence render a stronger case. The *volume* of an allusion refers to the number of verbatim word repetitions, but also to the prominence of the source text.[128] Genesis 1–3 is extremely prominent. I will follow Richard Hays's counsel to "consider not only the degree of exact verbal correspondence but also the relative weightiness of the material cited."[129] Likewise, the criterion of *recurrence* shows that the collection of so many allusions to the same context, subtle as some may be, increases the plausibility of each individual allusion.

There is also a close thematic correspondence to the story of Adam. Unlike Ps 106, Gen 3 and Rom 1 chiefly relate to God as creator.[130] Paul's description of humankind's sin assumes God's truth is discernible in creation (Rom 1:19–20): "claiming to be wise they were made fools" (1:22). Wrongfully claiming wisdom is the precise sin Adam committed.[131] Dunn writes, "Paul also had in mind the figure of Adam and the narrative of the fall . . . it was hardly possible for a Jew to think of humanity's place in creation, his knowledge of God, and his loss of that knowledge in a (single) act of willful rebellion, without reference to Gen 2–3. Paul's indictment of humankind is also his description of Adam (= man)."[132] Behind the story of the collective futility of mankind in Rom 1:19–20 is the initial failure of the first man, who instituted a pattern of transgression. This is corroborated by Rom 8:18–23 when Paul describes *all creation* as experiencing futility because of Adam's sin.[133] Therefore, there are both literary allusions and conceptual links from Rom 1 to Gen 1–3. The sheer number makes denying the connection difficult. However, there is a third reason to see the link. The remainder of this chapter will show a consistent pattern of allusions to Adam across Romans. The explicit reference to Adam in Rom 5:14 is far from isolated; it is simply the clearest instance of a structural theme.[134]

I conclude that both Ps 106:20 and Rom 1:18–32 refer to the paradigmatic sin of idolatry of which Adam and Israel are both guilty. Adam exchanged[135] the glory of God (Gen 3), Israel worshipped the calf (Exod 32), which was then recounted in their songs as an exchange of their glory (Ps 106:20). N. T. Wright concludes, "Despite suggestions to the contrary, the line of thought in 1.18–25 has 'Adam' written all over it, even while it also alludes clearly to the primal sin of Israel (the golden calf)."[136] Paul uses the Adam tradition paradigmatically. The first man may have instituted sin, but humanity followed suit.

Following the opening indictment of humanity (Rom 1:18–3:20), Paul summarizes his indictment saying, πάντες γὰρ ἥμαρτον καὶ ὑστεροῦνται τῆς δόξης τοῦ θεοῦ ("For all have sinned and fallen short of the glory of God," 3:23). The aorist ἥμαρτον combined with the progressive aspect of ὑστεροῦνται indicates an initial sin leading to a continual falling short.[137] The portrayal fits Adam's sin in the garden. This is another probable allusion to Adam's initial unrighteousness exchanging glory for the lie (cf. Rom 1:23, 25).[138] We might paraphrase its significance as, "All have sinned—like Adam—and are falling short." According to Schreiner, "There is no reason to doubt that Paul reflects on Adam's loss of glory here."[139] Similarly, Steven Enderlein observes "Recognizing that Paul is speaking about humanity lacking the glory of God in Rom 3:23 suggests that Paul already has Adam and the detrimental consequences of his sin in mind much prior to chapter 5."[140] Dunn simply states that Rom 3:23 "almost certainly alludes to Adam's fall."[141] In other words, the standard for mankind—paradigmatically so in Adam's case—is *glory.*[142]

Romans 3:23 expands upon the nature of the initial exchange of glory (1:23, 25–26).[143] Whereas 1:23 describes exchanging God's glory for the worship of images resulting in corruption, 3:23 frames it as an ethical requirement. There is some ambiguity in the verb ὑστερέω which is a comparative term reflecting either a failure to reach a goal or falling from a once-occupied position.[144] Mankind was made to attain δόξα, but has collectively and individually fallen short.[145] It is thus unclear whether the reference is to a glory which Adam already possessed or whether sin prevented him from attaining the potential before him.[146] Sprinkle rightly notes that Paul's focus is not upon Adam, but mankind, "Whether or not Adam is in the mind of Paul is not essential to the main idea: the glory of God is a potential possession of mankind, and all without distinction still do not have it."[147] Blackwell argues that "falling short of glory" reflects the ethical failure which resulted in passing from a state of incorruption and life to a state of corruption and death.[148] Adam certainly possessed incorruption in Eden, but not incorruptibility in the manner of the glory in believers' future. If Adam did at one time possess a measure of glory (cf. 2 Cor 3:18), it should not be equated with the permanence of eschatological glory nor was it a standard he was able to maintain.

Thus, when Paul writes Rom 5, he has already set the stage to discuss glory in terms of a standard set before man which has yet to be attained. In Rom 1–4 Paul's focus is mankind's exchange of God's glory and the accompanying loss of righteousness; in Rom 5–8 he focuses on its reclamation. It is no accident that Paul begins Rom 5 pointing to a hope in the *glory* of God and concludes Rom 8 saying that believers will be glorified. The explicit mention of Adam in Rom 5:14 is far from random. It is merely the clearest instance of a theme he has developed from the start and continues to develop throughout Romans 5–8 and to which he returns in 16:20. Paul clarifies in Rom 5 that this reversal is a function of Christ's work *as the last Adam.*[149] Mankind's unrighteousness began with Adam and ends with Christ. He was created with the hope and standard of glory and that hope is restored through Jesus's work as last Adam.

Not only does a series of allusions to Gen 1–3 begin Paul's argument in Romans, there is an allusion to Adam at its conclusion.[150] As he closes, Paul gives a final warning against enemies of the faith (16:17–20a) and a parting assurance that the church will triumph: "the God of peace [cf. 5:1; 8:6.] will crush Satan (τὸν σατανᾶν) under your feet in short time." The trampling of Satan likely alludes to the fulfillment of the protoevangelium (Gen 3:15).[151] What was promised to be accomplished through the singular seed (cf. Gal 3:16) is here shown to include believers. Through their incorporation into Christ, believers conquer in him (cf. Rom 8:37–39). Reciprocally, 16:20 identifies the adversary as the singular enemy (ὁ Σατανᾶς), in context, however, that enemy is inclusive of "those who cause divisions and stumbling" (τοὺς τὰς διχοστασίας καὶ τὰ σκάνδαλα, 16:17). Thus, the opponents of the gospel are shown to be in league with Satan while believers are linked with Christ in his victory. These groupings represent the outflow of Paul's theology of Adam and Christ employed throughout the epistle. Christ's victory is in the world through his people, and over the world, its ruler, and his subjects.

If the reader will grant the presence of Adamic allusions in Rom 16:20 and 1:18–32, then the epistle is bounded by references to the Adam tradition. It begins the epistle referencing Adam's transgression which led to the sinful inversion of the created order in the worship of created things, including ἑρπετῶν (meaning "reptiles" or even "serpents"). It concludes with Satan, who is often identified with the serpent of Gen 3 (cf. Wis 2:24; Rev 20:2),[152] being crushed underneath the feet, not of Christ the singular seed (Gal 3:16; cf. Gen 3:15), but of the saints themselves.[153]

Each of these echoes of Adam becomes more likely in company with the others.[154] A substructure of Adam-theology is woven throughout the epistle. The Adam-Christ parallels (life and death, flesh and spirit, slavery and freedom) have their basis in the soteriological-covenantal narrative Paul articulates.[155] As I examine Rom 5 and Rom 8 in more detail in subsequent chapters, we will see Paul's sustained dependence upon Adamic theology which forms the background and contrast to the work of Jesus Christ.

## CONCLUSION

In conclusion, Paul makes use of the Adamic tradition explicitly, but there is reason to see a wider implicit use of an Adamic theology throughout Romans. Subsequent chapters will argue that allusions to Adam in Rom 5 and 8 interlock with Paul's use of an Israel motif to show how Christ fulfills both by establishing the eschatological people of God though Christ. Thus, Paul employs *Urzeit* to understand *Endzeit.* I have argued that Paul is not alone in such a practice; several strands of Second Temple Jewish writings did the same. The sectarians at Qumran projected the end of the exile to involve the restoration of Adam's glory. Similarly, Sirach described the δόξα of Israel's patriarchs as a measure of participation in God's majesty, listing Adam as most glorious of all. They look forward to the restoration of that same glory in Israel's restoration from exile. This overlap of Israel's future with Adam's past is not entirely novel to Second Temple writings. Corporate Israel functions as an Adam-like type in the Hebrew Bible as well. Its eschatological hope is a continuation of Edenic potential. Israel received blessings and the partial fruition of aspects of the Adamic commission through Yahweh's promise to Abraham. Most importantly, Israel was called God's son (Exod 4:22; Deut 1:31; 8:5; 14:1; 32:5; Hos 11:1). Like Adam before, Yahweh created Israel out of chaos (תֹהוּ; cf. Gen 1:2; Deut 32:10–11), placed him in a paradisiacal land (cf. Gen 2:8; Isa 51:3; Ezek 36:35; Joel 2:3), commanded him to reflect his holiness (Exod 19:6; Deut 7:6), and promised blessings for obedience and curses for disobedience (cf. Gen 1:28–30; 2:17; Deut 28:1–14, 15–68). Also like Adam, Israel failed in its commission and forfeited the land. Adam's loss in Eden was the loss of life, land, and God's presence in that land. Israel's infidelity led to its exile, which is also described as its death. Later Judaism would consider Adam's expulsion from Eden to be the pattern which Israel follows.[156] In the following chapters, I will argue that Paul employs this overlap to proclaim the eschatological restoration of God's sons[157] through Christ.

## NOTES

1. The first man, אָדָם, was a representative figure. He embodied human potential for good or evil. Even in his name, Adam represents the rest of humanity. He is the

anthropological prototype. The perennial concept of "the one and the many" plays a part in how Gen 1:26–4:1 portrays הָאָדָם. As Robin Scroggs puts it, "it is clear that Gen. 1 is concerned more about 'man' than about Adam" (*The Last Adam: A Study in Pauline Anthropology* [Philadelphia: Fortress, 1966], 24).

2. G. C. Berkouwer, *Man: The Image of God* (Grand Rapids: Eerdmans, 1962), 114–7. Cf. D. J. A. Clines, "The Image of God in Man," *TynBul* 19 (1968): 90–2.

3. The exact number of explicit references to Adam is uncertain because of the semantic interplay between the common noun, הָאָדָם, the man, and the proper noun, הָאָדָם, Adam. Still, outside the early chapters of Genesis there are only a few scattered references to Adam. (According to the ESV translation, only 1 Chr 1:1 and the disputed reference in Hos 6:7.)

4. This paragraph follows David VanDrunen, "Israel's Recapitulation of Adam's Probation under the Law of Moses," *WTJ* 73 (2011): 303–24, esp. 305.

5. See, for example, N. T. Wright, *The Climax of the Covenant: Christ and the Law in Pauline Theology* (Edinburgh: T&T Clark, 1991), 20–2.

6. It is noteworthy that unlike Adam, Abraham—who does not receive the inheritance in his lifetime—is required to sojourn for a time before his descendants actually receive their inheritance.

7. Canaan is repeatedly compared to Eden in the Hebrew Bible: Isa 51:3, Ezek 36:35; Joel 2:3 (cf. Ezek 28:14; 40:2).

8. Gordon J. Wenham, *Story as Torah: Reading the Old Testament Ethically* (Edinburgh: T&T Clark, 2000), 37.

9. G. K. Beale, *A New Testament Biblical Theology: The Unfolding of the Old Testament in the New* (Grand Rapids: Baker Academic, 2011), 48.

10. Likewise, the tenth plague focused on the firstborn son (Exod 11:4–6). Cf. Deut 1:31; 8:5; 14:1–2; 32:4–6; Ps 80:7, 15, 16, 17, 19; Jer 3:19–20; Hos 1:10; 11:1–5; cf. Also Sir 4:10; Wisdom 2:18; *Ps. Sol.* 13:8; 18:4.

11. Although Genesis does not explicitly describe Adam as God's "son" (cf. Luke 3:38), this is the implication of Gen 5:1–3 where Adam is made in God's likeness and Seth is made in Adam's likeness.

12. John J. Schmitt, "Israel as Son of God in Torah," *BTB* 34 (2004): 69, 77.

13. Ibid., 76–7.

14. See Brandon D. Crowe, *The Obedient Son: Deuteronomy and Christology in the Gospel of Matthew,* BZNW 188 (Berlin: De Gruyter, 2012), 104–6.

15. Ibid., 106–7.

16. Ibid.

17. Meredith G. Kline, *Kingdom Prologue: Genesis Foundations for a Covenantal Worldview* (Eugene, OR: Wipf & Stock, 2000), 30.

18. See Paul Morris, "Exiled from Eden: Jewish Interpretations of Genesis," in *A Walk in the Garden: Biblical, Iconographical and Literary Images of Eden*, ed. Paul Morris and Deborah Sawyer, JSOTSup 136 (Sheffield: JSOT Press, 1992), 117–68. Consider the following comparison from *Gen. Rab.* (cited in ibid., 124):

Adam: "I brought the first man to the Garden of Eden (Gen. 2.15), I commanded him (2.16) but he broke my commandment (3.11). I sentenced him to be . . . driven out (3.23)" (*Gen. Rab.* 3:9).

Israel: "The same is for his [Adam's] descendants. I brought them to the Land of Israel (Jer. 2.7), I commanded them (Lev. 24.2), but they broke my commandment (Dan. 9.11). I sentenced them to be . . . driven out (Jer. 15.1)" (*Gen. Rab.* 19:9).

19. Israel does *not* have the representative function Adam had as head of humanity, nor does Israel share the expectation of *absolute* sinlessness (as this was impossible). Nevertheless, God called Israel to be holy (Exod 19:6).

20. William J. Dumbrell, "Genesis 2:1–17: A Foreshadowing of the New Creation," in *Biblical Theology: Retrospect and Prospect*, ed. Scott J. Hafemann (Downers Grove, IL: InterVarsity Press, 2002), 61–3.

21. On expanding the garden, see G. K. Beale, *The Temple and the Church's Mission: A Biblical Theology of the Dwelling Place of God,* NSBT 17 (Downers Grove, IL: IVP; Leicester, England: Apollos, 2004), 81–6.

22. Richard B. Gaffin Jr., "Glory, Glorification," *DPL* 348.

23. Scroggs, *Last Adam*, 98.

24. Brandon D. Crowe, *The Last Adam: A Theology of the Obedient Life of Jesus in the Gospels* (Grand Rapids: Baker Academic, 2017), 56.

25. Meredith G. Kline, *Images of the Spirit* (Eugene, OR: Wipf & Stock, 1980), 30.

26. Admittedly, the notion of the potential for blessing beyond what Adam enjoyed in Eden is disputed. For example, strands of Lutheran theology hold to a return to Eden as consummate. Some literature from the Second Temple period of Judaism does the same. Qumran, for example, hopes in the restoration to Eden and the glory of Adam (1QS IV, 23; CD III, 20; 1QH XVII, 15). Likewise, John L. Sharpe argues that eschatological New Creation "will be a restoration of man's prelapsarian state" ("Second Adam in the Apocalypse of Moses," *CBQ* 35 ([1973]), 43).

27. Berkouwer, *Image of God,* 103–4.

28. The Hebrew reflects an apparently deliberate play on words between the "nakedness" (עָרוֹם) of Adam and Eve (2:25) and the "cunning" (ערום) of the serpent (3:1) (Claus Westermann, *Genesis 1–11: A Continental Commentary,* trans. John J. Scullion [Minneapolis, Fortress, 1994], 237–9). Apart from the Masoretic pointing, the words are identical (Kline, *Kingdom Prologue,* 130; Carlos Bovell, "Genesis 3:21: The History of Israel in a Nutshell?," *ExpTim* 115 [2004]: 362). Despite man being an image-bearer, he remains a creature, just like the serpent.

29. For example, in classical Greek, Demosthenes, [*Neaer.*], 63. See "ἐκβάλλω," *TDNTTE* 2:131; Hauck, "ἐκβάλλω, ἐκ-, ἐπιβάλλω," *TDNT* 1:527–29.

30. "ἐκβάλλω," *TDNTTE* 2:131.

31. MT: שלך.

32. Crowe, *Last Adam*, 24, 74.

33. Hauck, "ἐκβάλλω, ἐκ-, ἐπιβάλλω," *TDNT* 1:527–9.

34. On the redemptive-historical reversal accomplished in Christ's resurrection, see C. Marvin Pate, *The Reverse of the Curse: Paul, Wisdom, and the Law*, WUNT 2/114 (Tübingen: Mohr Siebeck, 2000). The salient points are summarized in idem, "Paul: The Reverse of the Curse," in *The Story of Israel: A Biblical Theology*, ed. C. Marvin Pate et al. (Downers Grove, IL: IVP, 2004), 206–31.

35. See the discussion in chapter 5.

36. C. Marvin Pate, *Adam Christology as the Exegetical and Theological Substructure of 2 Corinthians 4:7–5:21* (Lanham, MD: University Press of America, 1991), 33.

37. Frank J. Matera, *Romans*, Paideia Commentaries on the New Testament (Grand Rapids: Baker Academic, 2010), 127.

38. Scroggs, *Last Adam,* 35.

39. I will argue this point below.

40. All translations of Sirach are my own. Any Greek text comes from the Göttingen critical edition.

41. John R. Levison, *Portraits of Adam in Early Judaism: From Sirach to 2 Baruch*, JSPSup 1 (Sheffield: Sheffield Academic, 1988), 45.

42. Sir 44:1, 2, 7, 13, 19; 45:2, 3 (2x), 7, 20, 23, 26; 46:2, 12; 47:6 (2x), 8, 11, 20; 48:4, 6; 49:5, 8, 12, 16; 50:5, 7, 11 (2x), 13.

43. See, Crispin H. T. Fletcher-Louis, *All the Glory of Adam: Liturgical Anthropology in the Dead Sea Scrolls*, STDJ 42 (Leiden: Brill, 2002), 91.

44. Text and translation from Colson, LCL unless otherwise noted.

45. See Gary M. Anderson, "Celibacy or Consummation in the Garden: Reflections on Early Jewish and Christian Interpretations of the Garden of Eden," *HTR* 82 (1989): 121–48; Robert G. Hamerton-Kelly, "Sacred Violence and Sinful Desire: Paul's Interpretation of Adam's Sin in the Letter to the Romans," in *Conversation Continues: Studies in Paul and John in Honor of J. Louis Martyn* (Nashville: Abingdon, 1990), 35–54.

46. Cf. Rom 1:23, ἀλλάσσω, and 1:25, μεταλλάσσω.

47. Translation by C. D. Yonge (*The Complete Works of Philo*, trans. C. D. Yonge [Peabody, MA: Hendrickson, 1993]). Loeb Classical Library translates the section more idiomatically as follows: "And this desire begat likewise bodily pleasure, that pleasure which is the beginning of wrongs and violation of law, the pleasure for the sake of which men bring on themselves the life of mortality and wretchedness in lieu of that of immortality and bliss."

48. The scholarly recognition of this correspondence is typically assigned to Hermann Gunkel, *Schöpfung und Chaos in Urzeit und Endzeit: Eine religionsgeschichtliche Untersuchung über Gen 1 und Ap Joh 12* (Göttingen: Vandenhoeck & Ruprecht, 1895), 367–70. Cf. Ernest Best, *The Temptation and the Passion: The Markan Soteriology*, 2nd ed., SNTSMS 2 (Cambridge: Cambridge University Press, 1990), xvi and literature cited in n.7.

49. For clarity, I will refer to the Greek version of by its traditional name *Apocalypse of Moses*. The Latin version will be referred to as *Vita Adae et Evae*.

50. All translations of *Apocalypse of Moses* and *Vita Adae et Evae* by Johnson, *OTP* 2.

51. Preston M. Sprinkle, "The Afterlife in Romans: Understanding Paul's Glory Motif in Light of the Apocalypse of Moses and 2 Baruch," in *Lebendige Hoffnungewiger Tod?!: Jenseitsvorstellungen Im Hellenismus, Judentum, Und Christentum*, ed. Michael Labahn and Manfred Lang, ABG 24 (Leipzig: Evangelische Verlagsanstalt, 2007), 206–7.

52. Sharpe, "Second Adam," 38.

53. Following Philip R. Davies, *The Damascus Covenant: An Interpretation of the "Damascus Document,"* JSOTSup 25 (Sheffield: JSOT Press, 1983), 76.

54. Michael O. Wise, "4QFlorilegium and the Temple of Adam," *RevQ* 15 (1991): 125.

55. On the interpretative and textual issues, see Davies, *The Damascus Covenant*, 76–95.

56. Ibid., 90; Wise, "Temple of Adam," 126.

57. Wise, "Temple of Adam," 126–7.

58. Ibid., 132.

59. John J. Collins, "Interpretations of the Creation of Humanity in the Dead Sea Scrolls," in *Biblical Interpretation at Qumran*, ed. M. Henze, Studies in the Dead Sea Scrolls and Related Literature (Grand Rapids: Eerdmans, 2005), 29–43.

60. The seven generations between Adam and Enoch is likely meant to highlight Enoch's importance (Richard J. Bauckham, *Jude, 2 Peter,* WBC 50 [Waco, TX: Word Books, 1983], 96).

61. L. Joseph Kreitzer, "Christ and Second Adam in Paul," *CV* 32 (1989): 55–6. Peter J. Scaer argues that Jesus's connection to Adam is meant to highlight his obedience in contrast to Adam's disobedience ("Lukan Christology: Jesus as Beautiful Savior," *CTQ* 69 [2005]: 70–2).

62. See Crowe, *Last Adam,* 161.

63. Yongbom Lee argues for a biblical theological connection among the breath of life to the resurrection of the army of Israel in the valley of dry bones via the breath of God (Ezek 37:9) to the Spirit's empowering presence in Christ (*The Son of Man as the Last Adam: The Early Church Tradition as a Source of Paul's Adam Christology* [Eugene, OR: Pickwick, 2012], 129–31).

64. For example, Joel B. Green, *The Gospel of Luke*, NICNT (Grand Rapids: Eerdmans, 1997), 189; Norval Geldenhuys, *Commentary on the Gospel of Luke*, NICNT (Grand Rapids: Eerdmans, 1951), 153; Lee, *The Son of Man,* 127.

65. Jeremias argues that Mk 1:12–13 is the *only* instance of Adam typology in the Gospels ("ἀδάμ," *TDNT* 1:141–3). There is an interesting disagreement between Hans-Josef Klauck, *Vorspiel im Himmel?: Erzähltechnik und Theologie im Markusprolog*, BibTS 32 (Neukirchen-Vluyn: Neukirchener, 1997), 55–60, and Dieter Lührmann, *Das Markusevangelium*, HNT 3 (Tübingen: Mohr Siebeck, 1987), 39, where the former argues for a first and second Adam typology in Mark 1:12–13 and the latter rejects the notion arguing instead that Jesus restores Adam's lost glory. I argue that these are not mutually exclusive elements of Jesus's work.

66. Crowe calls any comparison of Adam to Christ in secondary literature on the Gospels the "exception rather than the rule" (*Last Adam,* 24).

67. See below.

68. Ibid., 155.

69. On the relationship of Adam's divine sonship to his temptation, see Berkouwer, *Image of God* and Beale, *We Become What We Worship: A Biblical Theology of Idolatry* (Downers Grove, IL: IVP Academic, 2008), 132–3.

70. Crowe, *Last Adam*, 156.

71. Ibid., 155.

72. Ibid., 153–7.

73. David M. May, "The Straightened Woman (Luke 13:10–17): Paradise Lost and Regained," *PRst* 24 (1997): 245–58.

74. Matthew David Litwa, "Behold Adam: A Reading of John 19:5," *HBT* 32 (2010): 129–43. It should be noted that the phrase is omitted by several MSS (most significantly $\mathfrak{P}^{66*}$).

75. For example, Crowe, *Last Adam;* Yongbom Lee, *The Son of Man*; Joel William Parkman, "Adam Christological Motifs in the Synoptic Traditions" (PhD diss., Baylor University, 1994).

76. Parkman, "Adam Christological Motifs," 55.

77. Lee, *The Son of Man.*

78. Dan G. McCartney, "Ecce Homo: The Coming of the Kingdom as the Restoration of Human Vicegerency," *WTJ* 56 (1994): 2.

79. Ibid., 2n5.

80. Pauline authorship of the nine letters beyond the *Hauptbriefe* (Romans, 1–2 Corinthians, and Galatians) is debated. However, most scholars allow the Pauline origin of 1 Thessalonians, Philippians, and Philemon, but omit 2 Thessalonians, Colossians, Ephesians, 1–2 Timothy and Titus. While I am persuaded Paul wrote all thirteen epistles, such debates will have little impact upon the present study.

81. On the foundational role of protology in Pauline thought, see Wilhelm Dittmann, *Die Auslegung der Urgeschichte (Genesis 1–3) im Neuen Testament* (Göttingen: Vandenhoeck & Ruprecht, 1953), 156–92.

82. James D. G. Dunn has argued for a broader Adamic substructure in, for example, *Christology in the Making: A New Testament Inquiry into the Origins of the Doctrine of the Incarnation*, 2nd ed. (Grand Rapids: Eerdmans, 1996), 98–128; idem, *The Theology of Paul the Apostle* (Grand Rapids: Eerdmans, 1998), 90–101.

83. Ernst Käsemann, *Commentary on Romans,* trans. Geoffrey W. Bromiley (Grand Rapids: Eerdmans, 1980), 142.

84. Gordon D. Fee, *Pauline Christology: An Exegetical-Theological Study* (Peabody, MA: Hendrickson, 2007), 516.

85. The previous generation of scholars suggested that Paul appeals to the so-called myth of the "primal man" which goes beyond a Hebrew Bible or Second Temple Jewish background to draw upon Gnostic speculation or mystery religions (e.g., Egon Brandenburger, *Adam und Christus: Exegetisch-Religions-geschichtliche Untersuchung zu Röm. 5 12–21 (1.Kor. 15)*, WMANT 7 [Neukirchen: Neukirchener Verlag, 1962], 157; Scroggs, *Last Adam,* ch. 1); however, this is an unnecessary appeal, stemming from a *religionsgeschichtliche* ideology. Fee calls it a "scholarly mythology" without any hard data to support it (Fee, *Pauline Christology*, 377n23). As Stephen J. Hultgren notes, Paul derives his doctrine of two Adams from Gen 2:7 *exegetically* ("The Origin of Paul's Doctrine of the Two Adams in 1 Corinthians 15.45–49," *JSNT* 25 [2003]: 369–70 [for his critique of Hellenistic backgrounds, see 344–57]). Continued investigation into the background of Paul's use of the Adam tradition has not shown a departure from Jewish tradition, but a more profound grasp of it (Seyoon Kim, *The Origin of Paul's Gospel*, WUNT 2/4 [Tübingen: Mohr Siebeck, 1984], 159–92).

86. Geerhardus Vos, *The Eschatology of the Old Testament*, ed. James T. Dennison (Phillipsburg, NJ: P&R, 2001), 74.

87. Thanks to Dr. Carlton Wynne for bringing this sequence to my attention.

88. 𝔓[46] omits this second instance of Ἀδάμ.

89. Benjamin L. Gladd, "The Last Adam as the 'Life-Giving Spirit' Revisited: A Possible Old Testament Background of One of Paul's Most Perplexing Phrases," *WTJ* 71 (2009): 297–309.

90. Several MSS list the subjunctive, φορέσωμεν (𝔓[46], A, C, D, F, G, K, L, P).

91. Josephus uses this same word to describe priestly garments (*Ant.* 3:153).

92. See, for example, Hultgren, "Paul's Doctrine of Two Adams," 367; Dunn, *Christology in the Making,* 105–6.

93. See Jacob Jervell, *Imago Dei: Gen 1, 26 f. Im Spätjudentum, in Der Gnosis Und in Den Paulinischen Briefen*, FRLANT 76 (Göttingen: Vandenhoeck & Ruprecht, 1960), 217–9. Yet, Ridderbos criticizes this distinction in light of 1 Cor 11:7 where man is called *the* image [Herman Ridderbos, *Paul: An Outline of His Theology*, trans. John Richard De Witt (Grand Rapids: Eerdmans, 1997), 72n92].

94. Jervell, *Imago Dei,* 200, cited in Ridderbos, *Paul*, 71.

95. See, for example, Wright, *Climax of the Covenant,* 90–7; Sahlin, "Adam-Christologie im Neuen Testament," 26; Seyoon Kim, *The Origin of Paul's Gospel*, WUNT 2/4 (Tübingen: Mohr Siebeck, 1984), 139; Dunn, *Christology in the Making,* 113–25; Hooker, *"Adam Redivivus*: Philippians 2 Once More," in *The Old Testament in the New Testament: Essays in Honour of J. L. North*, ed. Steve Moyise and J. L. North, JSNTSup 189 (Sheffield: Sheffield Academic, 2000) 220–4; Oscar Cullmann, *The Christology of the New Testament,* trans. Shirley C. Guthrie and Charles A. M. Hall (Philadelphia: Westminster Press, 1963), 174; Fee, *Pauline Christology*, 375–401.

96. Fee, *Pauline Christology*, 376. Emphasis his.

97. Lee, *The Son of Man,* 45.

98. Ibid., 50.

99. Kim, *Origin*, first quote, 196, second quote, 197. See also, Ridderbos, *Paul*, 72.

100. Ridderbos, *Paul*, 72.

101. Kim, *Origin*, 193.

102. This is a central premise of Kim's argument.

103. See, Hultgren, "Paul's Doctrine of Two Adams," 369–70. The development of Paul's thought is not our direct focus, but merely the connection between εἰκών and Adamic Christologies.

104. For the initial argument, see N. T. Wright, "Adam in Pauline Christology," *Society of Biblical Literature 1983 Seminar Papers,* SBLSP 22 (Atlanta: Society of Biblical Literature, 1983), 359–89. This was later refined as chapter 2, "Adam, Israel and the Messiah" of idem, *Climax*, 18–40.

105. Wright, *Climax,* 20.

106. Idem, "Adam in Pauline Christology," 366–7.

107. Lee, *The Son of Man,* 8.

108. Richard B. Gaffin Jr., *"By Faith, Not by Sight": Paul and the Order of Salvation* (Bletchley, U.K.; Waynesboro, GA: Paternoster, 2006), 47. Emphasis his.

109. Ibid.

110. See, for example, Dunn, *Theology of Paul*, 79–101; C. Marvin Pate, *The Glory of Adam and the Afflictions of the Righteous: Pauline Suffering in Context* (Lewiston: Mellen, 1993), 143, 147; Wright, "Adam in Pauline Christology," 371.

111. The text also parallels Jer 2:11 and Deut 4:15–19 to a lesser degree.

112. Allen C. Leslie writes, "Romans i. 18 ff. is in fact Paul's analysis of the sin of his time not only in terms of the fall of Adam but also in terms of Israel's experience in the wilderness. His description of the contemporary scene not only portrays the sin of humanity as the fall of Adam all over again, but also as a repetition on a larger scale of Israel's sin against her covenant-God" ("The Old Testament in Romans I–VIII," *VE* 3 [1964], 15).

113. English versification will be followed throughout, unless specified otherwise. Other systems will be noted when necessary.

114. See, for example, Adolf Schlatter, *Romans: The Righteousness of God*, trans. Siegfried Schatzmann (Peabody, MA: Hendrickson, 1995) 41. Also see the recent monograph on the subject, Alec J. Lucas, *Evocations of the Calf?: Romans 1:18–2:11 and the Substructure of Psalm 106 (105)*, BZNW 201 (Berlin: De Gruyter, 2015). Lucas notes an association between the respective manuscript traditions where the grammatical voice of the verb is adjusted in both Romans and Psalms MSS to reflect a greater conformity (ibid., 126).

115. C. E. B. Cranfield, *A Critical and Exegetical Commentary on the Epistle to the Romans*, 2 vols., *ICC* (Edinburgh: T&T Clark, 1975), 1:120; Morna D. Hooker, "Adam in Romans 1," *NTS* 6 (1969), 297n2.

116. O. Palmer Robertson, *The Flow of the Psalms: Discovering Their Structure and Theology* (Phillipsburg, NJ: P&R, 2015), 174–5.

117. For a discussion on the literary relationship with Wis 13–15, see Jonathan A. Linebaugh, "Announcing the Human: Rethinking the Relationship between Wisdom of Solomon 13–15 and Romans 1.18–2.11," *NTS* 57 (2011): 214–37, and Gerhart Herold, *Zorn und Gerechtigkeit Gottes bei Paulus: Eine Untersuchung zu Röm. 1, 16–18,* EH 14 (Bern: Peter Lang, 1973), 188–209.

118. Initially, Niels Hyldahl, "Reminiscence of the Old Testament at Romans 1:23," *NTS* (1956): 285–8. Most notably, Hooker, "Adam in Romans 1," 297–306, and idem, "Further Note on Romans 1," *NTS* 13 (1967): 181–3. See also, A. J. Wedderburn, "Adam in Paul's Letter to the Romans," in *StudBibl 1978: Papers on Paul and other New Testament Authors*, vol. 3, JSNTSup (Sheffield: JSOT, 1980), 413–30 (esp. 414, 19); Jervell, *Imago Dei*, 115–6, 321–31; Dunn, *Theology of Paul,* 91–3; idem, *Romans 1–8,* 70–5; idem, *Christology in the Making,* 101–2; Brian Kidwell, "The Adamic Backdrop of Romans," *CTR* 11 (2013): 111–5; Douglas J. W. Milne, "Genesis 3 in the Letter to the Romans," *RTR* 39 (1980): 10–18; Thomas R. Schreiner, *Romans*, BECNT (Grand Rapids: Baker Books, 1998), 81; Benjamin C. Blackwell, "Immortal Glory and the Problem of Death in Romans 3.23," *JSNT* 32 (2010): 302n46.

119. Hooker, "Adam in Romans 1," 300.

120. Moo describes the view as "theologically attractive" but unconvincing (*Romans*, 109n85). Similarly, Stanley Stowers has vigorously disputed the argument

for finding Adam in Rom 1:18–32 (*A Rereading of Romans: Justice, Jews, and Gentiles* [New Haven: Yale University Press, 1994], 86).

121. Hooker, "Adam in Romans 1," 297–300.

122. Hyldahl, "Reminiscence," 285–8.

123. Ibid., 287–8. Hyldahl goes on to remark, "If it could be proved that the δόξα of God signifies not only the Glory of God but also in a way the God-likeness of man, which he has lost, then we would have a reference in ἡ δόξα τοῦ ἀφθάρτου θεοῦ to Gen. i. 27 κατ' εἰκόνα θεοῦ." (288n1).

124. Kidwell, "Adamic Backdrop," 112.

125. Edward Adams, *Constructing the World: A Study in Paul's Cosmological Language*, SNTW (Edinburgh: T&T Clark, 2000), 153.

126. Ibid.; Milne, "Genesis 3 in Romans," 11; Moo allows this *may* be an allusion to Gen 3 (*Romans,* 109n85).

127. Thayer comments that the term is chiefly used in secular writings (e.g., Homer) to refer to serpents ("ἑρπετόν," *A Greek-English Lexicon of the New Testament*, BibleWorks10, *s.v.)* Moreover, ἑρπετόν is a regular word used to refer to the serpent in Eden in the Second Temple period (e.g., *Jub.* 3:23).

128. Richard B. Hays, *Echoes of Scripture in the Letters of Paul* (New Haven: Yale University Press, 1989), 29–33.

129. Idem, *Conversion of the Imagination: Paul as Interpreter of Israel's Scripture* (Grand Rapids: Eerdmans, 2005), 37.

130. Dunn, *Theology of Paul,* 91.

131. Idem, *Romans 1–8*, 92.

132. Ibid., 72.

133. There is considerable debate regarding the identity of τὸν ὑποτάξαντα ("the one who subjected") creation to futility in Rom 8:20. God is ultimately the source of that judicial act, but I will argue that Paul refers to Adam's paradigmatic sin. See the discussion in chapter 5.

134. Further allusions to Adam in Romans (e.g., 3:23; 5:1–11, 12–21; 6:1–11; 7:7–13; 8:17–39; 16:20) render the background of Gen 1–3 in Rom 1 all the more likely.

135. Philo also describes the fall of Adam and Eve in terms of a sinful "exchange" (ὑπαλλάσσω) of the immortal condition for one that is mortal and full of misfortune (*Creation* 152).

136. N.T. Wright, *Paul and the Faithfulness of God*, COQG 4 (Minneapolis: Fortress, 2013), 769.

137. Dunn*, Romans 1–8*, 168.

138. Samuel Byrskog, "Christology and Identity in an Intertextual Perspective: The Glory of Adam in the Narrative Substructure of Paul's Letter to the Romans," in *Identity Formation in the New Testament* (Tübingen: Mohr Siebeck, 2008), 5.

139. Schreiner, *Romans*, 187.

140. Steven E. Enderlein, "To Fall Short or Lack the Glory of God?: The Translation and Implications of Romans 3:23," *JSPL* 1 (2011): 215.

141. Dunn, *Romans 1–8,* 168. *Pace* Fitzmyer, who argues that Paul is referring to a sharing in God's glory through communion not a glory of humankind lost by

Adam (*Romans: A New Translation with Introduction and Commentary,* AB 33 [New York: Doubleday, 1993], 347). To the contrary, Fitzmyer's position forges a false dichotomy. The Edenic condition of man and the eschatological hope of sharing in the glory of God are not mutually exclusive.

142. Other scholars who affirm an allusion to Adam's sin in Romans 3:23 include: C. K. Barrett, *A Commentary on the Epistle to the Romans* (New York: Harper & Brothers, 1957), 74; Scroggs, *Last Adam,* 73, 73n43; Cranfield, *Romans,* 1:205–6; Douglas A. Campbell, *The Rhetoric of Righteousness in Romans 3.21–26*, JSNTSup 65 (Sheffield: JSOT Press, 1992), 172–3; Christian Grappe, "Qui me délivrera de ce corps de mort?: L'esprit de vie! Romains 7,24 et 8,2 comme éléments de typologie Adamique," *Bib* 83 (2002): 481.

143. Carey C. Newman, *Paul's Glory-Christology: Tradition and Rhetoric*, NovTSup 69 (Leiden: Brill, 1992), 225; Schreiner, *Romans,* 187.

144. "ὑστερέω," *BDAG*, BibleWorks 10, s.v. The distinction is due to the ambiguity of the verb form which can be middle or passive. If middle, the interpretation would be "fall short." If passive, it would be "lack."

145. For further discussion on Rom 3:23 and the reference to Adamic glory, see Enderlein, "To Fall Short or Lack the Glory of God?," 213–23. See also Porter and Cirafesi's critique and Enderlein's rejoinder: Stanley E. Porter and Wally V. Cirafesi, "ὑστερέω and πίστις Χριστοῦ in Romans 3:23: a Response to Steven Enderlein," *JSPL* 3 (2013): 1–9; Steven E. Enderlein, "The Faithfulness of the Second Adam in Romans 3:21–26: A Response to Porter and Cirafesi," *JSPL* 3 (2013): 11–24. Dunn has also argued for an Adam motif in both texts, see *Theology of Paul,* 93–4, 98–100 and literature cited.

146. Dunn, *Theology of Paul,* 93–4.

147. Sprinkle, "Afterlife," 224–5.

148. Blackwell, "Immortal Glory," 300.

149. There is likely another allusion to Adam in Romans 7:7–13. Only Adam was fully alive before the commandment was given. Only he experienced the effect of passing from life to death as a result of sin. The deception of sin was central to Adam's paradigmatic fall (Käsemann, *Romans,* 196). Indeed, the resonance is so strong that Käsemann wrote, "there is nothing in this passage which does not fit Adam and *all of it only fits Adam*" (ibid. My emphasis). The resonance is especially high in light of the Adamic discussion in Rom 5— which original hearers would have heard moments before. Byrskog writes, "to the extent that the one man through whom sin came into the world is Adam according to chapter 5, the 'I' who experienced death according to chapter 7 also resembles Adam" (Byrskog, "Christology and Identity," 11–2). Proponents of this view include: Käsemann, *Romans,* 192–8; Dunn, *Theology of Paul,* 98–100; Grappe, "Qui me délivrera," 472–92; Pate, *The Glory of Adam*, 147–8; W. D. Davies, *Paul and Rabbinic Judaism: Some Rabbinic Elements in Pauline Theology*, 4th ed. (Philadelphia: Fortress, 1980), 32; F. F. Bruce, *Paul: Apostle of the Heart Set Free* (Grand Rapids: Eerdmans, 1977), 194; Wedderburn, "Adam in Romans," 420; Francis Watson, *Paul, Judaism, and the Gentiles: Beyond the New Perspective* (Grand Rapids: Eerdmans, 2007), 151–3. For a recent survey of this debate, see Richard Longenecker, *The Epistle to the Romans*,

NIGTC, ed. Marshall, I. Howard and Donald Hagner (Grand Rapids: Eerdmans, 2016), 651–60.

150. I take the canonical text of Romans to be the original form, including chapter 16 and the doxology of 16:25–27.

151. For a thorough investigation of the Genesis background of Rom 16:20a, see Jan Dochhorn, "Paulus und die polyglotte Schriftgelehrsamkeit seiner Zeit: eine Studie zu den exegetischen Hintergründen von Röm 16,20a," *ZNW* 98 (2007): 189–212. For a more recent defense of Rom 16:20a as alluding to Gen 2–3, see Wesley Crouser, "Satan, the Serpent, and Witchcraft Accusations: Reading Romans 16:17–20a in Light of Allusions and Anthropology," *JSPL* 4 (2014): 215–33; James Hamilton, "The Skull Crushing Seed of the Woman: Inner-Biblical Interpretation of Genesis 3:15," *SBTJ* 10 (2006): 33, 42; Donald L. Berry, *Glory in Romans and the Unified Purpose of God in Redemptive History* (Eugene, OR: Pickwick Publications, 2016), 129–30. Some commentators describe this allusion as certain, for example, Murray, *The Epistle to the Romans*, NICNT (Grand Rapids: Eerdmans, 1968), 237; Peter Stuhlmacher, *Paul's Letter to the Romans: A Commentary,* trans. Scott J. Hafemann (Louisville, KY: Westminster John Knox, 1994), 253–4; others consider it likely, for example, Moo, *Romans*, 932–3; Käsemann, *Romans,* 418; James D. G. Dunn, *Romans 9–16,* WBC 38b (Waco, TX: Word Books, 2003), 905; Schlatter, *Romans*, 277.

152. See, for example, Michael E. Stone, "Satan and the Serpent in the Armenian Tradition," in *Beyond Eden: The Biblical Story of Paradise (Genesis 2–3) and Its Reception History* (Tübingen: Mohr Siebeck, 2008), 141–86; and Crouser, "Satan, the Serpent, and Witchcraft Accusations," 215–33.

153. This is not to argue that these references form the only or controlling inclusio of Romans. The "obedience of faith" inclusio from 1:5 to 16:26 is clearly at the heart of Paul's argument. Rather, it is noteworthy that Paul maintains a consistency of allusions to Gen 1–3 throughout.

154. Again, based on Richard Hays's criteria of recurrence and thematic coherence (*Echoes*, 30). See also, Michael B. Thompson, *Clothed with Christ: The Example and Teaching of Jesus in Romans 12.1–15.13*, JSNTSup 59 (Sheffield: JSOT Press, 1991), 35.

155. Douglas J. Moo, "Israel and the Law in Romans 5–11: Interaction with the New Perspective," in *The Paradoxes of Paul*, vol. 2 of *Justification and Variegated Nomism*, ed. D. A. Carson, Peter T. O'Brien, and Mark A. Seifrid (Grand Rapids: Baker Academic, 2004), 194–5.

156. See Morris, "Exiled from Eden," 117–68.

157. I use the masculine, "sons" rather than "children," to highlight the theme of sonship from Adam to Israel to Christ to the new "sons" who are led by God's Spirit (Rom 8:14).

# *Chapter 4*

# The Restoration of Adam and Israel in Romans 5

The previous chapters surveyed the background in the Hebrew Bible and early Jewish usage of various Adam traditions and the metanarrative of Israel's exile and hope for restoration. We saw that not only did the Hebrew Bible testify to an exile that was not fully resolved for Israel, even after Ezra and Nehemiah, but hope for restoration continues to be significant throughout the Second Temple period. The present chapter will show that Paul interweaves allusions to Adam and prophecies of Israel's restoration throughout Rom 5. Although he only explicitly mentions Adam in Rom 5:14, his exposition of eschatological advancement through Christ mingles the reversal of Adam's sin with the idea of restoration. Just as Paul alludes to both Adam and Israel to show universal guilt in Rom 1:18–32,[1] so does he employ both in Rom 5 to describe humanity's estrangement from God because of sin and reconciliation through Christ. As the last Adam, Jesus reverses the curse of humanity and its separation from God. As the true Israel, Jesus restores the true people of God from their former exile. Paul sees a unity in the history of redemption. The evidence that Paul sees humanity's archetypal exile in Adam and Israel's typological exile as reversed through Christ is chiefly found in his use of the Jewish Scripture.

Romans 5 consists of two parts, the first of these (5:1–11) functions to transition from Paul's opening argument (1:18–4:25) to the second major argument of the letter (5:1–8:39). The second part (5:12–21) introduces Adam's and Christ's typological relationship as the foundation of the dichotomies of "life and death" and "flesh and spirit" throughout Rom 5–8. I will examine each of these sections in turn to demonstrate Paul's use of both Adam and Israel in the substructure of his argument as a whole.

## RECONCILIATION AS THE REVERSAL OF MANKIND'S EXCHANGE

There is a notable symmetry in the structure of Rom 1:18–5:11. Paul begins with humanity's exchange of God's glory and ends with God's choice to bear the consequence of that exchange and reconcile humanity to himself. Romans 5:1–11 functions as a literary bridge; it concludes the first argument and begins the second.[2] Paul concludes themes from his opening argument and introduces the subjects he will develop in the following chapters.[3] The use of ἀλλάσσω-terminology is the hinge upon which the discussion turns.[4] The first argument of Romans begins with men exchanging ([μετ]αλλάσσω, Rom 1:23, 25, 26) God's glory which results in God handing them over (παραδίδωμι, Rom 1:24, 26, 28) to futility. The threefold repetition of "exchange" corresponds to the threefold result. The solution and reversal comes through a righteous substitute who bears the iniquity of the spiritual children of Abraham (Rom 4:13, 23–25). Paul concludes his first argument in Rom 4:25 referencing how it began saying [Ἰησοῦς] παρεδόθη διὰ τὰ παραπτώματα ἡμῶν καὶ ἠγέρθη διὰ τὴν δικαίωσιν ἡμῶν ("[Jesus] *was handed over* on account of our transgression and raised on account of our justification"). Whereas "man"—enriched by allusions to both Adam and Israel—exchanged God's glory and was handed over to sin, Jesus Christ was handed over for τὰ παραπτώματα ἡμῶν. Paul's initial use of παράπτωμα, which will shortly be used to describe Adam's sin (cf. 5:15–20), and deliberate repetition of παραδίδωμι depict Christ's reversal of his people's curse by bearing it himself.

Paul Phrases Rom 4:25 in terms allusive of the Fourth Servant Song of Isaiah:

**Table 4.1 Isaiah 53 in Romans 4:25**

| *Isaiah 53:4–6, 11, 12*[a] | *Romans 4:25* |
|---|---|
| ... οὗτος τὰς ἁμαρτίας ἡμῶν φέρει (v. 4)<br>... αὐτὸς δὲ ἐτραυματίσθη διὰ τὰς ἀνομίας ἡμῶν καὶ μεμαλάκισται διὰ τὰς ἁμαρτίας ἡμῶν (v. 5)<br>... καὶ κύριος παρέδωκεν αὐτὸν ταῖς ἁμαρτίαις ἡμῶν (v. 6)<br>... δικαιῶσαι δίκαιον εὖ δουλεύοντα πολλοῖς καὶ τὰς ἁμαρτίας αὐτῶν αὐτὸς ἀνοίσει (v. 11)<br>...καὶ αὐτὸς ἁμαρτίας πολλῶν ἀνήνεγκεν καὶ διὰ τὰς ἁμαρτίας αὐτῶν παρεδόθη (v. 12) | Ἰησοῦν... ὃς παρεδόθη διὰ τὰ παραπτώματα ἡμῶν καὶ ἠγέρθη διὰ τὴν δικαίωσιν ἡμῶν. |
| Isa 53:11 MT יַצְדִּיק צַדִּיק עַבְדִּי לָרַבִּים[b] | |

*Note*: Solid underlines indicate parallels.
[a]There is debate as to the specific text to which Paul refers, whether it is some recension of the LXX, or a Hebrew *Vorlage*. There is insufficient space to address that question here. For an investigation of the OT background of Rom 4:25, see Hermann Patsch, "Zum Alttestamentlichen Hintergrund von Römer 4:25 und 1 Petrus 2:24," *ZNW* 60 (1969): 273–9, and literature he cites.
[b]Dunn argues that Rom 4:25 reflects dependence upon both Hebrew and Greek renderings of Isaiah (*Romans 1–8,* 241).

There is a notable literary and thematic connection between these texts making the allusion strong.[5] It is a significant dependence. Paul identifies Jesus Christ as the servant of the Yahweh who accomplishes two actions in parallel: (1) dying for τὰ παραπτώματα ἡμῶν and (2) being raised for justification, which results in reconciliation with God (Rom 5:1–11). Chapter 2 discussed the Isaianic identity of Israel's exile as Deuteronomic curse and demonstrated that it would be reversed through the singular work of the servant of Yahweh. Paul now claims that Jesus is that servant. His work reverses the effect of the threefold exchange (ἀλλάσσω) for those who believe. God gave Jesus over, instead of his people (ἡμῶν), to bear their sins (Rom 4:25) and so reconcile (καταλλάσσω) humanity to himself (Rom 5:10). I argue that Paul saw Jesus reversing Israel's exile, as Isaiah's servant. As Rikki Watts notes, "Isa. 53 is concerned primarily with Yahweh's planned redemption of his rebellious people from exile and its attendant curses."[6]

Paul's use of the ἀλλάσσω-root in his transitional paragraph links the reconciliation accomplished by Christ with the exchange (ἀλλάσσω) of God's glory described in Rom 1:18–32. The significance of Paul's use of καταλλάσσω should not be missed. It repeats the martyr tradition of 2 Maccabees, which viewed reconciliation (καταλλάσσω) as the end of Deuteronomic exile (cf. 2 Macc 1:5; 7:33, 8:29).[7] Indeed, as we will see below, the descriptions of the new era as one of peace, righteousness, and the outpouring of the Spirit all indicate the fulfillment of restoration promises.[8]

## ROMANS 5:1–11

Paul's opening paragraph (5:1–11) recalls the previous argument and introduces themes which will be developed throughout the next several chapters, particularly in Rom 8. The use of terms "justified" (δικαιόω, 5:1, 9), "boast" (καυχάομαι, 5:2, 11), and "glory of God" (δόξα τοῦ θεοῦ, 5:2) continue Paul's discussion from 3:21–4:25. More broadly, the continuation of the glory theme suggests that this was the very glory man exchanged (1:23) and the standard of righteous glory from which man initially and continually falls short (3:23). Schreiner writes, "Those who scorned God's glory (Rom. 1:21–23) and have fallen short of it (3:23) are now [i.e., in Rom 5] promised a future share in it."[9] Thus, the opening sentence in 5:1, Δικαιωθέντες οὖν ἐκ πίστεως εἰρήνην ἔχομεν[10] πρὸς τὸν θεὸν διὰ τοῦ κυρίου ἡμῶν Ἰησοῦ Χριστοῦ . . . καὶ καυχώμεθα ἐπ' ἐλπίδι τῆς δόξης τοῦ θεοῦ ("Therefore, because we have been justified by means of faith we have peace with God through our Lord Jesus Christ . . . and we boast on the basis of hope for the glory of God"), recalls humanity's unrighteous exchange of glory and foresees its attainment. I have shown in the previous chapter that both Adam's archetypal sin and Israel's repetition from it were connected to Paul's exposition of the nature of human sin in Rom 1–4. In Rom 5, that trend continues.

## Israel in Romans 5:1–11

Paul's triumphant declaration that "we" have been justified by faith (Rom 5:1) brings the Roman recipients of his letter into clear focus. Jew and Gentile alike are the spiritual children of Abraham and so inherit the promise and become heirs of the world (4:13, 16, 23–25). Yet within the vocabulary of Paul's opening paragraph there are clear echoes of God's former dealings with and promises to Israel. The era Christ inaugurates is depicted with the same terminology by which Israel's future restoration from exile was described in Isaiah.[11] Israel's restoration is indicated in at least three ways: the announcement of the outpouring of the Spirit (Rom 5:5), the use of καταλλάσσω to describe its result, and repeated allusions to Isaianic restoration.

### *Isaiah in Romans 5:1–11*

As he describes the new era Christ inaugurates, Paul echoes Isaianic descriptions of Israel's future redemption.[12] For instance, Frank Thielman notes an especially high correspondence in terms between the restoration prophecy of Isaiah 32:15–17 and Rom 5:1–11.[13] There is a possible allusion to Isa 32:17 in Rom 5:1 based upon the underlined words below.[14] These echoes are hardly convincing independently of one another, but as they follow Rom 4:25, there is a higher likelihood that Paul is writing in reference to Isaiah. According to Isaiah 32, the exile would endure:

> ἕως ἂν ἐπέλθῃ ἐφ' ὑμᾶς πνεῦμα ἀφ' ὑψηλοῦ . . . 16 καὶ ἀναπαύσεται ἐν τῇ ἐρήμῳ κρίμα, καὶ δικαιοσύνη ἐν τῷ Καρμήλῳ· 17 καὶ ἔσται τὰ ἔργα τῆς δικαιοσύνης εἰρήνη, καὶ κρατήσει ἡ δικαιοσύνη ἀνάπαυσιν, καὶ πεποιθότες ἕως τοῦ αἰῶνος·[15]
>
> until the spirit comes upon us from above . . . and judgment will rest in the wilderness and righteousness will dwell in Carmel. 17 And the works of righteousness will be peace and righteousness will cling to rest and they will be at ease forever.

Similarly, Rom 5:6, 8b are reminiscent of Isa 53:8.[16]

**Table 4.2 Isaiah 53:8 in Romans 5:6, 8b**

| *Isaiah 53:8* | *Romans 5:6, 8b* |
|---|---|
| … ὅτι αἴρεται ἀπὸ τῆς γῆς ἡ ζωὴ αὐτοῦ, ἀπὸ τῶν ἀνομιῶν τοῦ λαοῦ μου ἤχθη εἰς θάνατον. | Ἔτι γὰρ Χριστὸς ὄντων ἡμῶν ἀσθενῶν ἔτι κατὰ καιρὸν ὑπὲρ ἀσεβῶν ἀπέθανεν… [8b]ὅτι ἔτι ἁμαρτωλῶν ὄντων ἡμῶν Χριστὸς ὑπὲρ ἡμῶν ἀπέθανεν. |
| Because his life is being taken from the earth, on account of the acts of lawlessness of my people he was led to death. | For while we were yet weak, at the appointed time Christ died for the ungodly . . . [8b]that while we were yet sinners, Christ died for us. |

*Note*: Solid underlines indicate parallels.

Romans 5:6 and 5:8 are syntactically parallel and explain the significance of God pouring out his love in the Spirit upon his people.[17] Another potential allusion in 5:1 and especially the previous allusion to Isa 53 in Rom 4:25 increase the likelihood that Paul is consciously alluding to Isa 53 in Rom 5:6 and 8. Paul sees Christ's death as fulfilling Isa 53 and, hence, he uses that language to describe the reality it foresaw.[18] The descriptions of peace with God (5:1), righteousness (5:1, 9), reconciliation (5:10–11), a future hope of glory (5:2), and, perhaps most importantly, the outpouring of the Spirit (5:5) all recall Isaianic expectations (cf. Isa 32:15–17, above). Indeed, Rom 5:1–11 is bounded with the notion of "peace," as the term καταλλάσσω (5:10–11) also denotes renewed, relational peace.[19] Paul refers to eschatological peace with God, which God promised to his covenant people in the last days (Isa 9:6–7; 32:15–17; 48:20–22; 54:10; cf. Ezek 34:25; 37:26). It is noteworthy that several of these texts promise peace in the context of a future restoration.

### *The Outpouring of the Spirit as Marking Israel's Restoration*

The second indication that Paul announces Israel's restoration is the outpouring (ἐκκέχυται) of the Holy Spirit in Rom 5:5. While this point is not immediately clear in the context of Rom 5 alone, it is established when viewed alongside the use of Ezek 36–37 in Rom 8:1–11 (which will be argued in the next chapter).

G. K. Beale has noted a dual significance of the outpouring of the Spirit as marking the restoration of Israel (Isa 32:15; Ezek 39:28–29; Joel 2:28; cf. Zech 12:10) and the inauguration of the last days (Acts 3:18, 22–26; 4:25–28; 13:27–29, 46–48; 15:14–18; 26:22–23).[20] The Abrahamic promise was given to Israel, but has broadened to all Abraham's spiritual children (Rom 4:13,

16, 23–5).[21] The outpouring of the Spirit inaugurates God's renewed presence among his people. The Spirit's "coming" (ἐπέρχομαι) in Isa 32:15 is followed by righteousness (δικαιοσύνη), dwelling (κατοικέω), and resting (ἀναπαύω) in a fruitful place forever (Isa 32:16). The MT describes the wilderness itself becoming fertile.[22] Similarly, the outpouring of the Spirit comes at the beginning of the new age of life through Christ, which he contrasts with the previous age of death in Adam. In Rom 8, Paul will clarify that the Spirit works spiritual life through resurrection for those in Christ and that this ultimately leads to the redemption of the body and of creation itself (Rom 8:9–11, 14–17, 18–23). The expansion in Rom 8, however, demonstrates how the process of restoration is not immediate but will be achieved in glory (8:17). Likewise, in Rom 5:1–2, present justification results in future glory.

The parallel prophecy in Ezek 39:28–29 is linguistically similar to Rom 5:5. While the other two prophecies of the outpouring of the Spirit (Isa 32:15; Joel 2:8) point to the same event, Ezekiel's text stands closest to Paul's. The Spirit's coming is not the main clause of Ezek 39:28–29, but indicates the timing of renewed relationship. The promise is that at that time God will no longer "hide his face from them" (καὶ οὐκ ἀποστρέψω οὐκέτι τὸ πρόσωπόν μου ἀπ' αὐτῶν), a typical description that highlights the sundered relationship in exile (cf. Deut 31:17–8; Ps 44:24; 104:29).[23] Zimmerli describes the Spirit's coming as the "final irrevocable union of Yahweh with his people."[24] Indeed, that Paul is describing a renewed relationship is confirmed by his use of καταλλάσσω ("reconciliation," 5:10–11), προσαγωγή ("access," 5:2), and εἰρήνη ("peace," 5:1).[25] Each term underscores a renewed relationship.[26] Of the outpouring in Ezekiel, Daniel I. Block writes, "the pouring out of the Spirit of Yahweh upon his people signified the ratification and sealing of the covenant relationship. It represented the guarantee of new life, peace and prosperity. But it signified more than this. It served as the definitive act whereby he claimed and sealed the newly gathered nation of Israel as his own."[27] Thus, the Spirit's outpouring marks God's return to his people.

In Rom 5:5 Paul uses the same verb that Ezekiel employs (ἐκχέω) to demonstrate the end of Israel's exile. The coming of the Spirit marks the dawn of the new age, which Paul declares is begun in Christ, the last Adam. Furthermore, Ezekiel's prophecy is not for a universal presence of the Spirit, instead the Spirit will come ἐπὶ τὸν οἶκον Ισραηλ ("upon the house of Israel," Ezek 39:29). Paul describes exactly that reality. The Spirit has come upon true Israel in the spiritual children of Abraham, Jew, and Greek. The Spirit's vivifying presence becomes the key distinction between those κατὰ σάρκα versus those κατὰ πνεῦμα (Rom 8:5–11). Thus, the coming of the Spirit marks the end of the exile, the time when God will turn his face back to his people.

We should note, however, that Ezek 39:28–29 is complicated by differences in the textual tradition. Whereas the MT claims that Israel will be restored because God has poured out his *Spirit* (רוּחַ), the Göttingen LXX claims it will be restored because God poured out—and thus satisfied—his *wrath* (θυμός). Space will not allow for a full text-critical treatment.[28] However, I will simply observe that Paul speaks in Rom 5:5 of the outpouring of the *Spirit*, as opposed to the *wrath* of God.[29] As mentioned above, this allusion is rendered more likely by the use of Ezek 36–37 in Rom 8:1–11.[30] Moreover, Ka Leung Wong has noted that the word רוּחַ can connote the idea of anger. He argues that that θυμόν is likely an interpretive translation of the original Hebrew.[31] Despite this textual obstacle, it remains likely that Paul considered the Spirit's outpouring in Rom 5:5 to be the fulfillment of Ezekiel's restoration prophecy.

### *Reconciliation to God as the Inauguration of Restoration*

Paul's description of Christ's work as reconciliation (καταλλάσσω and καταλλαγή, Rom 5:10–11) also lends support to the thesis that he describes the end of Israel's exile in Rom 5:1–11. G. K. Beale has shown that Paul's use of καταλλάσσω in 2 Cor 5–7 was informed by Isaianic restoration prophecies.[32] Based upon his exegesis of the background of 2 Cor 5–7 in the Hebrew Bible, Beale writes, "it is plausible to suggest that 'reconciliation' in Christ is Paul's way of explaining that Isaiah's promises of 'restoration' from the alienation of exile have begun to be fulfilled by the atonement and forgiveness of sins in Christ."[33] While Isaiah does not employ identical terminology, Otfried Hofius observes that καταλλάσσω and καταλλαγή are easily derived from Hellenistic Judaism and would accurately communicate the notion of restoration in Paul's first-century context (e.g., 2 Macc 1:5; 5:20; 7:33; 8:29).[34] It has already been mentioned that the martyr tradition in 2 Maccabees considered the suffering of the Jewish people to be a function of Deuteronomic exile and that reconciliation would bring it to a close. Thus, Paul's terminology plausibly points to the end of exile. Yet, while the terminology likely comes from the martyr tradition, Hofius argues that the subject matter (*die Sache*) of Pauline reconciliation is derived from the fourth servant song, which we have already seen is concerned with restoration.[35] This is all the more likely when it is remembered that Paul has just identified Christ as Isaiah's servant in Rom 4:25 (and perhaps 5:1, 6, 8b). If Rom 5:1–11 is read in light of the earlier text 2 Cor 5:17–21 where Paul also develops the concept of reconciliation to God the connection is further strengthened.

Not only is reconciliation a central point of both Rom 5 and 2 Cor 5, but it is shown in both to be the result of justification through Christ's vicarious death (cf. Rom 5:1, 8–10; 2 Cor 5:2). Second Corinthians clarifies that justification in Christ is an act of new creation (2 Cor 5:17). Jesus Christ stands at the head of a new humanity, recreated through his death and resurrection. But, as Beale has shown, this new humanity is also the fulfillment of Isaiah's promise to restore Israel.[36] Thus, Paul's similar use of καταλλάσσω in Rom 5, in conjunction with his announcement of the outpouring of the Holy Spirit, strongly suggests that Jesus has initiated Israel's restoration.

Hofius concurs that Pauline reconciliation is "decisively shaped" by Isa 40–55 (specifically Isa 52:13–53:12).[37] He argues that reconciliation should be divided into God's act of reconciliation (*Versöhnungstat*) and its announcement (*Versöhnungswort*).[38] It is often noted that the accomplishment of reconciliation occurred upon the cross, but the act of reconciliation results in a message to be announced.[39] In light of these findings, it is appropriate to paraphrase Paul's statement in 2 Cor 5:19 in which he calls the gospel a message of reconciliation (καταλλαγῆς), instead a message of *restoration.* As Constantineanu puts it, "For Paul, reconciliation is nothing else but the great restoration of God's people, of humanity, of creation itself, to the initial purposes of God. By alluding to the story in Isaiah, Paul wants to point beyond the story of Israel to the story of God and the world."[40]

### *The Timing of Restoration in Romans 5:1–11*

Despite the indicators that restoration has begun, it remains incomplete. Restoration is both "already" and "not yet." Just after Paul boasts in peace with God and renewed hope in glory (Rom 4:25–5:2), he explains that the full realization of that hope will come after suffering (Rom 5:3–5). The nature of that suffering is due to the two-stage process of reconciliation. Paul argues that whereas humanity was separated from God spiritually and physically, in Christ they are first spiritually reconciled. The physical element of separation, however, remains in place. Romans 8 will clarify that believers (and creation with them) still await the redemption of the body (8:23).

This already-not yet redemption results in a life shared between ages and between kingdoms. Believers are reconciled to God and so participate in the age to come, but remain in the present fallen age ruled by Sin and Death.[41] This leads to yet another connection to Israel's exile and restoration in Paul's description of the present condition as one of "afflictions." Present justification does not result in present glory, but the assurance of *future* glory. Immediately after Paul explains that redemption results in a renewed hope of glory (5:2), he launches into the *catena* of Rom 5:3–5:

> 3 οὐ μόνον δέ, ἀλλὰ καὶ καυχώμεθα ἐν ταῖς θλίψεσιν, εἰδότες ὅτι ἡ θλῖψις ὑπομονὴν κατεργάζεται, 4 ἡ δὲ ὑπομονὴ δοκιμήν, ἡ δὲ δοκιμὴ ἐλπίδα. 5 ἡ δὲ ἐλπὶς οὐ καταισχύνει, ὅτι ἡ ἀγάπη τοῦ θεοῦ ἐκκέχυται ἐν ταῖς καρδίαις ἡμῶν διὰ πνεύματος ἁγίου τοῦ δοθέντος ἡμῖν.

> 3 And not only that, but also we boast in afflictions, because we know that the affliction produces perseverance, 4 and perseverance character, and character

hope. 5 And hope will not be shamed, for the love of God has been poured into our hearts through the Holy Spirit who has been given to us.

The term, θλῖψις, sometimes bears an eschatological significance for both Judaism and the early church.[42] Silva notes "the θλῖψις of the LXX is often the *distinctive oppression* experienced by Israel and regarded by the faithful as part of salvation history."[43] It acquires a theological significance in the LXX (as the chosen translation for multiple Hebrew terms) in that it primarily denotes the persecution of Israel or righteous individuals who represent God's people.[44] This reflects the belief sometimes called the "messianic woes" that in the last days there would be a time of heightened suffering for God's faithful before the Eschaton.[45] However, Israel's exile is also regularly described as θλῖψις. In Deut 28, θλῖψις is used three times in short succession to describe the misery that will come upon Israel from a foreign oppressor (Deut 28:53, 55, 57; cf. Deut 4:30; 31:17; Isa 8:22–23; 30:6). Each time Deut 28 mentions the θλῖψις that will come upon his covenant breaking people the term occurs is paired with στενοχωρία ("distress"). The location of the affliction is still within their land (e.g., 28:55, 57: "your cities") but the inevitable end is exile (28:64–68).[46] When it is recognized that Paul describes believers' persecution in the world in Rom 8:35 as θλῖψις and στενοχωρία the identification of believers' afflictions with exile is further strengthened.[47]

However, there is another layer to Paul's message. The reconciliation-hinge upon which Paul's argument shifts is the reversal of more than just the curse against Israel, but against the whole world. In light of Paul's dependence upon Isaiah, it is appropriate to recall Yahweh's speech to his servant in Isa 49:6: "It is too trivial for you to be my servant to raise up the tribes of Jacob and to restore the preserved of Israel; I will give you for a light to the Gentiles that my salvation might reach the ends of the earth."[48] While it can be said that Israel was intended to be a light to the nations (Isa 42:6; cf. 49:6; Zech 8:23),[49] it cannot be granted that the condemnation of the world is due to Israel. The world is under curse because of Adam. Paul explains in 5:12–21 that Jesus Christ, whom he has already identified as the servant of Yahweh, reverses the work of Adam. The explanation in 5:12–21 depends upon the juxtaposition of Jesus with Adam and the various polarities of "life" and "death," or "spirit" and "flesh" that arise from it.

## Adam in Romans 5:1–11

The discussion of sin, law, death, dominion, and transgression in Rom 5:12–21 is full of references to Adam's role in Gen 1–3, all of which is made explicit in 5:14 when Paul names him: ἐβασίλευσεν ὁ θάνατος ἀπὸ Ἀδὰμ μέχρι Μωϋσέως ("death reigned from Adam until Moses") and again Ἀδὰμ ὅς ἐστιν τύπος τοῦ μέλλοντος ("Adam, who is a type of the one to come").

However, less attention has been given to the previous paragraph, Rom 5:1–11. I argue that Rom 5:1–11 also reflects Adam's influence in its substructure. Theologically speaking, Adam's first sin lies behind the *need* for humanity's reconciliation to God (3:23; 5:12, 16, 18). The structure of Rom 1–5 indicates this. The exchange ([μετ]αλλάσσω) of God's glory could only be resolved by God reconciling (καταλλάσσω) man to himself. Once that theme concludes in Rom 5:1–11, Paul immediately begins to explain (Διὰ τοῦτο, Rom 5:12) these events in *Adamic* terms (5:12–21).[50] However, the chief evidence for an Adamic substructure in Rom 5:1–11 is the δόξα motif.

Within the limits of Paul's second argument (5:1–8:39), Rom 5:1–2 serves as an introductory statement to the *Leitmotif* of hope in glory which Paul will expand in Rom 8:17–30. Thus far in Romans, δόξα has functioned to describe the worship of God as creator that man exchanged for idolatry (1:23; cf. 3:7; 4:20) and the ethical standard of divine righteousness from which man continually falls short (3:23; cf. 2:7, 10).[51] In each of these previous instances, there are allusions to Adam's created state and first sin. In Rom 5:1–2, Paul explains that Christ renews the hope τῆς δόξης τοῦ θεοῦ through justification. Believers presently stand in a position of grace instead of a position of wrath, but they *will* attain δόξα in the future.[52] Thus the two-stage progression of salvation is clearly laid out: justification and reconciliation are not the end of redemption, but attaining δόξα.[53] This δόξα should be understood as a participation in divine glory as it is communicated to those in communion with him. Moreover, in the next paragraph, Paul will clarify that it is Christ's work *as the last Adam* that renders the attainment of glory certain (5:12–21). Hence, several scholars have argued the δόξα τοῦ θεοῦ of 5:2 is a restoration of Adam's lost glory.[54]

The *renewed* hope τῆς δόξης τοῦ θεοῦ raises the question, at what point in time did man previously hope in the glory of God (cf. Rom 1:23; 5:2)? Only Adam in his Edenic incorruption realistically hoped in or, to a degree, enjoyed the glory of God. Adam initially exchanged God's glory (Rom 1:23; 3:23 cf. *Apoc. Mos.* 20:1–5; *Vita* 11:2–3), and Israel followed in the Adamic example by worshiping the image of the golden calf (Ps 106:20). Recall Sirach's claims that none had so much δόξα as Adam (49:16). Although the notion of the "glory of Adam" is typically considered an extra-biblical category, there is good reason to conclude this is the concept Paul has in mind. By "Adamic glory," I mean the Edenic potential of humanity, the original state of incorruption and immortality, and the likeness Adam shared with his creator as image-bearer.

Paul argues that because righteousness is restored, glory will soon be bestowed upon renewed humanity through Christ. Indeed, with one exception (Rom 6:4), Paul's use of the δόξα word group in Rom 5–8 always refers to humanity's participation in eschatological glory with God (Rom 5:2; 8:17,

18, 21, 30).[55] If these uses of the glory-motif are applied to the interpretation of the hope of glory in Rom 5:2 several conclusions can be rendered:

(1) Glory is the inevitable result of justification (Rom 8:30).
(2) Glory will come after suffering with Christ (Rom 8:17).
(3) Glory will come at the end of the age (Rom 8:18).
(4) Glory is defined as the δόξης <u>τῶν τέκνων τοῦ θεοῦ</u> ("the glory of the children of God," Rom 8:21), which is itself related to adoption as God's children (8:15–16). That adoption will initially take place spiritually (Rom 8:15), but it will be consummated physically with the redemption of the body (Rom 8:23).
(5) Glory is the end result of the Spirit's work to conform believers to the image of the Son of God (Rom 8:29–30).

Thus, glory is the consummation of God's purpose in humanity and is related to the restoration of the previously obscured divine image. Despite the image persisting in fallen humanity in an ontological sense (cf. Gen 5:1–3; 9:6; Rom 8:29; 1 Cor 11:7; Eph 4:24, Col 3:10; James 3:9), likeness to God was obscured. Thus, while it must be articulated with qualification, in the context of Rom 1–5 as a whole, the glory of God in which humanity has a renewed hope is the same glory Adam lost through transgression. This glory should not be simplistically equated with the excesses of the rabbis or other Second Temple interpretations. For Paul, however, the glory in which believers boast in Rom 5:2 was first something held out to Adam. Whether it is the restoration of glory Adam actually possessed in Eden or, more likely, the attainment of something that remained future for him had he been obedient,[56] the conclusion that the future glory in which believers have certain hope was once lost by Adam's transgression seems inescapable. Christian Grappe writes,

> Or elle [la gloire d'Adam] se retrouve en Rm 1–8 où, si tous ont, à l'image d'Adam, perdu la gloire de Dieu (3,23), les croyants ne s'enorgueillissent pas moins dans l'espérance de cette même gloire (5,2), gloire à venir (8,18), mais qui s'est manifestée déjà dans la résurrection du Fils (6,4) et au bénéfice de laquelle se trouveront (8,17.21) et se trouvent dès maintenant, dans un présent revêtant une forte coloration eschatologique, les fils, prédestinés, appelés et justifiés (8,30).[57]

When Paul returns to the ἀλλάσσω-root in Rom 5:10–11, he does so to demonstrate that Christ has reversed the effects of humanity's departure from God and restored the Edenic hope of participation in God's glory. The glory of

Rom 5:2 is the inevitable result of reconciliation to God and the Christian's boast (cf. 8:31–39).

Thus, having completed his initial argument (1:18–4:25) and transitioned to the next (5:1–11), Paul turns to clarify the nature of the new age in comparison to the previous.

## ROMANS 5:12–21

The second paragraph of Rom 5 is one of the most studied and disputed passages in the Pauline corpus.[58] Its central point is the notion that Adam is the head of the original humanity and led to its curse, but Christ stands as the head of a new, eschatological humanity and ensures its blessing.[59] However, the apostle twice breaks his flow of thought to clarify what he has just said. Adam is introduced as a negative type of Christ (5:12), but the comparison is temporarily dropped to explain the situation of sin between Adam and the giving of the law (5:13–14). Paul then clarifies how Adam is *unlike* Christ (5:15–17), before returning to the subject of 5:12 and explaining the comparison more fully in 5:18–19. Finally, he concludes with a reflection on the law in redemptive history (5:20–21).[60] Thus, 5:13–17 should be seen as beside Paul's main point to show parallels between Adam and Christ.[61]

This paragraph is the clearest example of Paul's Adamic theology in Romans. Although Paul does not use the proper noun Ἀδάμ until 5:14, there should be no doubt that ἑνὸς ἀνθρώπου in 5:12 refers to the historical Adam. Scholars have questioned the origin of Paul's Adamic theology and its function. Yet, few studies have employed Paul's earlier allusions to Adam in Romans as a guide. As a noteworthy exception, A. J. M. Wedderburn notes that Paul begins this paragraph "in a manner that seems to assume that his readers are well aware of what he is describing. He refers simply and allusively to the narrative of Gen. iii by the words δι' ἑνὸς ἀνθρώπου."[62] This observation supports the thesis that Paul has been referring to Adam throughout. Douglas J. W. Milne suggests that Paul's argument in Rom 1:18–32, as it was in part based upon Adam's fall, is an "intentional prelude" to Rom 5.[63]

The most straightforward interpretation of Διὰ τοῦτο in Rom 5:12 is that it introduces an explanation.[64] Of course, that raises the question: What has already been said that Paul could explain by juxtaposing Adam and Christ in 5:12–21?[65] I argue that Paul has regularly alluded to the early chapters of Genesis to raise the anthropological problem of the Adamic curse. All humanity suppresses the truth in unrighteousness (Rom 1:18). All humanity has exchanged the glory of God (1:23). All humanity has fallen short of God's glory (3:23). But as Paul first implies and finally explains, it was

Adam who first fell and, by virtue of his God-given authority over the world, allowed Sin and Death to rule in his place (5:12–14). The explicit reference to Adam in Rom 5:12–21 strengthens the argument for an Adamic substructure throughout Rom 1–5. In turn, the previous allusions to Adam indicate Paul's intention to clarify the ways in which Christ both reverses the curse which had fallen upon the Adam-age and to show how Christ moves humanity forward toward glory.

Three stories intertwine throughout Rom 5–8: the stories of Christ, Adam, and Israel.[66] But Israel is not given equal prominence. There are not three ages, but two.[67] There is the Adam-age ruled by Death to which Israel belonged and there is the Christ-age, the life into which the new people of God has been brought. As Richard Gaffin notes, Adam is not only "last" but "second" (cf. 1 Cor 15:47); there is no one between them.[68] Paul's use of the Israel motif should not be seen as wholly distinct or a "new Adam," but as a type.[69] Israel did not share Adam's representative capacity. Both Adam and Israel typologically point forward to the true Son of God who would bring glory where they had fallen from it.

## Adam in Romans 5:12–21

Unlike other portions of Romans, the presence of the Adamic narrative rises above the surface in this paragraph and needs no defense. My goal in this section is to consider how Paul's explicit use of Adam contributes to the thesis that Adam's sin resulted in an archetypal exile. In other words, I will argue that Paul considered a consequence of Adam's transgression to be the physical and relational separation of humanity from God.

While it is the conclusion of this study overall, this thesis is not self-evident. One may object that Adam's curse was death (Gen 2:17), not exile. While Paul discusses Adam's transgression and the death that followed in Rom 5:12–21, he does not explain that Adam was "exiled" from God's presence or from Eden. Yet, from a theological standpoint are these so different?

It must be granted that a fully convincing case cannot be made from Rom 5 alone. The thesis depends upon Paul's hermeneutical development of themes from Rom 5 in Rom 8 and the contexts in the Hebrew Bible upon which he relies. My conclusion is derived from various angles, arising out of the redemptive-historical relationship between Adam and Israel, Paul's description of the *result* of Jesus's work as *last Adam* in terms drawn from passages which speak of Israel's restoration (particularly in Rom 8, but also in Rom 5), and the fundamental nature of the curse of death as spiritual separation from God.

### *Adam's Loss in Romans 5:12, 18–19*

Having argued that humanity can once again be righteous in God's sight and reconciled to God in Christ (Rom 4:25–5:11), Paul finds it necessary to explain (Διὰ τοῦτο) the redemptive-historical problem Christ resolves (5:12–21). Like many Second Temple writers, Paul views Adam's sin as personally, corporately, and cosmically disastrous. Indeed, Paul's typological contrast, indicated in the opening conjunction ὥσπερ, fundamentally presupposes both the historicity of Adam,[70] and his representative capacity.[71] The first two clauses of 5:12 simply restate the facts of Gen 2:17b and 3:3, 19 (cf. Wis 2:24).[72]

Διὰ τοῦτο

(a) ὥσπερ δι' ἑνὸς ἀνθρώπου ἡ ἁμαρτία εἰς τὸν κόσμον εἰσῆλθεν
(b) καὶ διὰ τῆς ἁμαρτίας ὁ θάνατος,[73]

For this reason,

(a) just as through one man sin entered the world
(b) and death (entered the world) through sin,

The movement from (1) Adam to (2) sin's entrance into the world to (3) death shows the cosmic scale that Paul will return to in Rom 8:18–23. The phrase εἰς τὸν κόσμον (5:12a) refers to the realm over which Adam was given sovereignty, to both humanity and creation.[74] Paul will later describe all creation as being subjected to futility (ματαιότης) on account of Adam's transgression (Rom 8:20).[75] Whereas God reigns over heaven and earth, he appointed Adam over creation as a vice-regent. His failure led to the curse of all that was under his authority (cf. Rom 8:19–22). The remaining two clauses reflect Paul's interpretation of Adam's sin and its effects.

(c) καὶ οὕτως εἰς πάντας ἀνθρώπους ὁ θάνατος διῆλθεν,
(d) ἐφ' ᾧ[76] πάντες ἥμαρτον·

(c) and in this manner death came to all men,
(d) because all sinned.

"Death" δι' ἑνὸς ἀνθρώπου will go on to serve as the antithesis in Rom 5–8 to the "life" that comes through the Spirit of Christ.[77] The dialectic of death and life in Rom 5–8 goes beyond the physical sphere to include the eschatological potential of Eden. Adam possessed life before the fall, but hoped for a more consummate life when he would pass beyond the possibility of corruption.

This may be a component of why the offer to be "like God" (ὡς θεοί, Gen 3:5 LXX) was so tempting.[78] His death fundamentally involved separation from God which entailed separation from the land of God's presence.[79] It was the beginning of the reign of Death over humanity and creation.

The phrase πάντες ἥμαρτον ("all sinned") in 5:12d closely follows the earlier statement in 3:23 (πάντες γὰρ ἥμαρτον).[80] The parallelism between 3:23 and 5:12d supports the previous argument that 3:23 refers to all humanity's (i.e., Jew and Greek's) emulation of Adam's sin and forfeiture of God's glory. Douglas Campbell writes, "This precise recapitulation of 3.23 in 5.12 is almost certainly more than coincidental. It would seem that, as for much of Judaism, Adam and the universality of sin were ideas closely linked in Paul's mind."[81] Both 3:23 and 5:12d provide further insight to the claim in 1:23 that humanity exchanges God's glory. In light of 5:12d, even apart from the potential allusions to Gen 1–3, it can be stated that the sins of exchanging God's glory in 1:23 and falling short of God's glory in 3:23 are *Adamic* sins that emulate his transgression.

Adam's transgression brought condemnation (κατάκριμα, 5:18a) for those he represented, for many became sinners through that transgression (5:18a, 19a). The term κατάκριμα is legal, not relational or social.[82] It pairs with παράβασις in 5:14, which implies a specific law to be transgressed.[83] I argue that the specific law in question was detailed in the covenant of creation with Adam with the various positive commands (Gen 1:28; 2:15) and the one prohibition (Gen 2:17). The results from the respective disobedience and obedience of Adam and Christ as death and life point to the covenantal framework in which the law was given. Covenant obedience leads to justification and life (Rom 5:18–19, 21). Reciprocally, covenant disobedience resulted in death, the exclusion from life.[84] Just as Israel's exile was its spiritual death, so was Adam's spiritual death his exile.

The cosmic shift resulting from Adam's sin is illustrated by an "unusual density of verbs of 'reigning'" in Rom 5.[85] Roy Ciampa argues that Paul's personification of Sin and Death indicates the replacement of Adam's dominion through creation's subjection to sin. Βασιλεύω and κυριεύω occur a combined eight times between 5:14 and 6:14,[86] neither appears in Romans beforehand. Adam, himself, was commissioned to reign, but his transgression resulted in the reign of the specific consequence of the covenant curse.[87] Genesis 3:16–19 lays out various consequences the first transgression, its summary is found in Gen 2:17, "on the day you eat from it you will surely die." Both the MT (בְּיוֹם) and the LXX (δ' ἂν ἡμέρᾳ) clarify that death occurs at the specific time of Adam's sin.[88] Adam's spiritual death and spiritual separation from God, which occurred immediately, are followed by physical separation in removal from Eden (Gen 3:23–24) and subsequent physical death.[89] Similarly, the spiritual resurrection of believers in Christ will be followed by a future physical inheritance of the New Heavens and New Earth (Rom 8:9–11, 18–23). Peter Leithart argues that the central point of Rom 5:12–21 highlights "a transfer of authority, from Death to those who receive grace and the gift of righteousness. This indicates that the purpose of Jesus' reversal of Adam's sin is to put humanity back onto the path of fulfilling the Adamic commission, back on creation's throne [cf. 1 Cor 6:2–3]."[90]

In sum, Adam's transgression resulted in the rule of Death. But humanity's subjection to Death necessarily entails separation from God. Thus, when Sin and Death are defeated and individuals receive spiritual life, it follows that separation from God (i.e., exile) will come to an end as well. Likewise, Israel's covenant curse results in a corporate "death" (Deut 4:25–28; 28:20, 22, 51).[91] Israel's resurrection was the only possible means of restoration (Ezek 37:1–14).[92]

### *Adam as a Type in Romans 5:13–14*

After explaining that the problem of death came through Adam, Paul turns aside to explain (γάρ) the universality of sin, even in the absence of explicit law.[93] We will return to this explanation when we discuss Israel in Rom 5:12–21 below. For now, we will consider the typological contrast between Adam and Christ.

By τύπος, Paul indicates a theological and hermeneutical correspondence between Adam and Christ. L. Goppelt describes Adam as an "advance "presentation" and as having "linear, dynamic interconnection" with the figure of Christ.[94] The correspondence relates to the representative office only they occupy. Both hold an office God intended for good. The antithesis Paul draws between the two is partially due to Adam's failure to uphold his commission. But, as Nicholas Meyer notes, "the antithesis is premised on a shared identity."[95] The previous point about Paul's use of βασιλεύω and κυριεύω illustrates the significance of Adam as τύπος. Adam was meant to *reign*. Yet, he failed to exercise kingly dominion by upholding the law he had been given (Gen 1:28–29; 2:15–17).[96] Thus, as a type, Adam provides a negative example and foreshadows the coming positive figure. Adam became the prototype of a failed son of God, who disregarded God's law and failed to reflect the righteousness of God to the rest of creation. In Adam, humanity became subject to Death through the express violation of God's revealed law and by virtue of his failure to execute his office lawfully. Paul will clarify the frustrated purpose of humanity and creation under him in Rom 8:18–30, but the covenant headship of Adam is the basis of that discussion.

### *Christ as Reversing Adam and Surpassing Him in Romans 5:15–17*

After having claimed Adam is a type of Christ, in the next verses Paul clarifies ways in which they are dissimilar. The opening line asserts as much: Ἀλλ' οὐχ ὡς τὸ παράπτωμα, οὕτως καὶ τὸ χάρισμα ("But it is not a matter of 'As is the transgression, so also is the gracious gift,'" Rom 5:15a).[97] What follows from 5:15b–17 is a series of differences. First, the righteousness (τὸ χάρισμα) God bestows through Christ is not to be equated with Adam's sin (τὸ παράπτωμα, 5:15). Adam's trespass may have brought death, but grace in Christ abounds (περισσεύω, 5:15). Second, whereas Adam's one sin brought condemnation, Christ's gift brings justification for many sins (5:16). Finally, whereas Death reigned through one transgression, those who receive the abundance of God's gracious and righteous gift will, themselves, reign in life (5:17). In sum, Christ exceeds Adam in every way. Meyer rightly argues that it is insufficient to merely note the antithesis between Adam and Christ.[98] Christ's reversal of the curse does not merely restore things to how they were. While Christ does reverse the effects of Adam's sin, he does not merely bring the restoration, but also the consummation of God's purposes for humanity.

As noted above, Paul draws upon the notion of ruling from Adam's Edenic vocation, which became impossible to fulfill due to sin.[99] The "futility" (ματαιόω, ματαιότης, Rom 1:21; 8:20) to which Paul refers in man and creation is the frustration of an enduring creational purpose. Paul understands that "Adam's sin in the garden [was] the archetypal turning back from that vocation, resulting in the inversion of the pattern of power Adam was to exercise over creation."[100] From a redemptive-historical perspective, Christ's surpassing Adam is the result of his triumph over temptation and achievement of God's purpose for humanity. He achieved God's purpose for humanity in his own person in addition to accomplishing redemption. N. T. Wright rightly concludes, "Nor was the result a mere restoration of where Adam was before: in Christ, the human project began in Adam but never completed, has been brought to its intended goal."[101]

Paul goes on to detail the present and future benefits of resurrection in Rom 8, but 5:17 introduces several themes. One benefit Paul lists is that those who receive grace in Christ "will reign in life" (ἐν ζωῇ βασιλεύσουσιν, 5:17). Whereas death was the consequence of violating the covenant of creation, life was the promised blessing. Since Paul juxtaposes the last Adam with the first, it is likely that the "life" in view is the eschatological life represented by the tree of life in the center of the garden. If we recall that the tree was not magical but symbolic of the benefit of nearness to God, we may conclude that "life" entails restoration to God's presence.

This was implied in Paul's return to the ἀλλάσσω-root to show the resolution of Adam's transgression of exchanging God's glory. Here it is further confirmed that man is restored to the hope of God's glory which is variously represented in the tree of life and in participation in eschatological glory with God.

Thus, one of Paul's central concerns in 5:12–21 is to show that Christ far exceeds Adam. Yet, Adam is not the only example in Scripture of such a pattern. Israel made precisely the same choice and, likewise, conforms to the negative pattern.

## Israel in Romans 5:12–21

The figure of Adam in Rom 5:12–21 is clearly Paul's central focus.[102] However, several scholars have identified Israel's history in Paul's argument as well, particularly in 5:13–14 and 5:20–21.[103] Paul's reasoning in 5:13–14 depends upon the analogy between Adam and Israel.[104]

> ἄχρι γὰρ νόμου ἁμαρτία ἦν ἐν κόσμῳ, ἁμαρτία δὲ οὐκ ἐλλογεῖται μὴ ὄντος νόμου, [14] ἀλλ' ἐβασίλευσεν ὁ θάνατος ἀπὸ Ἀδὰμ μέχρι Μωϋσέως καὶ ἐπὶ τοὺς μὴ[105] ἁμαρτήσαντας ἐπὶ τῷ ὁμοιώματι τῆς παραβάσεως (Rom 5:13–14)
>
> for sin was in the world before the law, but sin is not reckoned when there is no law, [14] but death reigned from Adam until Moses even over those who did not sin in the likeness of the transgression of Adam

Romans 5:13–14 functions as an explanation (γάρ) for the universality of sin prior to the giving of the Mosaic law. All humanity fell under Adam's federal representation, thus Death ruled over humanity before God gave Israel the Mosaic law.

James Dunn argues that the insertion of "law" into a discussion about Adam's sin introduces Israel into Paul's discussion: "We need simply note that here again Paul sees Israel's own experience of sin and death as in some sense paradigmatic for humanity as a whole."[106] Similarly, Thielman argues that the mention of the timing that sin is "reckoned" actually obscures Paul's argument if Israel is not a key component. Rather, "the story of Israel's violation of the covenant at Sinai was so close to the surface of Paul's thinking at this point in his discourse that, almost in the manner of a Freudian slip, it broke through."[107] Although I agree in part, Thielman seems to suggest Israel is inadvertently present in Paul's argument. To the contrary, it is more likely that Paul includes Israel because Israel's restoration and Adam's redemption are united in Christ's restoration of the sons of God.

The giving of the law to Israel at Sinai marks the time when the period in which there was no law ended (ἀπὸ Ἀδὰμ μέχρι Μωϋσέως, 5:14). The obverse of "sin is not reckoned when there is no law" obviously is that sin *is* reckoned in the presence of law. Thus, whereas Death ruled over those between Adam and Moses, the two specific scenarios in which an explicit law was present were Adam in Eden and Israel at Sinai bound for Canaan. Paul invokes the history of Israel in 5:14 in contrast to the period when there was no explicit law. The giving of the law at Sinai meant that subsequent sins—in the light of stated commandments—distinctly were in the likeness of Adam's transgression.[108] Thus, Israel *did* sin ἐπὶ τῷ ὁμοιώματι τῆς παραβάσεως Ἀδὰμ ("in the likeness of the transgression of Adam"). Although Death had reigned since Adam over all men, Israel is identified as following Adam's *likeness* by transgressing an explicit law. Thus, just as Adam is the predominant type of Christ. So also is Israel a type. The specific use of the term ὁμοίωμα may recall the previous usage in Rom 1:23 where Paul argued that humanity, and paradigmatically Adam *and Israel*,[109] exchanged God's glory and so were given over to corruption.

There is an analogy between the sin of Adam against God's clear command (Gen 2:17) and the sins of Israel under the law. Paul is here distinguishing himself from his Second Temple contemporaries. The election of Israel and its special position as Yahweh's chosen one was a matter of intense religious confidence. But Paul is able to see that Israel, for all its blessedness in being a recipient of God's law (Rom 3:1–2), was in Adam as well. The law came in and made explicit what had been in the world since Adam—the reign of Death. N. T. Wright correctly concludes, "The law, therefore, God's holy, just and good Torah, had come with a purpose: not to attempt to rescue Israel from its Adamic state, *but to draw out the force of sin all the more precisely in Israel,* in order that sin might be condemned."[110]

Much of Rom 5:12–21 is taken up by Paul clarifying how Adam and Christ are *not* similar (5:13–18a), but Paul returns again to the role of Israel in 5:20–21. Paul explains that the law came to increase the trespass (νόμος δὲ παρεισῆλθεν, ἵνα πλεονάσῃ τὸ παράπτωμα, 5:20). That is, sin is reckoned more strictly in the presence of law (cf. 4:15).[111] With respect to Israel, the presence of the law caused sin to increase, but in the opposite manner, grace increases through Christ. Paul employs the story of Israel and the addition of the law in order to confirm all people's identity in Adam.[112] In other words, the three stories do not represent equal figures, but two: Adam and Christ. They are the figureheads of the two redemptive-historical ages: the present age (ὁ αἰὼν οὗτος) and the age to come (ὁ αἰὼν ὁ μέλλων). Nygren writes, "In Adam and in Christ the two eons stand in sharp contrast to each other. As the old eon is the kingdom of death (ἡ βασιλεία τοῦ θεοῦ, cf. ἐβασίλευσεν ὁ θάνατος, vss. 14, 17, 21), so the new eon is the kingdom of life (ἡ βασλιλεία τῆς ζωῆς, cf. ἐν ζωῇ βασιλεύσουσιν vs. 17)."[113] The story of Israel is meant to confirm the reign of Death which came through Adam, which not even the law for all its goodness could reverse (cf. Rom 7:12). Indeed, Israel's law was never intended to save.[114]

## THE NEW AGE AS THE FULFILLMENT OF ISRAEL AND ADAM

How should we relate the stories of Adam, Israel, and Christ? I argue that Israel is an Adamic figure whose sin was clarified and confirmed by the law, but could not be removed by it. Death also reigned over Israel, for as Hofius puts it, all men "im Schatten Adams stehenden."[115] It is remarkable that Paul would discuss Israel at all in Rom 5:12–21, since his chief focus is the typological comparison of Adam with Christ. The example of Israel under the Mosaic law shows how closely related Adam's curse and Israel's stand in his thinking.[116] The analogies between Israel and Adam are close. They are both sons of God. They both sinned in the same likeness of violating a covenantal stipulation and being cursed with death. Both forfeited the land God had given them in that transgression. Moreover, the release from condemnation for both figures is equally achieved by reconciliation to God in Christ, the last Adam and the true Israel. The unity of salvation reflects the unity of humankind. Israel was also in Adam. The nation functions as a type of Christ, a recapitulation of Adam, but salvation and reversal would come through Christ himself.

In Rom 5, Paul begins a presentation that will remain consistent throughout Rom 5–8, in which two ages overlap. Whereas the Christ-age of eschatological consummation has begun in the Spirit, it is only a spiritual reality. The present evil age—or the Adam-age—endures in all its corruption, yet it has lost its power over the hearts of believers. Dunn writes, "As members of the first Adam, they belong to this age, they are dying; as members of the last Adam, they belong to the age to come, they experience the life-giving Spirit."[117] Paul portrays participation in Christ as a dying in Christ, which will give way to resurrection life in him.

## CONCLUSION

I have argued that Paul interweaves the stories of Adam and Israel into his description of life in the Spirit in Rom 5. The explicit reference to Adam in 5:12–21 confirms the implicit Adam theology up to that point. Although previous expositions of Rom 5:12–21 have reasonably focused upon interpreting the Adam-Christ typology, the paragraph's literary function as an explanation of reconciliation to Christ and the hope of glory in 5:1–11 is instructive. Following the excellent studies of Frank Thielman and David VanDrunen, I also argued that Paul interweaves the story of Israel into his typological comparison of Adam and Christ in 5:12–21, (esp. 5:13–14, 20–21). The two-age structure of Paul's thought remains intact, but Paul clearly develops an analogy between Adam and Israel. Both were guilty of transgressing an explicit law. Both were ruled by Sin and Death. However, Israel always functioned in the Adamic age and was sinful from the start. Thus, the nation functions under Adam and recapitulates his transgression.

I further argued that the explicit Adam typology in 5:12–21 is implicit in 5:1–11. The hope in the glory of God which Christ restores was a hope first held out to Adam. The theme of "glory" in Romans repeatedly occurs in conjunction with the Adamic substructure. Humankind—paradigmatically with Adam—exchanged God's glory in idolatry (1:23) and fell short of glory (3:23). Christ's substitutionary work as Isaiah's servant (cf. allusions to Isa 53 in 4:25; 5:1, 6, 8) renews that hope. Moreover, the future of Israel is a component of Paul's discussion in 5:1–11 both by virtue of the use of Isaiah's restoration prophecies and also in the depiction of a new humanity in Christ as the spiritual children of Abraham (4:13, 16, 24–25). The outpouring of the Spirit in Rom 5:5 indicates the fulfillment of Isa 32:15, Ezek 39:28–29, and Joel 2:28, all of which look forward to the end of Israel's exile. Thus, peace with God and reconciliation in Christ signal restoration. The new Israel of faith is restored through Christ. Beale writes, "By faith, people identify with and partake of the ultimate exile of death in Christ and his resurrection as the beginning of the new creation, which includes reconciliation and peace with God. Through Christ's redemptive actions he represented the nation in himself and so began to fulfill the Jewish scripture's hopes for the restoration of Israel by reconciling his people to God."[118] Thus, the backgrounds of both Adam and Israel inform Paul's exposition of the redemption accomplished by Christ. In Rom 8 Paul returns to the themes discussed in this chapter of the Spirit's coming, the hope of glory of God, and the end of the Adamic curse.

## NOTES

1. See chapter 3.
2. See discussion and literature cited in chapter 1.
3. Nils Alstrup Dahl, "Two Notes on Romans 5," *ST* 5 (1952): 37–48.
4. Against the possible critique that ἀλλάσσω and καταλλάσσω are different verbs and the suggested trajectory has no foundation, Leon Morris notes that ἀλλάσσω, διαλλάσσω, and καταλλάσσω all derive their basic meaning from

ἄλλος and "this basic meaning is modified *and confirmed* in the compounds" (*The Apostolic Preaching of the Cross* [Grand Rapids: Eerdmans, 1955], 187. My emphasis).

5. Shiu-Lun Shum, *Paul's Use of Isaiah in Romans: A Comparative Study of Paul's Letter to the Romans and the Sibylline and Qumran Sectarian Texts*, WUNT 2/156 (Tübingen: Mohr Siebeck, 2002), 189. See also, Cranfield, *Romans,* 1:251; Joseph A. Fitzmyer, *Romans: A New Translation with Introduction and Commentary*, AB 33 (New York: Doubleday, 1993); 389–90. Cf. Longenecker, *The Epistle to the Romans,* NIGTC (Grand Rapids: Eerdmans, 2016), 536–7. *Pace* Brendan Byrne, *Romans*, SP 6 (Collegeville, MN: Liturgical Press, 1996), 161–2, who argues that Paul is not alluding to Isa 53, but an early credal formula. There is not credible evidence for such a claim, especially in the presence of a much broader reliance upon Isaiah.

6. Rikki E. Watts, "Messianic Servant or the End of Israel's Exilic Curses?: Isaiah 53.4 in Matthew 8.17," *JSNT* 38 (2015): 89.

7. I. Howard Marshall, "The Meaning of 'Reconciliation,'" in *Unity and Diversity in New Testament Theology: Essays in Honor of George E. Ladd* (Grand Rapids: Eerdmans, 1978), 120–2; James M. Scott, "'For as Many as Are of Works of the Law Are under a Curse' (Galatians 3:10)," in *Paul and the Scriptures of Israel*, ed. James A. Sanders and Craig A. Evans, JSNTSup 83 (Sheffield: Sheffield Academic, 1993), 206.

8. Frank Thielman, "The Story of Israel and the Theology of Romans 5–8," *Society of Biblical Literature 1993 Seminar Papers,* SBLSP 32 (Atlanta: Society of Biblical Literature, 1993), 235–6.

9. Thomas R. Schreiner, *Romans,* BECNT (Grand Rapids: Baker Books, 1998), 254.

10. Several MSS have the subjunctive ἔχωμεν (א*, A, B*, C, D, K, L, 33, 81, 630, 1175, 1739*) instead of the indicative listed (א$^{1}$, B$^{2}$, F, G, P, Ψ, 0220$^{vid}$, 104, 365, 1241, 1505, 1506, 1739$^{c}$, 1881, 2464). The MSS evidence favors the subjunctive. However, most EVV and commentators favor the indicative reading on grounds of internal consistency. Neither reading will significantly affect the present study.

11. Thielman, "The Story of Israel," 235.

12. Corneliu Constantineanu, *The Social Significance of Reconciliation in Paul's Theology: Narrative Readings in Romans*, LNTS 421 (London; New York: T&T Clark, 2010), 111.

13. Thielman, "The Story of Israel," 235.

14. Shum, *Isaiah in Romans*, 193–4.

15. Cf. Rom 5:1 Δικαιωθέντες οὖν ἐκ πίστεως εἰρήνην_ἔχομεν πρὸς τὸν θεὸν διὰ τοῦ κυρίου ἡμῶν Ἰησοῦ Χριστοῦ.

16. Shum, *Isaiah in Romans*, 196.

17. Ibid.

18. Ibid.

19. See Michael Wolter, *Rechtfertigung und zukünftiges Heil: Untersuchungen zu Röm 5, 1–11*, BZNW 43 (Berlin: de Gruyter, 1978), 85, 97–8; Peter Stuhlmacher,

*Paul's Letter to the Romans: A Commentary,* trans. Scott J. Hafemann (Louisville, KY: Westminster/John Knox Press, 1994), 320; "ἀλλάσσω," *NIDNTTE* 1:245–9.

20. G. K. Beale, *A New Testament Biblical Theology: The Unfolding of the Old Testament in the New* (Grand Rapids: Baker Academic, 2011), 138, 744–7.

21. Some may object that Ezekiel's prophecy was given to *ethnic* Israel and that it would be an abuse of the original context to ascribe it to the NT church. Yet, the prophecy of the Spirit's outpouring should be read in light of Ezek 20:18–40 which limits the identity of the "house of Israel" to the faithful remnant, which is identified with church is identified in the NT (Beale, *NTBT*, 744n87).

22. There may be Edenic imagery in underlying the Hebrew term, כַּרְמֶל, which alternatively may be translated "garden, orchard" etc. See "I כַּרְמֶל," *HALOT*, s.v.

23. Note the additional correlation between exile and death in the progression of Ps 104:29 (103:29 LXX): "you hide your face, they are terrified; you take away their breath (רוּחַ; LXX: πνεῦμα), they die and return to their dust."

24. Walther Zimmerli, *Ezekiel 2: A Commentary on the Book of the Prophet Ezekiel, Chapters 25–48*, ed. Paul D. Hanson, trans. James D. Martin, Hermeneia (Philadelphia: Fortress, 1979), 321.

25. Preston M. Sprinkle, "The Afterlife in Romans: Understanding Paul's Glory Motif in Light of the Apocalypse of Moses and 2 Baruch," in *Lebendige hoffnungewiger Tod?!: Jenseitsvorstellungen im Hellenismus, Judentum, und Christentum,* ed. Michael Labahn and Manfred Lang, ABG 24 (Leipzig: Evangelische Verlagsanstalt, 2007), 226; Thielman, "The Story of Israel," 235.

26. Sprinkle (ibid., 226) notes that προσαγωγή consistently functions relationally in the Pauline corpus (cf. Eph 2:18; 3:12).

27. Daniel I. Block, "Gog and the Pouring out of the Spirit: Reflections on Ezekiel 39:21–29," *VT* 37 (1987): 257–70.

28. Though see J. Lust, "The Final Text and Textual Criticism: Ez 39,28," in *Ezekiel and His Book: Textual and Literary Criticism and Their Interrelation* (Leuven: Uitgeverij Peeters, 1986), 48–54, and Ka Leung Wong, "The Masoretic and Septuagint Texts of Ezekiel 39,21–29," *ETL* 78 (2002): 141–5.

29. The originality of רוּחַ is supported by the Targum and Vulgate. If Ezek 39:29 informs Paul's argument then he likely worked from the Hebrew.

30. Beale, *NTBT,* 252–4. See chapter 5.

31. Wong, "The Masoretic and Septuagint Texts of Ezekiel 39,21–29," 144.

32. G. K. Beale, "The Old Testament Background of Reconciliation in 2 Corinthians 5–7 and Its Bearing on the Literary Problem of 2 Corinthians 6:14–7:1," *NTS* 35 (1989): 550–81.

33. Ibid., 556.

34. Otfried Hofius, "Erwägungen zur Gestalt und Herkunft des paulinischen Versöhnungsgedankens," *ZTK* 77 (1980): 196. See also Otto Betz "Fleischliche und 'geistiche' Christuserkenntnis nach 2 Korinther 5:16," in *Jesus—der Herr der Kirche* (Tubingen: Mohr Siebeck, 1990), 114–28; Peter Stuhlmacher, "The Gospel of Reconciliation in Christ: Basic Features and Issues of a Biblical Theology of the New Testament," trans. George R. Edwards, *HBT* 1 (1979): 161–90.

35. Hofius, "Erwägungen," 194–9. Cf. Constantineanu, *Reconciliation in Paul's Theology,* 39–40.

36. Beale, "Old Testament Background," 552–8.

37. Hofius, "Erwägungen," 194–9 (quote from 199).

38. Ibid., 196.

39. For example, Morris, *Apostolic Preaching*, 198.

40. Constantineanu, *Reconciliation in Paul's Theology,* 114.

41. The personified forms of Sin and Death are capitalized but the common noun forms will be lowercase.

42. The similarity between the brief afflictions of believers before glory (cf. Rom 8:18) and the brief (βραχύν) suffering of the Maccabean martyrs is noteworthy (cf. 2 Macc 7:36).

43. "θλῖψις," *NIDNTTE* 2:462. My emphasis.

44. Heinrich Schlier, "θλίβω, θλῖψις," *TDNT* 3:140–2.

45. Stanley Porter writes, "The messianic woes refers to the kinds of travails to be experienced not only by the Messiah but by humankind in general in anticipation of the establishment of the messianic kingdom. The travails include various kinds of turmoil and evil" ("Tribulation, Messianic Woes," *DLNTD* 1180). Cf. Dubis, "Messianic Woes" *EDB* 890–1.

46. It should be remembered that as the culmination of the covenant curses "exile" can function as a general descriptor of the whole.

47. Thielman argues that the list of difficulties in Rom 8:35 is "largely drawn" from the covenant curses of Deut 28 and Lev 26 thus, "the suffering which Paul and other believers experience as the people of God . . . is strangely analogous to the suffering which the disobedient and unrestored Israel experienced because of their sins" ("Story of Israel," 239–40). See chapter 6 for the full discussion on the relationship between Deuteronomic afflictions and believers suffering in Christ.

48. My translation of the MT. The LXX also sets the servant as a light to the nations but does not diminish his role to Israel: Μέγα σοί ἐστι τοῦ κληθῆναί σε παῖδά μου.

49. Simon J. Gathercole observes that this theology of Israel as "light" is rooted in the Abrahamic covenant (Gen 12:1–3) and Deuteronomic theology (*Where Is Boasting?: Early Jewish Soteriology and Paul's Response in Romans 1–5* [Grand Rapids: Eerdmans, 2002], 200–1, see also the literature cited.

50. Michael Wolter, *Der Brief an Die Römer: Teilband 1: Rom 1–8*, vol. 1 of *EKKNT* VI (Vandenhoeck & Ruprecht, 2014), 345–6.

51. In addition to ethical righteousness based upon God's perfection, Benjamin C. Blackwell argues that δόξα in 3:23 is "an ontological statement related to incorruption and life" ("Immortal Glory and the Problem of Death in Romans 3.23," *JSNT* 32 [2010]: 300–1).

52. Righteousness and glory are closely related in Romans. Both have a qualitative and communicative sense. Righteousness is a legal status as well as a description of God's nature and attributes. Similarly, glory can refer to God's worthiness, incorruption, and radiant appearance and participation in his incorruption and likeness (Donald L. Berry, *Glory in Romans and the Unified Purpose of God in*

*Redemptive History* [Eugene, OR: Pickwick, 2016], 54–65). Cf. Ernst Käsemann, *Commentary on Romans,* trans. G. W. Bromiley (Grand Rapids: Eerdmans, 1980), 134.

53. Ibid., 70–1.

54. For example, Berry, *Glory in Romans*, 69; Käsemann, *Romans*, 133; C. E. B. Cranfield, *A Critical and Exegetical Commentary on the Epistle to the Romans*, 2 vols., ICC (Edinburgh: T&T Clark, 1975), 1:260; C. Marvin Pate, *The Glory of Adam and the Afflictions of the Righteous: Pauline Suffering in Context* (Lewiston: Mellen, 1993), 148–52; Schreiner, *Romans,* 254–5; Craig S. Keener, *Romans: A New Covenant Commentary*, NCCS 6 (Eugene, OR: Cascade, 2009), Kindle edition, *ad loc*. Rom 5:2.

55. Ibid., 69.

56. See Maurice Carrez, *De la souffrance à la gloire: De la δοξα dans la pensée paulinienne* (Switzerland: Delachaux & Niestle, 1964) 47; Berry, *Glory in Romans,* 69n2.

57. Christian Grappe, "Qui me délivrera de ce corps de mort?: L'esprit de vie! Romains 7,24 et 8,2 comme éléments de typologie Adamique," *Bib* 83 (2002): 481.

58. For helpful summaries of major interpretations, see Schreiner, *Romans,* 271–9 and Fitzmyer, *Romans,* 405–11.

59. Nicholas A. Meyer, *Adam's Dust and Adam's Glory in the Hodayot and the Letters of Paul: Rethinking Anthropogony and Theology*, NovTSup 168 (Leiden: Brill, 2016), 187; Anders Nygren, *Commentary on Romans*, trans. Carl C. Rasmussen (Minneapolis: Fortress, 1983), 210.

60. This is a typical structure accorded by numerous commentators, for example, John D. Harvey, *Romans*, EGGNT (Nashville, TN: B&H Academic, 2017), 137.

61. See John Murray, *The Imputation of Adam's Sin* (Grand Rapids: Eerdmans, 1959), 7; Cranfield, *Romans*, 1:289.

62. A. J. M. Wedderburn, "Theological Structure of Romans 5:12," *NTS* 19 (1973): 340.

63. Douglas J. W. Milne, "Genesis 3 in the Letter to the Romans," *RTR* 39 (1980): 11–2.

64. A. T. Robertson, *A Grammar of the Greek New Testament in the Light of Historical Research* (Nashville: Broadman Press, 1934), 965; Cranfield, *Romans,* 1:255; Schreiner, *Romans,* 247.

65. See Nygren, *Romans*, 209.

66. Thielman, "The Story of Israel," 236.

67. Notwithstanding the three eras Paul differentiates historically: (1) Adam to Moses, (2) Moses to Christ, and (3) Christ to the Eschaton. From the cosmic and covenantal perspective of Sin's rule, Israel belonged to the Adamic age.

68. Richard B. Gaffin Jr., *"By Faith, Not by Sight": Paul and the Order of Salvation* (Bletchley, UK; Waynesboro, GA: Paternoster, 2006), 47.

69. *Pace* N. T. Wright, "Adam in Pauline Christology," *Society of Biblical Literature 1983 Seminar Papers,* SBLSP 22 (Atlanta: Society of Biblical Literature, 1983), 359–89; idem, *The Climax of the Covenant: Christ and the Law in Pauline Theology* (Edinburgh: T&T Clark, 1991), 18–40.

70. J. P. Versteeg, *Is Adam a "Teaching Model" in the New Testament?: An Examination of One of the Central Points in the Views of H. M. Kuitert and Others,* trans. Richard B. Gaffin (Nutley, NJ: P&R, 1977), 8–9; Kasemann, *Romans,* 142.

71. Versteeg, *"Teaching Model,"* 8–14; Murray, *Imputation,* 36–41.

72. Cranfield, *Romans,* 1:279.

73. The phrase ὁ θάνατος is absent in the Western textual tradition (D, F, G, 1505, it, Ambst) but well attested elsewhere.

74. *Pace* Douglas Moo, who argues that κόσμον is a metonymy referring to all people (*The Epistle to the Romans,* NICNT [Grand Rapids: Eerdmans, 1996], 319n26). Cf. Fitzmyer, *Romans,* 411, who defines it as the "history of humanity."

75. See the discussion in chapter 5.

76. Fitzmyer lists eleven interpretations of ἐφ' ᾧ (*Romans,* 413–7). Robert Jewett (Robert Jewett and Roy David Kotansky, *Romans: A Commentary,* ed. Eldon Jay Epp, Hermeneia [Minneapolis: Fortress, 2007], 376) lists a 12th. Following Murray, *Imputation,* 19–21, I have translated ἐφ' ᾧ as equivalent to a causal conjunction. Fitzmyer lists an impressive number of scholars who do the same including: Achtemeier, Barrett, Brandenburger, Bruce, Bultmann, Byrne, Cranfield, Dibelius, Dodd, Dunn, Gaugler, Huby, Käsemann, Kuss, Lagrange, Lindeskog, Meyer, Michel, Moule, Moo, Pesch, Pray, Schlier, and Wilckens (*Romans,* 415), though he himself interprets it consecutively, "with the result that" ("The Consecutive Meaning of ἐφ' ᾧ in Romans 5:12," *NTS* 39 [1993]: 321–39).

77. See, for example, J. Christiaan Beker, "The Relationship Between Sin and Death in Romans," in *Conversation Continues: Studies in Paul & John in Honor of J. Louis Martyn* (Nashville: Abingdon, 1990), 55–61; C. Clifton Black, "Pauline Perspectives on Death in Romans 5–8," *JBL* 103 (1984): 413–33; A. Feuillet, "Le règne de la mort et le règne de la vie," *RB* 77 (1970): 481–521.

78. See the discussion in chapter 3.

79. Schreiner writes, "the account in Genesis indicates that death is fundamentally separation from God, and this alienation from God entered the world through Adam's sin" (*Romans,* 272).

80. J. R. Daniel Kirk, *Unlocking Romans: Resurrection and the Justification of God* (Grand Rapids: Eerdmans, 2008), 105.

81. Douglas A. Campbell, *The Rhetoric of Righteousness in Romans 3.21–26,* JSNTSup 65 (Sheffield: JSOT Press, 1992), 173.

82. "κατάκριμα," BDAG, BibleWorks 10, s.v.

83. Meyers, *Adam's Dust,* 185–7.

84. See John Calvin, *The Epistle of Paul the Apostle to the Romans,* trans. and ed. John Owen (repr., Grand Rapids: Baker, 2003), 212–3.

85. Roy Ciampa, "Genesis 1–3 and Paul's Theology of Adam's Dominion in Romans 5–6," in *From Creation to New Creation: Biblical Theology and Exegesis,* ed. Daniel Gurtner and Benjamin Gladd (Peabody, MA: Hendrickson, 2013), 107. The remainder of this paragraph refers to this citation.

86. βασιλεύω: Rom. 5:14, 17 (2x), 21 (2x); 6:12.
κυριεύω: Rom. 6:9, 14.

87. See Meredith G. Kline, *Kingdom Prologue: Genesis Foundations for a Covenantal Worldview* (Eugene, OR: Wipf & Stock, 2000), 42–6, who argues for

a connection between the kingship of man and the man as a son of God where both concepts are rooted in the investiture of the *imago Dei.*

88. Schreiner, *Romans,* 272–3.

89. Kline, *Kingdom Prologue,* 42. See also, Schreiner, *Romans,* 273.

90. Peter Leithart, "Adam, Moses, and Jesus: A Reading of Romans 5:12–14," *CTJ* 43 (2008): 263.

91. See Kenneth J. Turner, "Deuteronomy's Theology of Exile," in *For Our Good Always: Studies on the Message and Influence of Deuteronomy in Honor of Daniel I. Block,* ed. Jason S. DeRouchie, Jason Gile, and Kenneth J. Turner (Winona Lake, IN: Eisenbrauns, 2013), 189–220 (esp. 194).

92. Ibid., 190.

93. Moo, *Romans,* 329–32.

94. L. Goppelt, "τύπος," *TDNT* 8:252–3.

95. Meyer, *Adam's Dust,* 188.

96. Kline, *Kingdom Prologue*, 127.

97. My translation follows Cranfield, *Romans,* 1:269.

98. *Adam's Dust,* 189. Cf. B. J. Malina, "Some Observations on the Origin of Sin in Judaism and St Paul," *CBQ* 31 (1969): 28–31.

99. Meyer, *Adam's Dust,* 190.

100. Ibid.

101. Wright, "Romans," in *The New Interpreter's Bible: Acts – First Corinthians*, ed. Robert W. Wall and J. Paul Sampley (Nashville: Abingdon Press, 2002), 10:524. Geerhardus Vos explains that Christ completed both the "remedial" work of salvation and humanity's original eschatological purpose (*The Eschatology of the Old Testament,* ed. James T. Dennison [Phillipsburg, NJ: P&R, 2001], 74).

102. Pace Wright, who argues that Israel is central ("Romans," 512). He writes, "The context of [Paul's] thinking is the fairly widespread Second Temple Jewish belief not merely about Adam as the progenitor of the human race, and indeed the fountainhead of human sin (e.g., Wis 2:23–24; 2 Bar 17:3; 23:4; 48:42; 54:15 [but cf. 54:19]; 4 Ezra 3:7; 3:21; 7:118), but about Israel, as the new humanity the inheritors of "all the glory of Adam" (ibid., 524).

103. For example, Otfried Hofius, "Die Adam-Christus-Antithese und das Gesetz: Erwägungen zu Röm 5,12–21," in *Paul and the Mosaic Law: The Third Durham-Tübingen Research Symposium on Earliest Christianity and Judaism, Durham, September, 1994*, James D. G. Dunn, WUNT 89 (Tubingen: Mohr Siebeck, 1996), 165–206; idem, *The Theology of Paul the Apostle* (Grand Rapids: Eerdmans, 1998), 97; Thielman, "The Story of Israel," 233–49; David VanDrunen, "Israel's Recapitulation of Adam's Probation under the Law of Moses," *WTJ* 73 (2011): 306–10. Cf. Wedderburn, "Theological Structure," 352.

104. VanDrunen, "Israel's Recapitulation of Adam's Probation," 306.

105. Some MSS omit μή (614, 1739*, 2495*, d*, m, Or[pt], Ambst). The external evidence strongly supports the presence of the negative particle.

106. Dunn, *Theology of Paul,* 97.

107. Thielman, "The Story of Israel," 236–7 (quotation from p. 237).

108. Cranfield, *Romans,* 1:282–3; Schreiner, *Romans,* 279; VanDrunuen, "Israel's Recapitulation," 309.

109. Recall that the allusion to Ps 106 is stronger than the allusion to Gen 3. See chapter 3.

110. N. T. Wright, *Paul and the Faithfulness of God,* COQG 4 (Minneapolis: Fortress, 2013), 764. Emphasis his.

111. The *relative* interpretation of sin not being reckoned in 5:13 is widespread. See, for example, Cranfield, *Romans*, 1:282–3; Schreiner, *Romans,* 277–80.

112. See VanDrunen, "Israel's Recapitulation," 314.

113. Nygren, *Romans*, 217. This quote and the previous point.

114. Hofius writes, "Weil es sich dabei um die ureigentliche, von Gott gesetzte Aufgabe der Tora handelt, deshalb vermag sie weder der Sünde zu wehren noch gar dem Sünder den Weg zum Heil zu eröffnen" ("Die Adam-Christus-Antithese," 206).

115. Ibid., 206.

116. See VanDrunuen, "Israel's Recapitulation," 315.

117. Dunn, *Theology of Paul,* 482. Cf. Robert C. Tannehill, *Dying and Rising in Christ: A Study in Pauline Theology,* BZNW (Berlin: Töpelmann, 1967), 47, 70.

118. Beale, *NTBT,* 547.

## *Chapter 5*

# The Restoration of Adam and Israel in Romans 8:1–30

The previous chapter argued that the explicit mention of Adam in Rom 5:14 is not unexpected, but rather a confirmation of his tacit presence throughout the epistle. The Adam theology of Rom 5:12–21 corroborates and substantiates the previous pattern of allusions to Adam. Paul explains that Christ fulfills the commissions of Adam and of Israel (which was itself Adamic) by virtue of his righteous life and substitutionary death. It was my contention that the triumphant boast of mankind's restored hope in divine glory in Rom 5:1–5 is the renewal of mankind's Edenic potential to share in the glory of God.

We have seen that Rom 5 and Rom 8 are deliberately structured as "bookends" of Paul's argument. I will argue in this chapter that Paul returns to central themes from Rom 5 and further develops them in Rom 8, where he continues to interweave the stories of Adam and Israel. Paul's allusions to the Hebrew Bible and continuation of themes from Rom 5 indicate that Jesus launches eschatological Israel's restoration from exile. But the reversal goes beyond the borders of Israel and encompasses all of humanity. Jesus reverses the curse of Adam as well as Israel. However, that reversal takes place in two stages. First, mankind is spiritually restored to God's presence through the remission of sin. Second, both renewed humanity and creation will be physically restored to God at the last day.

The chapter will be divided into three sections. First, Rom 8:1–11 returns to the theme of the outpouring of God's Spirit from Rom 5:5, but develops the work of the Spirit to show his resurrecting power. Second, Rom 8:12–17 continues the focus on the Spirit, but shifts from the Spirit as the source of resurrection life to describe him as the guide toward believers' final inheritance. Third, Rom 8:18–30 then describes following the Spirit as a journey of struggle, ending with the complete restoration of God's sons and creation along with them. Each of these sections is informed by Adam and Israel themes as Paul describes Christ's reversal of the curse.

## ROMANS 8:1–11—RESURRECTED LIFE IN THE SPIRIT AS INAUGURATED RESTORATION

The opening paragraph (8:1–11) restates Paul's conclusion from 5:12–21 that those in Christ have had eternal life replace the rule of Death over them.[1] The reign of grace has begun and overlaps with the present age and the reign of death (cf. Rom 5:17). The chapter opens with the famous declaration: Οὐδὲν ἄρα νῦν κατάκριμα ("There is therefore now no condemnation," 8:1a). But the limitation is also clear: τοῖς ἐν Χριστῷ Ἰησοῦ ("for those who are in Christ Jesus," 8:1b).[2] Yet the focus in 8:1–11 is not specifically upon Christ, but upon the transformative power of the Spirit.[3] As opposed to continuing to refer to those ἐν Χριστῷ, Paul draws upon material from Rom 6–7 to describe the role of the Spirit in giving life.[4] A complementary reason for the emphasis upon the Spirit in Rom 8:1–11 is the background in the Jewish scripture that informs it. I argued in the previous chapter that the Spirit's outpouring in Rom 5:5 was the fulfillment of Ezek 39:28–29 (and Joel 2:8; Isa 32:15) which promised Yahweh's return to Israel in the last days through restoration from exile. In the following section, I will argue that Ezek 36–37 also parallels Rom 8:1–11.

### Identifying Ezekiel in Romans 8:1–11

Several scholars have noted a close relationship between Ezek 36–37 and Rom 8:1–11.[5] G. K. Beale argues that Paul's terminology throughout Rom 5–8 closely parallels Ezek 36–37.[6] John W. Yates argues the correspondence is particularly focused on Ezek 36:26–27 in Rom 8:4 and Ezek 37:1–14 in Rom 8:9–11.[7] Ezekiel prophesies a future restoration of Israel as an act of God done for his name's sake (36:22–38).[8] The subsequent vision of the valley of dry bones complements the prophecy and illustrates Israel's restoration to God as an act of new creation (Ezek 37:1–14).[9] John A. Bertone argues that Paul's description of life in the Spirit arises directly from the eschatological prophecies of Ezekiel:

> From Paul's Jewish heritage he understood that the Spirit that brings life was part of the promise for the future. It was the life-giving function of the Spirit that signaled the arrival of the messianic age. Ezekiel 36.26–28 announces a future time when God will grant his Spirit to his people which will result in an intimate relationship with God and obedience to him.[10]

Ezekiel 36–37 and Rom 8:1–11 are the prediction and inaugurated announcement of the same event. However, the link between the two passages goes beyond shared themes to include verbal parallels. There are three possible allusions to Ezek 36–37 in Rom 5–7, but these are corroborated by several more concentrated parallels in 8:1–11.[11]

(1) As I argued in chapter 4, the outpouring of the Spirit in Rom 5:5 is the fulfillment of Ezek 39:29 (and Joel 2:8; Isa 32:15). Both employ the verb ἐκχέω and describe the eschatological restoration of God to his people in the last days. The verse repeats the promise of the Spirit[12] from Ezek 36:26–27; 37:5–6, 9–10, 14.[13]
(2) In Rom 6, Paul describes Christian baptism in terms unique to Ezek 36:25–28, which speaks of God purifying Israel for its restoration by sprinkling it with clean water to result in a "new heart and a new spirit" (καρδίαν καινὴν καὶ πνεῦμα καινόν, 36:26).[14] Similarly, Paul explains in Rom 6:3–6 that baptism is a means by which believers die to their "old man" (ὁ παλαιός, 6:6)—a term which points to humanity's solidarity with Adam[15]—and replace it with "newness of life" (καινότητι ζωῆς, 6:4). Israel is baptized and given a new heart and spirit for its restoration. Believers in Christ are baptized into his death and raised to new life.[16]
(3) Paul re-echoes the promise for a new Spirit (πνεῦμα καινόν) from Ezek 36:26 in Rom 7:4–6 where he states that believers' union with the resurrected Christ enables serving him with newness of spirit (καινότητι πνεύματος) as opposed to oldness of letter (παλαιότητι γράμματος). The proximity to the baptism discussion in Rom 6:3–6, which itself immediately follows the Adam–Christ contrast in Rom 5:12–21, indicates Paul saw the coming of the Spirit as the remedy of death in Adam.

Thus, there are multiple parallels of Ezek 36–37, 39 in Rom 5–7. None is beyond doubt, yet each parallel phrase is rendered more probably an allusion in the presence of the others.[17] Moreover, our interest is not primarily whether Paul's Roman *readers* would have identified any allusions but as Yates argues, it is "in the likelihood that certain texts and traditions shaped the way Paul thought about the work of the spirit in an identifiable way."[18] However, after a series of clarifications and other topics in Rom 6–7, the case for Paul's dependence upon Ezek 36–37, 39 becomes more convincing in Rom 8. The apostle resumes the theme of the outpouring of the Spirit with terminology that echoes Ezek 36–37 in at least six ways:

(1) Both passages describe the entrance of the Spirit *into* God's people.[19] Paul's description of the Spirit as the source of eschatological life seems to arise directly from Ezek 36–37 in which the coming of the Spirit of life

(πνεῦμα ζωῆς, 37:5) resurrects dead Israel. Similarly, eschatological life comes via the indwelling of the Spirit in Romans. The law of the Spirit of life (τοῦ πνεύματος τῆς ζωῆς) has set believers free (Rom 8:2; cf. 7:6). The mind set on the Spirit is life (πνεύματος ζωή) as opposed to the mind set on the flesh, which is death (Rom 8:5, 6). Indeed, Ezek 37 is the only passage in the LXX which links πνεῦμα and ζωή/ζάω in an eschatological context.[20] Ezekiel makes that connection three times (37:5, 6, 14). The vision of Israel's resurrection describes a process where dead Israel will receive Yahweh's Spirit (πνεῦμα) and will live (ζήσεσθε, 37:6). Again in Ezek 37:14a, "I will give my spirit (πνεῦμά μου) to you and you will live (ζήσεσθε)." Thus, there is a shared vocabulary as well as a shared context in the eschatological resurrection of God's people.[21]

The resurrection of Israel in Ezek 37:1–14 by the coming of the Spirit is functionally the renewal of God's relationship with them and the restoration of his presence. The remainder of Ezek 37:14 indicates the close relationship between eschatological life and restoration: "you will live and I will place you in your land and you will know that I am the Lord" (Ezek 37:14b). Similarly, Paul will go on to describe new life as following the Spirit in a new exodus to receive their inheritance, which is the new heavens and new earth.[22]

(2) Another possible link to Ezekiel is Paul's parallel description of the Spirit as πνεῦμά θεοῦ in Rom 8:9 and πνεῦμα ζωή in 8:10. Ezekiel 37:5–6 also describes the Spirit as πνεῦμα ζωῆς and πνεῦμα μου.[23] While there are minor differences in form, both cases clearly identify the πνεῦμα ζωή/ῆς as the source of life in parallel with its identification as God's Spirit.
(3) Paul's dichotomy of flesh versus Spirit where οἱ κατὰ σάρκα are those in Adam and οἱ κατὰ πνεῦμα are in Christ also parallels Ezekiel. Only Ezek 36 and Rom 8 contrast unbelieving flesh with a divinely renewed human spirit (cf. Ezek 36:26–7; Rom 8:4–11).[24]
(4) There is a close parallel between Rom 8:4 where Paul explains that the Spirit's renovative work in believers enables them to walk according to God's righteous commandments and Ezek 36:27 where God promises to place his Spirit within Israel and cause its people to walk righteously.[25]
(5) The physically resurrected army of Israel in Ezek 37 is also paralleled in Rom 8:9–11. Ezekiel first prophesied to the bones; they reassembled and flesh and sinew grew upon them. But there was no πνεῦμα in them and so the bodies were not living (37:7–8). The prophet then calls upon the πνεῦμα to come and make them live (37:9). The Spirit comes, they live (ἔζησαν), and they stand (ἔστησαν) a very great multitude (συναγωγὴ πολλὴ σφόδρα, 37:10; MT: a very great *army* [דוֹלגָּ חַיִל מְאֹד־מְאֹד][26]). Likewise, Paul argues in Rom 8:11 that the Spirit who raised Christ will give

**Table 5.1 Ezekiel 36:27 in Romans 8:4**

| *Ezekiel 36:27* | *Romans 8:4* |
|---|---|
| καὶ τὸ πνεῦμά μου δώσω ἐν ὑμῖν καὶ ποιήσω ἵνα ἐν τοῖς δικαιώμασί μου πορεύησθε καὶ τὰ κρίματά μου φυλάξησθε καὶ ποιήσητε. | ἵνα τὸ δικαίωμα τοῦ νόμου πληρωθῇ ἐν ἡμῖν τοῖς μὴ κατὰ σάρκα περιπατοῦσιν[a] ἀλλὰ κατὰ πνεῦμα. |
| And I will put my Spirit in you and I will cause you to walk in my righteous requirements and keep my judgments and do *them*. | In order that the righteous requirement of the law might be fulfilled in us, who walk not according to the flesh but according to the Spirit. |

*Note:* Underlines indicate verbal links.
[a]At the time of the writing of Romans περιπατέω had replaced πορεύομαι in common usage. This observation further confirms an already likely allusion (Yates, *Spirit and Creation*, 144).

life to believers' physical bodies. The work of the Spirit culminates in physical resurrection.[27]

(6) Finally, the two-stage resurrection of Ezekiel is paralleled but reversed in Romans. Whereas Ezekiel describes the physical re-formation of dead Israel followed by the Spirit's vivifying entrance, Paul describes life as first coming through the Spirit, followed by a subsequent bodily resurrection (8:11).

In sum, there is sufficient dissimilarity to rule out explicit quotation. Nevertheless, These are highly probable allusions. Hans Hübner is doubtlessly correct to note the "theologische Koinzidenz."[28] In light of this *Koinzidenz* of repeated verbal and thematic correspondence, it may be concluded that Paul views the outpouring of the Spirit (Rom 5:5) and the spiritual resurrection of believers in Christ (Rom 8:1–11) to be the fulfillment of Ezek 36:16–37:14 and 39:29. This supports the conclusions of the previous chapter that the eschatological era of peace and reconciliation introduced through Christ (Rom 5:1–11) is the inauguration of Israel's restoration from exile. Beale concludes, "Paul views Christians in Rom. 6–8 to be the *actual fulfillment* of the prophesied spiritual resurrection of Israel that was to transpire in the latter days at the time of their restoration from exile."[29]

We will now examine Ezekiel's prophecy in its context before returning to Paul's use of it.

## The Old Testament Context of Ezekiel 36:16–37:14

Ezekiel prophesied a renewed era in which Yahweh would enable his people's obedience and would end their exile (Ezek 11:19; 36:27; 37:14, 24; 39:28–29).[30] Prior to the restoration prophecy of Ezek 36:16–37:14, the prophet pronounces several oracles of judgment against the nations (25–32) before concentrating upon the need for repentance (cf. 33:1–20 and 33:23–33). He reminds Israel that they belong to Yahweh, their shepherd (34:1–31), and shows his capacity to save as well as to judge in an oracle against Edom (35:1–15).[31] The formal restoration promise occurs in 36:16–38 and is followed by a prophetic vision depicting that restoration as God's resurrection of the army of Israel from decayed and dry bones in 37:1–14. The vision of Israel's resurrection is followed by an oracle of a divided Israel being fused into one people (37:15–28), which is itself followed by the prophecy of an eschatological battle and Yahweh's triumph over Gog (38:1–39:29). At the end of the final battle and to conclude the section, Yahweh repeats his promise to restore Israel in the last days (39:28–29; cf. 36:18, 28, 33–35, 38).

I mention the broader context in order to highlight symmetry in the LXX between Israel's initial scattering in exile and the promise of its restoration through eschatological resurrection. At the start, Yahweh explains that because of Israel's idolatry he "poured out his wrath upon them" (ἐξέχεα τὸν θυμόν μου ἐπ' αὐτούς, Ezek 36:18). The language repeats at the close of the Gog prophecy when God again announces Israel's restoration, saying "I will not hide my face again from them, when I pour out my wrath upon the house of Israel (ἐξέχεα τὸν θυμόν μου ἐπὶ τὸν οἶκον Ισραηλ, Ezek 39:29). I noted in the previous chapter that the MT of 39:29 claims God's רוּחַ will be poured out, not God's θυμός. Following the insightful work of Ka Leung Wong, I argued that θυμός is an interpretive translation of רוּחַ, which can sometimes connote wrath.[32] A further argument in favor of θυμός as an interpretive translation is the textual symmetry it creates showing Israel's exile beginning with God's wrath being poured out (Ezek 36:18) and its resolution in its reversal (Ezek 39:29).[33] Note the identical syntax:

> ἐξέχεα τὸν θυμόν μου ἐπ' αὐτούς (36:18)
>
> ἐξέχεα τὸν θυμόν μου ἐπὶ τὸν οἶκον Ισραηλ (39:29)

The symmetry is somewhat present in the MT:

> וָאֶשְׁפֹּךְ חֲמָתִי עֲלֵיהֶם (36:18)
>
> שָׁפַכְתִּי אֶת־רוּחִי עַל־בֵּית יִשְׂרָאֵל (39:29)

The LXX of 39:29 indicates that God exhausted his anger against Israel and thus will restore his people. The focus is upon *result*. The MT, however, demonstrates the timing and manner of restoration. The return of God's Spirit gives life (cf. 37:5, 6, 14) and functionally begins restoration from exile (as the core significance of exile is estrangement from God). Regaining and possessing the land is the inevitable fruit of that restored relationship. The translator(s) likely chose θυμός in 39:29 in order to highlight the beginning and end of the section promising eschatological restoration (36:18–39:29). Ultimately, however, the choice of θυμός over πνεῦμα obscures the connection between Ezek 37:1–14 and 39:29 and the prophetic indicator of the end of the exile through the coming of the Spirit. Thus, Ezekiel's restoration prophecy is bounded by the affirmation that exile begins with the outpouring of God's covenant wrath and is reversed by the outpouring of his Spirit in its place. This is precisely the argument that Paul makes in Rom 5–8.

For Ezekiel, the restoration of Israel is an eschatological event. Yahweh sets the timing of the restoration as ἐν ἡμέρᾳ (Ezek 36:33; MT: בְּיוֹם).[34] Zimmerli notes a "remarkably close factual parallel" to the eschatological restoration promise of Isa 43:22–28.[35] Both prophets assure the restoration of Israel, however, a unique contribution by Ezekiel is Yahweh's motivation. He does it διὰ τὸ ὄνομά μου τὸ ἅγιον ("for the sake of my holy name," Ezek 36:22; cf. 36:32). But note the result: cities are rebuilt (Ezek 36:33–34) and deserts are cultivated to be like the garden of Eden (36:35). Yahweh promises to increase Israel ὡς πρόβατα ἅγια ("like a flock *for sacrifices,*" 36:38). The "holy" sheep were sacrificial sheep as the remainder of the verse clarifies. They are for Jerusalem's festivals. Thus, they were "for slaughter." The similarity to Ps 44:22, which Paul quotes in Rom 8:36, is noteworthy. In Ps 44, the righteous in exile are ὡς πρόβατα σφαγῆς ("like sheep for slaughter," Ps: 44:22; cf. 44:11). Similarly, Ezekiel's restored people of Israel are depicted as consecrated to the Lord *for sacrifice.* This reading comports with the Pauline expectation that believers will suffer before glory (Rom 5:3–5; 7:14–24; 8:17, 18–23, 35–36; cf. Phil 2:17). Indeed, he calls them to proffer their bodies as a living sacrifice (θυσίαν ζῶσαν) knowing that their suffering (τὸ δοκιμάζειν) is an offering to God (Rom 12:1–2). Yet those sufferings are light and momentary in comparison to glory (Rom 8:18).

The vision of the valley of dry bones contains the final contextual parallel we will consider. The resurrected army of Israel is a restoration prophecy (cf. Ezek 37:12, 14). However, the manner of Israel's resurrection closely resembles the first creation of man. Indeed, the text of Ezekiel 37:5, 9 appears to directly allude to Gen 2:7 LXX (see Table 6, below).

In the Gen 2 creation narrative, God first formed the man/Adam (τὸν ἄνθρωπον; MT: הָאָדָם) from the dust of the earth (Gen 2:7a). Then God breathed εἰς τὸ πρόσωπον αὐτοῦ πνοὴν ζωῆς ("into his face the breath of life") with the result that the man/Adam became a living creature (Gen 2:7b). Derek Kidner captures the tenderness of the moment describing the formation of man as the work of a master craftsman and breathing into him as "warmly personal, with the face-to-face intimacy of a kiss and the significance that this was an act of giving as well as making; and self-giving at that."[36] Of all the myriad of created things, Yahweh only took such care with Adam, his son.

**Table 5.2 Genesis 2:7 LXX in Ezekiel 37:5, 9 LXX**

| *Genesis 2:7 LXX* | *Ezekiel 37:5, 9 LXX* |
|---|---|
| καὶ ἔπλασεν ὁ θεὸς τὸν ἄνθρωπον χοῦν ἀπὸ τῆς γῆς καὶ ἐνεφύσησεν εἰς τὸ πρόσωπον αὐτοῦ πνοὴν ζωῆς καὶ ἐγένετο ὁ ἄνθρωπος εἰς ψυχὴν ζῶσαν. | 37:5 τάδε λέγει κύριος τοῖς ὀστέοις τούτοις ἰδοὺ ἐγὼ φέρω εἰς ὑμᾶς πνεῦμα ζωῆς |
| | 37:9 καὶ εἶπεν πρός με προφήτευσον υἱὲ ἀνθρώπου προφήτευσον ἐπὶ τὸ πνεῦμα καὶ εἰπὸν τῷ πνεύματι τάδε λέγει κύριος ἐκ τῶν τεσσάρων πνευμάτων ἐλθὲ καὶ ἐμφύσησον εἰς τοὺς νεκροὺς τούτους καὶ ζησάτωσαν |

*Source:* Excerpt from *A New Testament Biblical Theology* by G. K. Beale, copyright © 2011. Used by permission of Baker Academic, a division of Baker Publishing Group.
*Note*: Solid underlining represents lexical parallels and dotted lines conceptual parallels.

The resurrection of the fallen army of Israel is clearly portrayed as an act of new creation. However, it corresponds in many ways to the first creation. Adam was formed physically *then* filled with πνοὴν ζωῆς (Gen 2:7) and finally placed in Eden (Gen 2:8). Likewise, the people of Israel are re-formed physically *then* filled with τὸ πνεῦμα (Ezek 37:10) and then restored to the land (Ezek 37:12, 14). As in Isaiah, the restoration of Israel in Ezekiel requires an act of new creation.[37] For, as has been noted, Israel's exile was its death.[38] In other words, exile was the enactment of the covenant curse upon Israel by separating the people from both God and the land of their inheritance. The reconstitution of Israel's army takes place in two stages, which correspond to the two-part formation of Adam. Zimmerli observes that the two-stage resurrection of Israel "takes as its hidden model the process of the primeval creation of man as this is reported in Gen 2:7."[39] The resurrection of Israel is, thus, a creative act. Once again, God breathes life into his son and intends to place him in "Eden" (Ezek 36:35; cf. Gen 2:7–8). Both Gen 2:7–8 and Ezek 37:1–14 follow the pattern of physical formation followed by the giving of life through the Spirit/breath then being planted in a land of rest.[40] In sum, although Ezekiel's promise of restoration is given to Israel, it has an Adamic shape. Paul will further develop the redemptive-historical theme to show that eschatological resurrection is the restoration of *all* of God's children. Adam and Israel will be restored when Christ reverses the curse.

## The Outpouring of the Spirit as the Already-Not Yet Restoration of Israel

Having now seen the background of Ezekiel's restoration promise, we can conclude that the new humanity in Christ is the object of the Spirit's new creation. Justification ensures the removal of condemnation and the indwelling of the Spirit marks the resurrection of God's formerly dead people. These spiritual children of Abraham (Rom 4:16) constitute eschatological Israel (Rom 9:6–7). In other words, Rom 8:1–11 confirms what I argued regarding Rom 5:5 in the previous chapter—that the outpouring of the Spirit marks the fulfillment of Ezekiel's restoration prophecy.

It should be noted that Paul presents eschatological resurrection in an already-not yet framework. Of course, Jesus's physical resurrection is the basis for the believers' later physical resurrection. However, initially, their resurrection is only spiritual. The body is not yet affected. Romans 8:10 shows the contrast clearly: εἰ δὲ Χριστὸς ἐν ὑμῖν, τὸ μὲν σῶμα νεκρὸν διὰ ἁμαρτίαν τὸ δὲ πνεῦμα ζωὴ διὰ δικαιοσύνην ("but if Christ is in you, the body is dead on account of sin, but the Spirit is life on account of righteousness"). Paul's use of the μέν . . . δέ construction highlights the antithesis. Death continues to affect the physical bodies of believers despite the life-giving work of the Spirit. That ζωή occurs in its noun form instead of as an adjective further indicates that πνεῦμα ζωὴ διὰ δικαιοσύνην refers to the indwelling presence of the Holy Spirit: "The (Holy) Spirit *is* life" as opposed to "the (human) spirit is alive."[41] Thus, the outpouring of the Spirit into believers' hearts (Rom 5:5) fulfills prophecies (Isa 32:15; Ezek 39:28–29; Joel 2:28; cf. Zech 12:10), but it does so spiritually and without an immediate effect upon the physical body (Rom 8:10–11) or external creation (8:19–22). Nevertheless, both Ezek 37:1–14 and Paul's argument in Rom 8 point forward to the physical manifestation of the Spirit's work. Ezekiel promises that God *will* restore their land. Paul refers to believers as heirs (κληρονόμοι, 8:17) and to the redemption of their bodies and subhuman creation (8:21, 23).

This two-stage process of the resurrection is paralleled in Ezek 37, where Ezekiel prophesies to the valley of dry bones (37:7) and sinews and flesh grow over the bones, but they are not yet alive (πνεῦμα οὐκ ἦν ἐν αὐτοῖς, 37:8). But God instructs Ezekiel to prophesy again ἐπὶ τὸ πνεῦμα and call him to come that the dead may live (37:9). Admittedly, the parallel is not exact. In Romans, resurrection begins with the indwelling of the Spirit. The second stage is the physical resurrection (Rom 8:11). Ezekiel's first stage is the reconstitution of the dead body and then the Spirit's entrance to make it live. The disparity is likely due to the prior background of Ezek 37 itself. Paul's purpose in Rom 8:1–11 is not to follow every detail of Ezekiel's text, but to explain the nature of life in the Spirit *before* the physical resurrection. His point is that this resurrection is an act of new creation of a new humanity in the last Adam which corresponds to the creational pattern of the first (Gen 2:7). Indeed, it should arrest our attention that Paul has shown such a close affinity to Ezek 36–37, but now reverses the order of events. I argue that he does so because the last Adam does not only *establish* a new humanity, but in fact *reverses* the curse that was brought upon the first humanity. This is the contribution of the notion of restoration to the overall new creation that Paul describes. The indwelling of the Spirit is the fulfillment of Ezekiel's prophecy and the inauguration of restoration from exile. However, the consummation of restoration will not take place until the complementary resurrection of the body and renewal of the land itself, which Paul calls believers' inheritance (8:17), the revelation of the sons of God (8:19) and the liberty of creation (8:21).

## Conclusion of Romans 8:1–11

In sum, Paul's focus upon the inner transformation accomplished by the presence of the Spirit in Rom 8:1–11 marks his return to and expansion of the motif of the outpouring of the Spirit in Rom 5:5. I argued in the previous chapter that Paul's use of the term "reconciliation" coupled with the announcement of the outpouring of the Spirit indicated the end of Israel's exile. Paul not only develops that notion in Rom 8, but indicates that the restoration of *Israel* will correspond to the first creation of *Adam.* Indeed, we have already seen that Paul interweaves the figures of Adam and Israel into his singular announcement of redemption in Rom 5. Thus, although Rom 8:1–11 focuses upon Israel's restoration by virtue of its connection to Ezekiel, we should remember that this restoration is accomplished by the last Adam.

Paul's foundational use of the Adam-Christ typology displayed in the dichotomies of flesh and Spirit, and the dependence of Rom 8, as a whole upon the themes introduced in Rom 5 indicates that Adam plays a role in Paul's thoughts there as well. Indeed, the universal scope of both the inheritance and redemption Paul envisions points to a background in Adam's headship and not Israel's influence alone. Moreover, Ezekiel's echo of Gen 2 in its prophecy of Israel's resurrection indicates that Paul is not drawing from two independent sources, but continuing a redemptive-historical trajectory. Like the first creation, the eschatological restoration of mankind takes place in two-stages.

The fruition of spiritual resurrection but it's still-pending physical consummation anticipates the remainder of Rom 8. Ezekiel's prophecy included both resurrection and land. Moreover, Israel was raised an *army* ready for battle (cf. Rom 8:37). In Rom 8:12–17, Paul transitions to describe the conflict with Sin and Death (8:12–13) but final triumph in glory (8:17). He further points to the renewal of subhuman creation (8:19–22) and the future reception of the inheritance of God's sons (8:23), which he has already indicated is the whole world (Rom 4:13; 8:17, 21).

## ROMANS 8:12–17—THE SPIRIT'S LEADING AS NEW EXODUS

The Spirit's presence links the second paragraph (8:12–17) to the previous one (8:1–11) as both develop the significance of the coming of the Spirit introduced in Rom 5:5. But the focus is no longer on the quality of the Spirit versus the flesh, but on the ethical obligation to follow the Spirit (cf. Gal 5:16–18).[42] Paul's direct address to his readers in 8:12, ἄρα οὖν, ἀδελφοί ("So then, brothers"), marks his shift from description to application (7:4–6; 8:4). This ethical obligation is directly related to the focus of 8:14–30 upon the notion of divine sonship.[43] Whereas we have seen restoration imagery in Rom 8:1–11, several scholars have identified exodus imagery in Rom 8:12–17, which they argue portrays life in the Spirit as a new exodus.[44] The proposed exodus allusions are focused in 8:14–17.

> ὅσοι γὰρ πνεύματι θεοῦ ἄγονται, οὗτοι υἱοὶ θεοῦ εἰσιν.[45]
>
> 15 οὐ γὰρ ἐλάβετε πνεῦμα δουλείας πάλιν εἰς φόβον ἀλλ᾽ ἐλάβετε πνεῦμα υἱοθεσίας ἐν ᾧ κράζομεν· αββα ὁ πατήρ.
>
> 16 αὐτὸ τὸ πνεῦμα συμμαρτυρεῖ τῷ πνεύματι ἡμῶν ὅτι ἐσμὲν τέκνα θεοῦ.
>
> 17 εἰ δὲ τέκνα, καὶ κληρονόμοι· κληρονόμοι μὲν θεοῦ, συγκληρονόμοι δὲ Χριστοῦ, εἴπερ συμπάσχομεν ἵνα καὶ συνδοξασθῶμεν.
>
> For as many as are *led by the Spirit of God*, these are *sons of God.* 15 For you did not receive a *spirit of slavery* [to fall] again to fear, but you have received the *spirit of adoption* by whom we cry, "Abba, Father." 16 The same spirit testifies with our spirit that we are *children of God.* 17 And because we are children, [we are] also *heirs*, *heirs of God*, and co-heirs with Christ, since we suffer with him in order that we also will be glorified with him.

The argument interprets the underlined words above as allusions to Israel's exodus from Egypt where Yahweh led Israel his firstborn son out of bondage and toward the promised land inheritance. Nevertheless, the position has been challenged. Douglas Moo, for example, writes, "[The] suggestion that the phrase ["as many as are led"] describes the Christian's path to eschatological fulfillment in imitation of the OT description of the people of God being led into the promised land is intriguing, but it lacks clear lexical support in the NT and LXX."[46] Despite objections, I will argue below that Paul does portray believers as participating in the eschatological exodus.

Before examining the evidence, we should recall that Paul has already displayed a pattern of dependence upon Isaiah, particularly Isa 40–55, in Romans.[47] In 4:25–5:11 alone Paul identified Jesus as Isaiah's servant,[48] echoed Isaianic descriptions of the eschatological age of peace, and declared that the Spirit had been poured out—an event prophesied in Isa 32:15.[49] The dominant motif of Isaiah 40–55's restoration prophecies was exodus (cf. Is 42:13–44:23, esp. 43:16–19; 48:20–21; 51:9–11; 52:11–12). The expectation was that God would restore Israel from exile with an ingathering of the Gentiles in a salvific work that was analogous to but greater than the first exodus.[50] As we turn to examine the evidence for allusions to the exodus, we should recall that Paul's overall agenda is to articulate the significance of the outpouring of the Spirit and the inauguration of the Isaianic age of peace. I argue that while Paul does allude to an exodus *like* the one from Egypt, this new exodus must be understood in light of Isaiah.

## Establishing the Exodus Allusions

The first point of evidence that Paul invokes the exodus tradition is the phrase πνεύματι θεοῦ ἄγοντα in 8:14a. For N. T. Wright, it unambiguously alludes to the wilderness wanderings of Israel, which was led by the *Shekinah* glory cloud.[51] Ignace de la Potterie has argued, "Le verbe ἄγειν (avec ses composés ἐξάγειν et εἰσάγειν) et son synonyme ὁδηγείν, sont devenus dans la Bible grecque des termes techniques du vocabulaire de l'Exode" (cf. Exod 3:11, 12; 6:6, 7, 26, 27; 15:22; Deut 8:2, 15; 29:5; 32:12; Josh 24:8).[52] This may overstate the case, as ἄγω is quite common. Nevertheless, the motif of "being led" from Egyptian bondage is a common way to describe the exodus throughout the Hebrew Bible.[53] In the Book of Exodus alone, some form of ἄγω or ὁδηγέω is used 41 times to describe the exodus deliverance.[54] Exodus 6:6, in which God promises to deliver Israel, is one example:

> Ἐγὼ κύριος, καὶ ἐξάξω ὑμᾶς ἀπὸ τῆς δυναστείας τῶν Αἰγυπτίων, καὶ ῥύσομαι ὑμᾶς ἐκ τῆς δουλείας, καὶ λυτρώσομαι ὑμᾶς (Exod 6:6)

> I am the Lord and I will lead you from the power of the Egyptians and I will deliver you from slavery and I will redeem you (Exod 6:6)

Yahweh leads (ἐξάγω) Israel from its δουλεία with the promise of redemption. Furthermore, following Martin Noth, Keesmaat observes that this phrase, with minor variations, becomes an early confession of Israel and self-designation for Yahweh.[55] For example, the preamble to the Decalogue in Exod 20:2 describes Yahweh as the one who led (ἐξάγω) Israel out of the land of Egypt and the house of bondage (δουλεία). Yahweh's self-designations in Deuteronomy also follow this pattern (Deut 5:6; 6:12; 7:8; 8:14; 13:6, 11). Yet this early confession is not only retrospective. We should also note that it occurs in Lev 26:45 as the basis for Israel's *future* deliverance from exile.[56] After Leviticus predicts Israel's covenant breaking and exile, when the people are in foreign lands, Yahweh promises "I will remember their former covenant when I led them out of Egypt out of the house of bondage" (μνησθήσομαι αὐτῶν τῆς διαθήκης τῆς προτέρας ὅτε ἐξήγαγον αὐτοὺς ἐκ γῆς Αἰγύπτου ἐξ οἴκου δουλείας, Lev 26:45). Paul also echoes second exodus language in Isa 49:22 which foresees the Gentiles as Yahweh's instruments for leading (ἄγω) Israel from exile. As elsewhere in the Hebrew Scriptures, the text of Isaiah also frequently uses forms of ἄγω to describe Yahweh leading Israel in the first exodus.[57] However, it uses such terminology more frequently to describe the manner of Israel's *future* eschatological deliverance.[58] Thus, Paul's ascription of NT believers as being led (ἄγω) by God's Spirit out of δουλεία describes their salvation experience with terminology that is redolent of the expected manner of Israel's restoration from Isaiah as well as Israel's first exodus.

The second point of evidence is the identification of those who are led as *sons* (8:14b). If leading by the Spirit recalls the exodus, the inclusion of sonship lends strong support. Keesmaat notes that the most common image associated with divine sonship is *Israel* as God's son.[59] We have already seen that Israel's status as Yahweh's firstborn was the basis of its redemption (Exod 4:22–23). Similarly, Paul connects the leading of the Spirit for NT believers with their status as sons. The careful insertion of sonship and the leading of the Spirit recall the exodus.[60] But they also identify believers with Christ's divine sonship. Thus far in Romans, Paul has exclusively referred to Christ as son (1:3, 4, 9; 5:10; 8:3). He was born κατὰ σάρκα, but declared "Son" by his resurrection (1:3–4). In Rom 5:10 Paul briefly mentioned that reconciliation to God is possible διὰ τοῦ θανάτου τοῦ υἱοῦ αὐτοῦ ("through the death of his son") before developing that thought in Rom 8:3: ὁ θεὸς τὸν ἑαυτοῦ υἱὸν πέμψας ἐν ὁμοιώματι σαρκὸς ἁμαρτίας καὶ περὶ ἁμαρτίας κατέκρινεν τὴν ἁμαρτίαν ἐν τῇ σαρκί ("by means of sending his own son in the likeness of sinful flesh and for sin he condemned sin in the flesh"). However, Paul has been building the case for believers' inheritance (4:13, 16; 5:17) and their incorporation into Christ and receiving his benefits through faith from the start (e.g., 1:5, 16; 3:22; 4:24–5; 5:1–2; 6:8). That Paul has finally stated the notion he has been developing indicates that he is near the conclusion of his argument. The combination of the notion of sonship with the leading of the Spirit recalls both the historical exodus and Isaianic expectations of a greater exodus.

The third point of evidence is the contrast in Rom 8:15 where Paul describes the nature of the indwelling Spirit. The Spirit is not a spirit of such "bondage" (πνεῦμα δουλείας) but of "adoption" (πνεῦμα υἱοθεσίας). As I argued above, the use of the word δουλεία corroborates the exodus allusions. While ἄγω (or one of its compounds) is often used in Yahweh's self-designations which formed early confessions for Israel, such credos invariably affirm that Yahweh's deliverance is from δουλεία.[61] "Slavery" in Rom 8:15 is the continuation of a theme begun with Paul's reference to redemption in Rom 3:24 (cf. Exod 6:6, above), but primarily expanded in Rom 6 where the slave-master is Adamic bondage to Sin and Death.[62] Paul repeatedly refers to believers' former slavery to Sin and Death (with the δουλός/δουλεία word group: Rom 6:6, 16, 17, 18, 19, 20, 22) or "captivity" to the law (κατέχω, 7:6) prior to their deliverance.[63] Thus, Paul's use of the term δουλεία along with the notions of leading by the Spirit and sonship recalls the first exodus, but frames the slave-master as *Adamic* bondage to Sin and Death as opposed to Egyptian slavery.

The final destination of the Spirit's leading is a fourth parallel to the exodus. Paul builds a deliberate logical progression from the Spirit's leading to sonship to its accompanying *inheritance* (εἰ δὲ τέκνα, καὶ κληρονόμοι, 8:17a). By mentioning the inheritance, Paul returns to the topic of God's promise that Abraham would be heir of the world (τὸ κληρονόμον αὐτὸν εἶναι κόσμου, 4:13). Paul is taking advantage of the ambiguity of the Hebrew term אֶרֶץ (land *or* earth).[64] While the promise was originally given with reference to Canaan, there was always an implicit broader meaning.[65] The full scope of the promise always went beyond physical limits of Canaan. Paul's cosmic interpretation of Abraham's inheritance is not unique to Paul, but is echoed in the Hebrew Bible (e.g., Deut 1:7–8; Ps 2:8) and Jewish literature (Sir 44:21; *Jub.* 17:3; 22:14; 39:19; *1 En.* 5:7; *2 Bar.* 14:13; 51:3).[66] Thus, the inheritance is far from immaterial. It is terrestrial *and* glorious (cf. 8:17).[67] Just as God promised Abraham אֶרֶץ, and Israel its own land, the Spirit leads believers toward a land of rest and blessing.[68] The cosmic scope of the inheritance, its description as "glory" (8:17–18), and Jesus's merit of it *as last Adam* indicates the land in question is a renewed and expanded Eden.

Finally, we should recall that Paul often introduces themes he will later resume and expand upon. J. Ross Wagner has convincingly argued that the events of the historical exodus form the backdrop of Rom 9:14–18.[69] While defending God's justice in election, Paul explicitly quotes Moses in Rom 9:15, "For he says to Moses, 'I will have mercy on whomever I will have mercy and I will have compassion on whomever I will have compassion'" (τῷ Μωϋσεῖ γὰρ λέγει· ἐλεήσω ὃν ἂν ἐλεῶ καὶ οἰκτιρήσω ὃν ἂν οἰκτίρω; cf. Exod 33:19) as well as explicitly referring to the hardening of Pharaoh's heart in Rom 9:17. I mention Paul's use of the exodus in Rom 9 to show the nearness of the exodus events to Paul's mind while he was writing Rom 8.

In sum, Moo's dismissive claim that there is no lexical support for an exodus allusion is a welcome caution against over-reading, but incorrect. The message of (1) the Spirit's leading of (2) sons of God (3) out of bondage and (4) toward a land of covenant inheritance is redolent with exodus themes, which Paul employs typologically[70] to describe believers' already, not yet restoration to God.

## New Exodus as Israel's Restoration

Israel's history is in the back of Paul's argumentation, but Israel's future is his focus. He frames the eschatological people of God as the heirs of God's promises to Israel and the fruition of the prophesied second exodus. Redemptive-historically conditioned, they *are* Israel by virtue of their union with Christ, who embodies true Israel. Like Israel, believers were not baptized (cf. Rom 6:3–4; 1 Cor 10:2–4) and instantly transported to the land of inheritance. Instead, they were given a new law (cf. Exod 19–24; Rom 8:2) and commanded to follow the Spirit (8:14–17).

The description of believers as *adopted* sons of God provides further support for viewing the eschatological work of Christ as restoration from exile. James M. Scott has demonstrated that many first-century Jews believed the "adoption formula" in 2 Sam 7:14 ("I will be to him a father and he will be to me a son") foretold the recovery of Israel's status of divine sonship in its eschatological restoration from exile.[71] Thus, Paul's description of believers' adoption (υἱοθεσία, 8:15), in combination with his prior development of Ezek 36–37 in Rom 8:1–11, leads Scott to conclude that Paul argues for the fulfillment of both in Christ. He writes, "the υἱοθεσία of believers recalls the 2 Sam. 7:14 tradition, which looks forward to the outpouring of the Spirit on the eschatological people of God who are adopted as sons of God with the Messiah."[72] Brendan Byrne also notes that the motif of Israel's divine sonship "came to be associated particularly with eschatological Israel, God's people destined to 'inherit' the promises of salvation (*1 En.* 62:11; *Jub.* 1:24–5; 2:20; *Pss. Sol.* 17:30; *As. Mos.* 10:3; *4 Ezra* 6:58; *2 Apoc. Bar.* 13:9; *Bib. Ant.* 18:6; 32:10; *Sib. Or.* 3:702; 5:202; 4QDibHam 3:4–6; 3 Macc 6:28; etc)."[73] Scott's logic is helpful. The Messiah is son first. God's eschatological people are incorporated into sonship with him. This is consistent with Paul's use of the notion of divine sonship throughout Romans. The introduction in Rom 1:3–4 showed Christ as the Davidic son κατὰ σάρκα, but declared *Son* in power in his resurrection from the dead (ἐξ ἀναστάσεως νεκρῶν, 1:4) by the Spirit. Scott suggests that Rom 1:3–4 implies Christ's resurrection is the first of many in the plural form νεκρῶν.[74] This implication is corroborated in Rom 8:29–30, which speaks of the predestination of the adopted sons.[75] The resurrection of Christ provides the certainty of the future glorification of adopted sons, who should be identified as the eschatological Israel, the heirs of Abraham. They are adopted as sons of God through the Spirit's resurrecting work who has been poured into their hearts and leads them out of their previous condition of exile from God's presence and toward their inheritance of land and glory.

If the argument thus far is correct and Paul's explicit description of life in the Spirit and reconciliation to God is implicitly the fulfillment of prophetic expectations of restoration from exile, his use of the exodus motif is fitting. We have seen him interweave Adam and Israel imagery in both Rom 5 and 8 toward the ultimate goal of demonstrating that Jesus Christ is the antitypical fulfillment of their roles. Each of these figures was called God's "son," whether the protological son in Adam or Israel as a typological, corporate son. Paul has demonstrated that through the victory of Christ the Son (Rom 1:3–4; 5:10) believers enjoy a renewed hope in the glory of God (Rom 5:2; 8:17), which Paul will further describe in Rom 8:21 as the glory of the *children of God* (τῆς δόξης τῶν τέκνων τοῦ θεου). Hence, it should come as no surprise to find Paul describing the eschatological redemption of God's *sons* in the terms of the prior salvation of God's typological son. The exodus was the paradigmatic act of salvation by which later prophets described future salvation.[76] Thus, the notion of divine sonship has been carefully developed and finally appears explicitly to link this stage of redemptive-history with the previous one.

I should clarify that Paul is *not* retelling Israel's story nor using the exodus as a rigid rubric.[77] Paul is not recapitulating an earlier chapter of redemptive-history, but telling a new one. It is, as it were, the *third* chapter of the sons of God. Jesus, the eschatological Son of God, received the same commission as the previous two: obey God and bless the world. In conjunction with that role, he functions as the redeemer of God's chosen people and suffers the curse of their disobedience. He was condemned, died, and was raised to new life. He fulfilled the role of divine son, received the inheritance, and proffers his inheritance to those he redeems (cf. Rom 1:3–4; 4:25; 5:12–21; 8:17, 37–39).

## New Exodus as Adam's Restoration

I have argued that Paul depicts believers being led by the Spirit on a new exodus as eschatological Israel in Rom 8:14–17. However, there are three overlapping reasons to see the new exodus not as *exclusively* the fulfillment of Israel's restoration from exile but *inclusively* as the new humanity's restoration from Adamic exile. These reasons are: (1) the cosmic scale of restoration, (2) the inheritance of glory as well as land, and (3) the redemptive-historical continuity of sonship.

First, the cosmic scale of restoration—in reversing the Adamic curse (5:12–21) and including subhuman creation (8:18–23)[78]—indicates a scope of redemption that goes well beyond the borders of Israel. Of course, it has already been noted that Jewish tradition had expanded the scope of the Abrahamic promise beyond Canaan (cf. Rom 4:13).[79] Yet, chapter 2 showed that Israel received Adam's commission via Abraham and that Israel's growth into a great nation is an early fulfillment of the Abrahamic promise (e.g., Exod 1:7, 12, 20). God's promise of a land of rest *for Israel* recalled the land Adam had forfeited. The reality of Israel living in the land was not identical to Adam in the garden,[80] but *mutatis mutandis,* Israel (the type of Adam) received its inheritance in Canaan (a type of Eden).[81] Paul's expansion of the scope of the inheritance of divine sons simply restores the size to where it began.[82]

A second indicator that Paul's new exodus is restoration from Adamic exile is the theme of *glory* (8:17, 18, 21, 30). Donald L. Berry argues that "by correlating the inheritance with glorification, Paul locates the promise to Abraham and Israel within the larger purpose of God for humanity, seen first in his intention for Adam, and then for Israel as a corporate Adam."[83] The glory motif reaches its climax in Rom 8. Mankind (paradigmatically in Adam) exchanged God's glory (Rom 1:23), and fell short of glory (Rom 3:23), but Jesus Christ, the last Adam, reconciles man to God and renews hope in his glory (5:10–11, 2). I argued in the previous chapter that this glory was originally offered to Adam. That Paul describes the inheritance as *glory* in Rom 8:17, in addition to the more obvious category of land, indicates the consummation of Adamic potential. It is the consummation of God's eschatological purpose for his image-bearer, which Adam failed to achieve. Paul says that for the duration of the journey there will be suffering *with Christ* (συμπάσχομεν) but that will give way to glory *with him* (συνδοξασθῶμεν). Participation in Christ is the prerequisite for these particular trials and eschatological glory. Thus, glory is the inheritance which Jesus earned and which believers receive by faith as co-heirs (συγκληρονόμοι).

Finally, I have argued that Paul's description of believers as adopted sons indicates his use of the exodus motif pointing to the restoration of Israel. In context, however, the image of sons of God inheriting glory points to Adam as well, perhaps even more clearly. David B. Garner writes,

> Bearing the theological weight beneath Israel's sonship is Adam's own sonship (cf. Luke 3:38), and Paul's filial-rich theology finds its deepest historical referent in the anticipated glory and inheritance associated with Adam's promised covenantal future as an obedient son (cf. 1 Cor. 15:20–49).[84]

The previous section demonstrates that Paul uses sonship terminology to describe the Spirit's leadership in a new and greater exodus. God is once again leading his sons out of slavery and toward rest. Yet, this is not merely a typological identification of NT believers with the Israel's exodus. The concept of divine sonship cannot be divorced from Adam, the protological son. Israel's sonship must be understood through Adam, not Adam's through Israel. This is why Paul refers to three *stories* (Adam, Israel, and Christ), but only two *ages* (Adam and Christ). The nearness of these two sons in Paul's mind has already been demonstrated in our analysis of the redemptive-historical substructure of Rom 5. Israel's place as son of God is directly derivative of Adam's such that we could discuss the implicit presence of the Adam motif in this passage based upon the sonship motif alone. The strength of that tacit connection is increased by Paul's repeated allusions to Adam throughout Rom 1–8 (e.g., 1:23; 3:23; 5:12–21; 7:7–13; Ezek 37:1–14 in Rom 8:1–11) and by his casting the conflict between sin and righteousness in terms derived from the Adam-Christ typology (e.g., flesh/Spirit). Thus, I argue that Paul is communicating the expansion of the redemptive-historical motif in the consummate sonship of Christ (Rom 1:4), who perfectly reflects the image of God. Jesus is the consummate image-bearer and mankind is restored to God in union with him (8:29–30), reversing Adamic separation.

## Conclusion of Romans 8:12–17

Paul portrays redemption in Christ as the second great salvation event of history, a new exodus greater than the first. It is the restoration of Israel and the undoing of the Adamic curse. However, the character of this new exodus is essentially one of struggle, as the inheritance has yet to be attained. Paul indicates that struggle in Rom 8:13 when he describes life κατὰ πνεῦμα as one of continually putting to death the deeds of the body. The language of "putting to death" picks up on Paul's discussion of baptism in Rom 6:1–11. The transfer from a position κατὰ σάρκα in Adam to κατὰ πνεῦμα in Christ is accomplished by being crucified with Christ (Rom 6:6). Tyler Stewart explains, "To be put to death 'through Christ's body' is to participate in his crucifixion (Rom 6:6; Gal 2:20) and thereby enter the Christ-age released from Adam-age-captivity."[85] Thus, a fundamental characteristic of life in the Spirit on the wilderness journey is to suffer with Christ. Ezekiel 37 implied the struggle before glory in the resurrection of the *army* of Israel. Paul will ultimately conclude that, in Christ, believers "prevail completely" (ὑπερνικάω, Rom 8:37)—a military term.[86] Paul's use of the exodus motif to describe restoration from God indicates that the not-yet of life in the Spirit will be marked by struggle.

## ROMANS 8:18–30—THE RESTORATION OF CREATION

Having described life in the Spirit as a new exodus in 8:12–17, Paul transitions to answer the related question: What will this exodus be like? Verses 18–30 answer that it will be a time marked by suffering and ending with glory. By returning to the pattern of *suffering then glory,* Paul resumes the language with which he began Rom 5 (e.g., 5:3–5).[87] In addition to Rom 5, Paul also returns to motifs and vocabulary from his opening argument in 1:18–32.[88] Suffering is due to the futility that began with Adam's exchange. It follows that Christ's perfect obedience will result in both mankind and creation being set free from that curse. The subjection of creation is the result of the "handing over" of 1:24, 26, 28.[89] The thesis of the description is found in 8:18:[90]

> Λογίζομαι γὰρ ὅτι οὐκ ἄξια τὰ παθήματα τοῦ νῦν καιροῦ πρὸς τὴν μέλλουσαν δόξαν ἀποκαλυφθῆναι εἰς ἡμᾶς.
>
> For I consider that the sufferings of the present time are not worthy of comparison to the glory about to be revealed to us.

The time period between the spiritual resurrection of believers through the outpouring of the Holy Spirit and their glorification will be characterized by *groaning.* The suffering which Paul has attributed thus far only to believers in Christ is shared by creation (8:19–22), believers (8:23–25), and the Spirit with them (8:26–27). Nevertheless, there is a certainty of deliverance concurrent with the future glory of God's children. Each of the three groanings represents a parallel movement. The interconnection among the groanings of Spirit, sons, and creation resonates with Paul's consistent application of the theology of curse and restoration we have seen throughout. The groaning of creation is the futility resulting from Adam's failed dominion over subhuman creation. The groaning of the Spirit reflects his intercession and support of believers before their bodily restoration.

### Adam in Romans 8:18–30

Whereas the previous section featured the history of Israel with Adam in the background, Rom 8:18–23 highlights Adam's influence and the affect of his transgression upon everything God had placed under his authority. The Adamic substructure of Paul's thinking in these verses is evidenced in at least three ways: (1) the distinction of ἡ κτίσις from believers in redemption, (2) creation's subjection to futility, and (3) the mechanism of the curse's reversal.

## *ἡ κτίσις* as Subhuman Creation in Romans 8:18–23

Paul has described suffering as belonging to the present age (Rom 5:3–5; 8:15–17, 18). Believers are the subjects of the tribulation predicted in Rom 5:3–5 and 8:17. Their co-suffering with Christ is the basis for confidence in glory. Now Paul claims that ἡ κτίσις also participates in those travails.[91] Creation *also* (καί, 8:21) eagerly awaits the revelation of God's sons (8:19). He goes on to explain τῇ γὰρ ματαιότητι ἡ κτίσις ὑπετάγη ("for creation was subjected to futility," 8:20). By fronting "futility," Paul emphasizes that creation also shares the suffering described.[92] It groans along with believers and the Spirit. Not only does creation's futility resume the theme of futility from 1:21, but these references to groaning likely also allude to a broader motif of groaning under curse beginning with Eve's pain in childbirth (Gen 3:16) and continuing in Israel's groaning in Egyptian slavery (Exod 2:23).[93] Thus, the groaning of creation recalls again the stories of Adam and Israel. In this context, groaning is the experience of curse; it is bondage resulting from Adam's abdication and the rule of Sin in his place.

The meaning of κτίσις is a central interpretive issue for this passage.[94] There is a diversity of interpretations.[95] The most widespread position, sometimes called the cosmic interpretation, identifies κτίσις as subhuman creation.[96] A second position views κτίσις as all creation inclusive of humanity.[97] A third position, famously held by Saint Augustine, views κτίσις as only humanity, excluding the rest of creation.[98] Ecologically motivated readings have also emerged which entirely isolate creation from human concerns.[99] Taking the majority position cited above, I argue that κτίσις is subhuman creation—everything over which Adam was given dominion in the covenant of creation. One surface-level reason for this conclusion is that Paul distinguishes ἡ κτίσις from believers in Rom 8:19, 21, 23. This observation weighs against viewing κτίσις inclusively. It is also difficult to see unbelieving humanity longing for the fuller realization of God's kingdom coming defined as "the freedom of the glory of God's children" (εἰς τὴν ἐλευθερίαν τῆς δόξης τῶν τέκνων τοῦ θεοῦ, 8:21).[100]

The redemption of mankind is the "anthropological hinge" upon which the eager expectation of creation turns.[101] Paul likely has Gen 2:5–9 and the connection between "Adam" and "ground" in his mind when writing 8:20–22.[102] The groaning of creation is centered on two allusions to Gen 3:14–19, which describes when creation's futility began. The first allusion to Gen 3:14–19 (and 5:29) occurs in Rom 8:20–1:

> τῇ γὰρ ματαιότητι ἡ κτίσις ὑπετάγη, οὐχ ἑκοῦσα ἀλλὰ διὰ τὸν ὑποτάξαντα, ἐφ' ἑλπίδι 21 ὅτι καὶ αὐτὴ ἡ κτίσις ἐλευθερωθήσεται ἀπὸ τῆς δουλείας τῆς φθορᾶς εἰς τὴν ἐλευθερίαν τῆς δόξης τῶν τέκνων τοῦ θεοῦ.

> For the creation was subjected to futility, not willingly but on account of the one who subjected, in hope 21 that the creation itself might be set at liberty from the slavery of corruption to the freedom of the glory of the children of God.

Although there is not a lexical parallel, the context is clearly pointing to the fall of Eden.[103] Like mankind in Adam, κτίσις itself was enslaved in τὴν δουλείαν τῆς φθορᾶς. Thus, futility (ματαιότης), bondage (δουλεία), and corruption (φθορά) are related results of the unrighteous exchange in 1:23 (which I argued in chapter 3 alludes to Adam's paradigmatic sin), while freedom (ἐλευθερία) and glory (δόξα) contrast with them (8:21).[104] The link between ματαιότης in 8:20 and ματαιόω in 1:21 strongly indicates that creation's "unwilling" subjection is related to the "giving over" of mankind.[105] C. K. Barrett traces the ματαιότης of creation to Adam's sin and authority over it (cf. Gen 3:17).[106]

The Adamic background points to the subhuman option and against unbelieving humanity. The use of the aorist, ὑπετάγη ("was subjected"), is likely a constative aorist suggesting that the subjection was accomplished in a singular event.[107] Most commentators conclude the aorist is a divine passive specifically referencing God's inclusion of creation in the consequences Adam's sin in Gen 3:17–18.[108] However, it has also been suggested that the διὰ + accusative construction indicates that διὰ τὸν ὑποτάξαντα should be identified as Adam.[109] This position was argued in the early church by John Chrysostom:

> Creation became corruptible. Why and for what reason? Because of you, O man! For because you have a body which has become mortal and subject to suffering, the earth too has received a curse and has brought forth thorns and thistles . . . but it has not been irreparably damaged. For it will become incorruptible once again for your sake.[110]

According to this position, just as Adam subjected himself to futility, so did his representative capacity ensure creation's liability to curse. Creation was forced into futility *because of* Adam (cf. *4 Ezra* 7:11–12). Just as ματαιότης recalls Rom 1:21, the phrase οὐχ ἑκοῦσα ("not willingly") may link to Paul's affirmation that God's invisible power is known τοῖς ποιήμασιν ("to the created things," 1:20). Further, Dunn suggests that Paul may be alluding to Ps 8:7 which also uses the verb ὑποτάσσω with reference to Adam (cf. Phil 3:21 where it is used of Christ, the last Adam).[111]

The more widespread position holds that the judicial referent of ὑποτάσσω leads to the conclusion that God alone could do the subjecting.[112] Yet, it is highly unusual for διὰ + accusative to express agency.[113] If God were the agent of subjection, we would expect διὰ + genitive or ὑπό + genitive.[114] I suggest that Paul intends both. God is the judge and ultimate cause of creation's subjection to futility, hence the use of the divine passive. However, Adam's transgression was the immediate cause making him τὸν ὑποτάξαντα. This would explain the quick repetition of ὑποτάσσω and the complexity of the choices. Dunn is likely correct in his conclusion:

> The reason for the difficulty is probably that Paul was attempting to convey too briefly a quite complicated point: that God subjected all things to Adam, and that included subjecting creation to fallen Adam, to share in his fallenness; the repetition of the ὑποτάσσω has the further welcome effect of emphasizing that creation's present condition is not the result of chance or fate but deliberately so ordered by God.[115]

The salient point is creation's subjection due to Adam's action, but its renewal through the consummation of sonship (i.e., conformity to Christ's glorified image, Rom 8:29–30). It may be concluded—particularly in light of the Adam substructure thus far in Paul's argument—that Paul considers Adam's transgression to be the basis for creation's futility (cf. Rom 5:14). This conclusion, however, is equally true of subhuman creation *and* unbelieving humanity. Yet, there is a second allusion to Gen 3 in Rom 8:21 which convincingly points to ἡ κτίσις as nonhuman creation.

Paul explains Rom 8:20–21 with Rom 8:22–23: οἴδαμεν γὰρ ὅτι πᾶσα ἡ κτίσις συστενάζει καὶ συνωδίνει ἄχρι τοῦ νῦν ("for we know that all creation groans and travails together until now"). Although συστενάζω is only used in Rom 8:22, the cognate στενάζω occurs six times in the NT and 27 in the LXX.[116] Most commentators rightly highlight the Second Temple Jewish tradition that "birth pangs" will precede the Eschaton.[117] However, surprisingly few scholars discuss the potential allusion in creation's "groaning" (συστενάζω) to Eve's groaning in childbirth (στεναγμός, Gen 3:16).[118] The basic meaning of στενάζω (to "sigh" or "groan") expresses misery due to undesirable circumstances.[119] Στεναγμός rarely refers to birth pains. The normal word is ὠδίν, which Paul also uses in Rom 8:22 (adjusting for the συν- prefix).[120]

There are only three occurrences in the LXX of στεναγμός as birth pains: Gen 3:16, Jer 4:31, and Isa 21:3.[121] Both Jeremiah and Isaiah use στεναγμός metaphorically to describe the experience of Israel's covenant curse. Isaiah 21:2–3 describes groaning as a result of Babylonian oppression. Jeremiah 4:31 portrays Zion's terror in response to advancing troops by personifying it as a woman experiencing birth pangs. Neither prophetic text refers to physiological labor pains, but to the "pain" of covenant discipline. This pattern may inform Paul's usage of the term in Rom 8:22. When it is recalled that Adam's curse and Israel's exile are intimately related as covenant curses against a failed son of God, the redemptive-historical connection is clear: in every instance when στεναγμός refers to birth pangs in the LXX, it describes covenant discipline. Thus, Paul's use of the same root to describe creation's experience of a curse that it endured "not willingly" (οὐχ ἑκοῦσα), but because of the choices of its covenant head, is fitting. The shared root (στεναγμός) recalls the curse that was pronounced upon both the man and the woman. The ground (ἡ γῆ) was cursed through Adam (Gen 3:17–8) and childbearing through Eve (Gen 3:16). The "eager expectation" (ἀποκαραδοκία) of creation fits neatly into the notion of groaning in childbirth.[122] Creation, like Eve and every subsequent woman in labor pains, anticipates the joy of new life.[123] It should be noted that creation's pain is not wholly positive. It is the result of futility, the frustration of creation's purpose. However, neither is it wholly negative, "helpless" pain.[124] Rather, the expectation is positive and the ordeal is necessary for glory (Rom 8:17–18).

It may be objected that Adam, Eve, and the serpent were cursed in Gen 3:14–19, but the ground was not. How could Paul be alluding to Gen 3, if the curse was not pronounced against creation, but upon Adam's *labor*? The ground produces thistles, not because it was cursed itself, but to curse human work.[125] Nevertheless, the reality is that the earth experiences the effects of Adam's sin.[126] The LXX reads ἐπικατάρατος ἡ γῆ ("cursed is the ground," Gen 3:17; MT: הָאֲדָמָה ארוּרָה). This is Paul's point in Rom 8:21–22 when he describes creation's role in its own futility. Like other Second Temple interpreters, Paul views Adam's sin to be the root cause of trouble for mankind *and* subhuman creation (e.g., *Jub.* 3:28–31; *2 Bar.* 54:15).

In light of the background of "groaning," it can be concluded that κτίσις in Rom 8:19–23 is a reference to subhuman creation over which Adam ruled. But, like Eve in Gen 3:16, its pain points to the imminent birth of new life, which for creation will be the new creation. The restoration of the created realm to its τέλος, thus, is intertwined with the return of humankind to its own.[127]

### *Subjection to Futility as Covenant Curse*

The question of the nature of creation's groaning is directly related to the cause of its subjection. The return to the term ματαιότης (8:20; cf. 1:21) implies that Paul sees Adam's initial exchange of glory as the cause of creation's participation in futility. The term denotes the frustration of purpose or incapability of reaching a desired end.[128] Its antonym is τέλος.[129] Paul's use of the rare term ματαιότης is noteworthy as one of only three instances in the NT (cf. Eph 4:17; 2 Pet 2:18). Outside of Septuagintal Greek, ματαιότης is extremely rare in the remainder of the Greek-speaking world.[130] Within the LXX, 39 of all 54 instances of ματαιότης occur in Ecclesiastes and it is the only Greek term used to translate הֶבֶל.[131] Steve Moyise has argued that Paul's use of ματαιότης is partially grounded in the book of Ecclesiastes. Qohelet's *Leitmotif* of הֶבֶל is translated with ματαιότης in the LXX.[132] O. Bauernfeind argues that Paul likely uses ματαιότης as "a valid commentary on Qoh[elet]."[133] This is an intriguing possibility as it fits perfectly with the argument of Romans, where the coming of God's Spirit reverses futility. Although most scholars interpret Qohelet's use of הֶבֶל as a reference to "vanity" or "breath," it can also be used as the contrasting term of רוּחַ, the breath of life.[134] The semantic field of הֶבֶל also includes the notions of "emptiness," which can also be represented by the Heb. synonyms רִיק (cf. Isa 30:7) and תֹּהוּ (cf. Isa 49:4).[135] We have already seen that the latter of these two functions in the Heb. Bible describe the disorder and chaos out of which God draws Adam (Gen 1:2) and Israel (Deut 32:10). Thus, Romans 8:20 describes a futile state of affairs which intruded into the world and will pass away such that, "before its [i.e., the state of futility] beginning and beyond its end is God, and a κτίσις without ματαιότης."[136]

The connection to Ecclesiastes is probable, but there is no doubt that Paul describes the effects of humanity turning from God. This description highlights Adam's primacy. It was *Adam's* sin that led to futility for mankind (Rom 1:21, 23) and for nonhuman creation (Rom 8:19–23; cf. Gen 3:17–18; Eccl 7:29). The reign of death over humanity also extends to the nonhuman realm, which experiences futility and participates in τὰ παθήματα τοῦ νῦν καιροῦ. Its groaning is a longing for the realization of its own purpose, which is intimately related to humanity's (8:23).

However, because Christ justifies and restores humankind's reign in life (Rom 5:1–2, 17), it follows that creation will also be restored. Creation's unwilling subjection to futility (i.e., the curse of the ground, Gen 3:17–18) will be replaced by blessing. Paul explains, ὅτι[137] καὶ αὐτὴ ἡ κτίσις ἐλευθερωθήσεται ("because creation *also itself* will be set free," 8:21). The use of both καί and αὐτή functions to emphasize the notion that creation will be set free in addition to God's sons.[138] That point becomes clear when we recall that the new exodus in which believers' journey will culminate in restoration to a land of inheritance. The deliverance of creation from futility is the restoration of creation to its Edenic purpose. It represents the renewal and perfection of the inheritance God's sons will receive. It is the land, the *cosmos*, the children of Abraham were promised.

## *The Adamic Background in the Mechanism of Restoration*

We have seen that Paul employs Adamic theology in the distinction of believers from the remainder of creation and in creation's subjection to futility. The third indicator of Paul's Adamic theology in Rom 8:18–30 is the mechanism by which groaning finally gives way to joy, freedom, and glory. The mechanism of restoration is believers' conformity to the image of Christ (8:29). Even subhuman creation will be renewed by humanity's return properly to reflect God's likeness.

The phrase ὅτι καὶ αὐτὴ ἡ κτίσις ("that the creation also itself," 8:21) indicates that Paul's focus has always been upon the sons.[139] Indeed, creation and sons together long for the adoption of the sons, which is defined as τὴν ἀπολύτρωσιν τοῦ σώματος ἡμῶν ("the redemption of our body," 8:23). The mention of the body recalls Rom 8:10 where Paul has just explained that the resurrection will take place in two stages. The Spirit is life, but the body remains dead. Hence, Paul's reference to the redemption of the body refers to the physical aspect of the resurrection, namely the passing of the body to incorruption. Donald Berry explains,

> By exchanging the 'glory of the incorruptible (ἀφθάρτου) God' for the 'image of corruptible (φθαρτοῦ) man' (1:23), humanity became subject to corruption and death. But the eschatological hope of glory involves a share in God's own incorruptible nature, both for the new humanity (cf. 2:7) and for creation over which they are to rule. This is the 'freedom of the glory of the children of God' for which creation groans.[140]

Thus, the future redemption to which Paul refers is the physical aspect of the resurrection. Recalling Rom 5:2, Paul explains that believers were saved in that hope (8:24a). But he goes on to describe the nature of hope as unseen (8:24b–5). The difficulty with the not-yet aspects of salvation is precisely the unrealized nature of the promise. Believers remain in bodies of death (Rom 7:24; 8:10). This condition is the cause of their weakness (ἀσθένεια, 8:26). But, the Spirit helps them. A chiasm in Rom 8:26 clarifies the nature of the Spirit's help:[141]

A τὸ πνεῦμα συναντιλαμβάνεται ("The Spirit helps")
  B τῇ ἀσθενείᾳ[142] ἡμῶν ("in our weakness")
  B´ τὸ γὰρ τί προσευξώμεθα καθὸ δεῖ οὐκ οἴδαμεν ("for we do not know what to pray for as we ought")
A´ ἀλλ' αὐτὸ τὸ πνεῦμα ὑπερεντυγχάνει στεναγμοῖς ἀλαλήτοις ("but the Spirit intercedes with unspoken groanings")

The Spirit's help is with believers' weakness to know how to pray in accordance with God's will as they suffer through τὰ παθήματα τοῦ νῦν καιροῦ. Because the body remains affected by sin and restoration is assured but incomplete, the Spirit's leading (8:14) is also in the realm of prayer. Specifically, he searches hearts (8:27) and draws out believers' unspoken prayers (i.e., their groans).[143] However, the Spirit's intercession *with groanings* is related to the creation's groaning and to believers' (8:22, 23). It is an anxious anticipation for the consummation of redemption, the fullness of adoption.

I stated above that Rom 8:18 gives Paul's theme for the section. Suffering will give way to glory. The curse of Adam and Israel will be undone and the new humanity will inherit the restored creation. Paul reiterates this precise point with Rom 8:28, πάντα συνεργεῖ εἰς ἀγαθόν ("all things work together for good"). In other words, sufferings will give way to glory. Then Paul explains: ὅτι οὓς προέγνω, καὶ προώρισεν συμμόρφους τῆς εἰκόνος τοῦ υἱοῦ αὐτοῦ ("for those whom he foreknew, he also predestined to be conformed to the image of his son," 8:29). It is no accident that Paul returns to use the word εἰκών for the first time here since Rom 1:23. The Adamic curse is reversed by mankind rightly reflecting the true image of God. The restoration of the image results in δόξα (8:30).

In conclusion, the influence of Adam upon Rom 8:18–30 is evidenced by the cosmic scope of the effects of sin upon subhuman creation resulting in its futility when creation itself had not transgressed but Adam alone. Additionally, the restoration of mankind to glory by conformity to the image of the son also points to Adam's original dereliction of his divine sonship and failure to reflect the image of God in his actions.

## Israel in Rom 8:18-30

I argued above that the Pauline motif of groaning alludes to Eve's groaning in childbirth in Gen 3:16. However, if we expand the focus, it is likely that he references the broader redemptive-historical motif, which echoes in the history of Israel. The theme of groaning first recurs as an expression of Israel's misery in Egypt, but it continues in the prophets. Just as Eve's groans would be the result of her subjection to the power of sin, Israel was also said to groan (καταστενάζω, Exod 2:23) in its bondage in Egypt. Exodus 6:5 states that Yahweh heard τὸν στεναγμὸν τῶν υἱῶν ("the groaning of the sons") and he remembered the covenant and responded because they were sons (Exod 4:22). Thus, there are numerous connections between Israel's deliverance from Egypt and the eschatological deliverance of believers in Rom 8.

The groaning motif continues in the prophets. Jonathan Moo has argued that it is "nearly certain" that Paul exhibits the influence of Gen 3 in Rom 8, but that this influence is filtered through the prophets.[144] Specifically, Moo notes a focused correspondence between Isa 24–27 and Paul's interconnection of the groaning of creation, the suffering of God's people, and the hope of glory.[145] He notes a series of thematic and verbal parallels between Rom 8 and Isa 24–27.[146]

There are numerous thematic links in Rom 8:19–23 to Isa 24–27. Like Rom 8:22, the land itself is said to suffer because of the sins of its inhabitants. The oracle opens with a broad statement announcing Yahweh's judgment against the land (24:1–13).[147] He promises to scatter its inhabitants (24:1) and utterly empty the land (24:3). Watts notes that the judgment against the land recalls the Adamic and Noahic curses. The basic problem was the ground had innocent blood spilled upon it (Isa 24:6).[148] Isaiah 24:5 is particularly instructive in its similarity to Rom 8:19–23. The MT reads: "and the earth was defiled under its inhabitants, because they passed over its laws, transgressed its statute, *they broke the eternal covenant*" (my emphasis). The LXX makes the land itself the transgressor: "And the earth behaved lawlessly because of the ones who inhabit it, because they transgressed the law and exchanged (ἤλλαξαν) the commands of the eternal covenant." By either reading the land suffers because of the sins of its people.[149]

The connections are further strengthened on the basis of verbal parallels. As Moo notes, Isa 24 begins describing Yahweh "ruining the world" (καταφθείρει τὴν οἰκουμένην, Isa 24:1) such that it is "corrupted with corruption" (φθορᾷ φθαρήσεται ἡ γῆ, Isa 24:3). Similarly Paul describes creation as in bondage to φθορά (Rom 8:21).[150] There is also a verbal link between the descriptions of "mourning." While the initial mention of the land groaning uses the verb πενθέω (Isa 24:4), the second instance uses the rarer form στενάζω to speak of the mourning of the wine and vine (Isa 24:7).[151] Paul uses a form of the same verb to describe the threefold groaning in Rom 8:22, 23, and 26.

There is verbal parallelism between Paul's description of creation's "labor pains" and Isaiah's description of God's people in Isa 24:16–18. In Isa 26:17, they are said to "groan" like a "woman in labor," both using forms of the verb ὠδίνω (cf. Rom 8:22).[152] The next verse, Isa 26:18, is especially intriguing. The MT describes the people's labor pains and giving birth to רוּחַ. Most translations render רוּחַ as "wind" suggesting that this was a failed birth.[153] The LXX, however, renders the Hebrew positively: ὠδινήσαμεν καὶ ἐτέκομεν πνεῦμα σωτηρίας σου ἐποιήσαμεν ἐπὶ τῆς γῆς ("we were in labor and we gave birth, we produced a spirit of your salvation upon the land").[154] In either case, the next verse points to the ultimate solution in the defeat of death by resurrection. Isaiah 26:19 repeats the earlier promises that death will be defeated on the last day (i.e., 24:21; 25:9; 26:1; cf. 27:1, 2, 12, 13) and promises that God's dead will be raised up (ἀναστήσονται οἱ νεκροί καὶ ἐγερθήσονται οἱ ἐν τοῖς μνημείοις). Thus, Isa 24:16–18 describes the curse that comes upon God's people through violating the eternal covenant as "labor pains" that will be resolved through the birthing of רוּחַ and their resurrection.

In sum, Paul's description of life in the Spirit before glory not only alludes to the curse of Gen 3, partly through Isa 24, but also to a pattern of affliction

Israel experienced in Egypt and again in exile. The effects of the curse included both Israel and the land, both of which wait for redemption through the resurrection of the dead.

### Conclusion of Romans 8:18–30

It is not difficult to see why creation would "eagerly await" the end-time revelation of God's sons. Subhuman creation experiences the curse because of human unrighteousness. If the curse against humanity is lifted, so too will the curse against the remainder of creation be removed.[155] Jonathan Moo writes, "Paul considers material creation itself to be caught up in the drama of salvation by virtue of having its fate tied to humankind. The story of Adam and the story of Israel, brought to a climax in the story of Christ, is also the story of God's purposes for all creation."[156]

The reference to τὴν ἀποκάλυψιν τῶν υἱῶν τοῦ θεοῦ ("the revelation of the sons of God," 8:19) indicates the eschatological unveiling of God's glorified children (8:30). Just as Christ was born κατὰ σάρκα but was later declared "Son" (Rom 1:3-4), the revelation of the sons is a redemptive-historical advancement. The sonship of believers is already a hidden reality (Rom 8:15), but it will be known openly at the last day (8:23). The public declaration of sonship will be glorification.[157] That advance reflects the reversal of the Adamic curse. Bryan writes, "we are speaking of the recovery of Adam's glory. Humanity, created in the 'image' of God (LXX Gen. 1.26–27), failed to manifest that image faithfully. Now that image is manifested in Christ, who, in Paul's view, is 'the image of God' (2 Cor. 4.4), and into whose 'image' we are being transformed in our turn (2 Cor. 3.18)."[158] Thus, God freely offers to humanity what humanity had refused to give him (cf. Rom 1:21).[159]

## CONCLUSION

We have seen Paul return to the themes of Rom 5 and continue to develop them in Rom 8:1–30. The histories of both Adam and Israel inform the new chapter of redemption he announces. In Rom 8:1–11 Paul focuses upon the eschatological resurrection of God's people by the Spirit, which fulfills the dual expectations of Ezek 36:18–37:14 of the resurrection of God's eschatological people *and* their restoration from exile. Restoration is effected by resurrection. We saw that this restoration would take place as a second exodus in Rom 8:14–17 where God's Spirit leads his sons from Adamic bondage to glory and inheritance once again. I argued that this exodus is not merely an allusion to Israel's first exodus, but is the fulfillment of Isaiah's second exodus in which Israel would return from exile. Finally, we saw in Rom 8:18–30 that the glory and inheritance toward which the Spirit leads involves the restoration of the created realm and the glorification of God's sons after a period of suffering. While the threefold groaning of creation, believers and Spirit in Rom 8:18–30 echo Israel's experience of wilderness and exile, we saw that Adamic subjection to curse is the root cause of futility and the sufferings of the present time. Adam's influence is evidenced by the experience of subhuman creation over which he was given authority, the cosmic scope of the curse, and by conformity to the image of God as the mechanism of its reversal. The restoration of creation fulfills Ezekiel's expectation that new Israel would be placed in an Edenic land (Ezek 36:35). Paul concludes in 8:28–30 affirming the certainty of the glorification of God's sons, for all who are called run the full course of God's plan from predestination to glorification.

In the next chapter we will see Paul's triumphant boast that nothing can separate believers from the love of God, not even the sufferings that come before glory. However, within his boast, Paul clearly warns that sufferings will come that will seem to threaten separation from God. I will argue that the descriptions of these sufferings have their origin in exilic suffering and that they provide further evidence that Paul sees Christ as restoring humanity from the curse of exile.

## NOTES

1. Most commentators put an argument break between 8:11 and 8:12 (e.g., C. E. B. Cranfield, *A Critical and Exegetical Commentary on the Epistle to the Romans*, 2 vols., ICC [Edinburgh: T&T Clark, 1975], 1:372; James D. G. Dunn, *Romans 1–8*, WBC 38A [Dallas, TX: Word Books, 2003], 414–5; Ernst Käsemann, *Commentary on Romans*, trans. G. W. Bromiley [Grand Rapids: Eerdmans, 1980], 212). Note the aural repetition which would begin the two sections: 8:1 (ἄρα νῦν*), 8:12 (Ἄρα οὖν).

2. Some MSS add the words μὴ κατὰ σάρκα περιπατοῦσιν to the end of 8:1 (A, D[1], 81, 365, 629), and some also add ἀλλὰ κατᾶ πνεῦμα (א[2], D[2], K, L, P, 33[vid], 104, 630, 1175, 1241, 1505) to the phrase above. These variant readings are likely due to the assimilation of 8:4 as the evidence they are not original is compelling (א*, B, D*, F, G, 6, 1506, 1739, 188, etc.). Also, the word νῦν is absent from a few MSS in the Western tradition (D*, sy[p]), but the majority of external evidence points to its originality.

3. Romans 5–8 is well known for its emphasis upon the Spirit. The term πνεῦμα occurs 21 times in Rom 8 alone.

4. Douglas Moo, *The Epistle to the Romans*, NICNT (Grand Rapids: Eerdmans, 1996), 471.

5. Hans Hübner, *Die Theologie des Paulus und ihre neutestamentliche Wirkungsgeschichte,* vol. 2 of *Biblische Theologie des Neuen Testaments* (Göttingen: Vandenhoeck & Ruprecht, 1990), 301–6; John W. Yates, *The Spirit and Creation in Paul*, WUNT 2/251 (Tübingen: Mohr Siebeck, 2008), 143–51; G. K. Beale, *A New*

*Testament Biblical Theology: The Unfolding of the Old Testament in the New* (Grand Rapids: Baker Academic, 2011), 252–4; John A. Bertone, "The Function of the Spirit in the Dialectic Between God's Soteriological Plan Enacted But Not Yet Culminated: Romans 8.1–27," *JPT* 7 (1999): 75–97 (esp. p. 82); James M. Scott, *Adoption as Sons of God: An Exegetical Investigation into the Background of υἱοθεσία in the Pauline Corpus*, WUNT 2/48 (Tubingen: Mohr Siebeck, 1992), 263–5. Cf. Cranfield, *Romans,* 1:384–5.

6. Beale, *NTBT,* 252–4.

7. Yates, *Spirit and Creation,* 143.

8. Ezekiel's one-sided *perspective* should not be interpreted as dissonant with the Deuteronomic theology of restoration, which requires repentance. Preston M. Sprinkle rightly notes the contrast, but wrongly implies these perspectives are incompatible by describing them as distinct "programs of restoration" (Sprinkle, *Paul and Judaism Revisited: A Study of Divine and Human Agency in Salvation* [Downers Grove, IL: IVP Academic, 2013], 38–67).

9. Ezek 37:1–14 is linguistically and conceptually linked to 36:26–27. See Leslie C. Allen, "Structure, Tradition, and Redaction in Ezekiel's Death Valley Vision," in *Among the Prophets: Language, Image and Structure in the Prophetic Writings,* ed. Philip R. Davies and David J. A. Clines, JSOTSup 144 (Sheffield: JSOT Press, 1993), 140–1.

10. Bertone, "The Function of the Spirit," 82.

11. The following points are adapted from Beale, *NTBT,* 252–4.

12. Due to Paul's allusions to Ezek 36–37 in Rom 5–8 to describe the coming of the Holy Spirit, I have chosen to translate רוּחַ as a reference to the third person of the Trinity.

13. Zimmerli argues that Ezekiel repeatedly affirms the promise of the Spirit from 36:27 and 37:14 with "different terminology" as well as remarking that Joel advances the same message (*Ezekiel 2: A Commentary on the Book of the Prophet Ezekiel, Chapters 25–48*, ed. Paul D. Hanson, trans. James D. Martin, Hermeneia [Philadelphia: Fortress, 1979], 421).

14. Beale, *NTBT,* 253.

15. Dunn, *Romans 1–8,* 332; Moo, *Romans,* 374; Herman Ridderbos, *Paul: An Outline of His Theology*, trans. John Richard De Witt (Grand Rapids: Eerdmans, 1997), 62–4.

16. Qumran also developed its practice of proselyte baptism in connection with Ezek 36 (Otto Betz, "Die Proselytentaufe der Qumransekte und die Taufe im Neuen Testament," *RQ* 1 [1958/59]: 213–34). When describing the eschatological purification of mankind I QS IV, 20–1 says "God will refine . . . cleansing [man] with the spirit of holiness [ברוח קדוש] from every wicked deed. He will sprinkle over him the spirit of truth" (text and translation from Florentino García Martínez and Eibert J. C. Tigchelaar, eds., *The Dead Sea Scrolls Study Edition*, 2 vols. [Leiden: Brill, 1997]). This sprinkling and cleansing of the Spirit was directly related to their hope for restoration from exile. As was discussed in chapter 2, the sectarians viewed themselves as an exilic community and hoped for an imminent restoration.

17. This is the criterion of recurrence. See Richard B. Hays, *Conversion of the Imagination: Paul as Interpreter of Israel's Scripture* (Grand Rapids: Eerdmans, 2005), 37.

18. Yates, *Spirit and Creation,* 146.

19. Ibid., 145.

20. Beale, *NTBT,* 253.

21. Hübner, *Biblische Theologie,* 2:301–2.

22. See the next section.

23. Yates, *Spirit and Creation in Paul,* 145.

24. Beale, *NTBT*, 253.

25. Scott argues this is a conscious allusion (*Adoption as Sons,* 263–5). Yates also argues that the connection is "apparent" (Yates, *Spirit and Creation*, 144). Cf. Cranfield, *Romans,* 1:384–5.

26. Cf. Rom 8:37, "more than *conquerors*".

27. Yates, *Spirit and Creation,* 145.

28. Hübner, *Biblische Theologie*, 2:301–6, quotation, p. 301.

29. Beale, *NTBT,* 254. My emphasis.

30. Jason Gile, "Deuteronomy and Ezekiel's Theology of Exile," in *For Our Good Always: Studies on the Message and Influence of Deuteronomy in Honor of Daniel I. Block* (Winona Lake, IN: Eisenbrauns, 2013), 287.

31. Verse divisions according to Zimmerli, *Ezekiel 1: A Commentary on the Book of the Prophet Ezekiel, Chapters 1–24*, ed. Frank Moore Cross and Klaus Baltzer, trans. Ronald E. Clements, Hermeneia (Philadelphia: Fortress, 1979), 52–67 and idem, *Ezekiel 2,* vi.

32. Wong demonstrates that רוּחַ can refer to wrath (K. L. Wong, "The Masoretic and Septuagint Texts of Ezekiel 39,21–29," *ETL* 78 [2002]: 144). It should further be noted that the typical object of שָׁפַךְ in Ezekiel is חֵמָה ("wrath"). Cf. Ezek 7:8; 9:8; 20:8, 13,21; 22:22, 30:15; 36:18 (See J. Lust, "Ezekiel 36–40 in the Oldest Greek Manuscript," *CBQ* 43 [1981]: 529n62).

33. This argument stands regardless of the original order of Ezek 36–39. J. Lust has argued that Ezek 37 originally followed Ezek 39. Either way, the initiation of exile and its resolution are marked by God's pouring out wrath and returning his Spirit ("Ezekiel 36–40," 517–33).

34. For a discussion on the latter days in the Hebrew Bible, see Beale, *NTBT,* chapter 3 (for Ezekiel, see p. 107).

35. Zimmerli, *Ezekiel 2,* 247–8, 50.

36. Derek Kidner, *Genesis: An Introduction and Commentary,* TOTC 1 (Downers Grove: InterVarsity Press, 1967), 60.

37. Zimmerli remarks that this restoration oracle is "remarkably close" to the restoration oracle in Isa 43:22–28 (*Ezekiel 2*, 247).

38. Kenneth J. Turner, *The Death of Deaths in the Death of Israel: Deuteronomy's Theology of Exile* (Eugene, OR: Wipf & Stock, 2011), *passim,* e.g., 225.

39. Zimmerli, *Ezekiel 2,* 257.

40. There is a key difference. Whereas Gen 2 outlines the giving of life which obviously was mutable and could be forfeited, the eschatological life described in Ezekiel

eschatological and, hence, irreversibly given. The difference may be implied by the coming of the Spirit (πνεῦμα) in Ezekiel, but the giving of breath (πνοήν) in Gen 2:7.

41. Cranfield, *Romans,* 1:390.

42. Nils Alstrup Dahl, "Two Notes on Romans 5," *ST* 5 (1952): 37–8.

43. Some scholars take 8:14–30 as one section which centers upon the notion of sonship. See, for example, Peter von der Osten-Sacken, *Römer 8 als Beispiel paulinischer Soteriologie*, FRLANT 112 (Göttingen: Vandenhoeck & Ruprecht, 1975), 143–4; J. J. J. van Rensburg, "The Children of God in Romans 8," *Neot* (1981): 160.

44. The magisterial study is Sylvia C. Keesmaat, *Paul and his Story: (Re)-Interpreting the Exodus Tradition*, JSNTSup 181 (Sheffield: Sheffield Academic, 1999), who argues that exodus allusions compose the substructure of Rom 8:14–39 (pp. 54–153). See also the article-length summary: idem, "Exodus and the Intertextual Transformation of Tradition in Romans 8:14–30," *JSNT* 54 (1994): 29–56. Cf. Ignace de la Potterie, "Le Chrétien Conduit Par l'Esprit Dans Son Cheminement Eschatologique (Rom 8,14)," in *The Law of the Spirit in Rom 7 and 8*, ed. Lorenzo de Lorenzi (Rome: St. Paul's Abbey, 1976), 209–41; N. T. Wright, "Romans," in *The New Interpreter's Bible: Acts - First Corinthians*, ed. Robert W. Wall and J. Paul Sampley (Nashville: Abingdon Press, 2002), *passim*, e.g., 511, 539; idem, "The New Inheritance According to Paul: The Letter to the Romans Re-Enacts for All Peoples the Israelite Exodus from Egypt to the Promised Land-from Slavery to Freedom," *BR (Washington, D.C.)* 14 (1998): 16, 47; idem, "New Exodus, New Inheritance: The Narrative Substructure of Romans 3–8," in *Romans and the People of God: Essays in Honor of Gordon D. Fee on the Occasion of His 65th Birthday*, ed. Sven K. Soderlund and N. T. Wright (Grand Rapids: Eerdmans, 1999), 26–35; Dunn, *Romans 1–8,* 395; Schreiner, *Romans,* 423.

45. The word order of the phrase υἱοὶ θεοῦ εἰσιν varies in the textual tradition, but the NA[28] reading has considerable support (א, A, C, D, 81, 630, 1506, 1739, ar, b).

46. Moo, *Romans,* 498n11. Cf. John Byron, *Slavery Metaphors in Early Judaism and Pauline Christianity: A Traditio-Historical and Exegetical Examination,* WUNT 2/162 (Tübingen: Mohr Siebeck, 2003), 217.

47. See chapters 2, 4.

48. Rom 4:25 alludes to Isa 53:4–6, 11, 12.

49. See chapter 4. Furthermore, Romans 1–3 and 9–15 also demonstrate significant influence from Isaiah. On Rom 1–3, see Robert C. Olson, *The Gospel as the Revelation of God's Righteousness: Paul's Use of Isaiah in Romans 1:1–3:26*, WUNT 2/428 (Tübingen: Mohr Siebeck, 2016). On Rom 9–15, see J. Ross Wagner, *Heralds of the Good News: Isaiah and Paul "in Concert" in the Letter to the Romans*, NovTSup 101 (Leiden: Brill, 2002).

50. "Exodus, Second Exodus," *DBI* 253–5.

51. Wright, "Romans," 593.

52. de la Potterie, "Le chrétien," 221.

53. Keesmaat, "Exodus in Romans 8:14–30," 41–2.

54. ἄγω: Exod 3:10. ἐξάγω: Exod 3:8, 10, 11, 12; 6:6, 7, 26, 27; 7:4, 5; 12:17, 42, 51; 13:3, 9, 14, 16; 16:3, 6, 32; 18:1; 20:2; 29:46; 32:1, 7, 11, 12, 23; 33:1. εἰσάγω: Exod 3:8; 6:8; 13:5, 11; 15:17; 23:20, 23; 33:3. ὁδηγέω: Exod 13:17; 15:13; 32:34.

55. Ibid., 42. Cf. Martin Noth, *A History of Pentateuchal Traditions*, trans. Bernard W. Anderson (Englewood Cliffs, NJ: Prentice-Hall, 1971), 47–9.

56. Ibid.

57. ἄγω: Isa 48:21; 63:12, 13, 14. ἐξάγω: 48:21. ὁδηγέω: Isa 63:14.

58. ἄγω: Isa 42:16; 43:5, 6 (2x); 49:10, 22; 66:20. ἐξάγω: Isa 42:7; 43:8; 65:9. εἰσάγω**:** Isa 14:2; 56:7.

59. Keesemaaat, "Exodus and Romans 8:14–30," 38. See Exod 4:22; Deut. 14:1; 32:6, 7, 20, 43; Hos 2:2 (LXX); 11:1; Isa 1:2, 4; 43:5–7; 45:11; Jer 31:9 (LXX 38:9); 31:20 (LXX 38:20); Sir 36:4; Wis 9:7; 12:6, 21; 14:3; 16:10, 26; 18:4, 13; 19:6; *Pss. Sol.* 13:9; 17:27; 18:4; *Jub.* 1:24, 25; *Sib. Or.* 3.702; *T. Mos.* 10.3.

60. This is not to say that the notion of sonship is exclusively Jewish. Indeed, Paul may have appropriated the term υἱοθεσία from the Greco-Roman sociological context (Richard Longenecker, *The Epistle to the Romans*, NIGTC, ed. Marshall, I. Howard and Donald Hagner [Grand Rapids: Eerdmans, 2016], 704–5). However, the sonship of Israel is intimately related to exodus, which renders this juxtaposition significant.

61. Keesmaat lists: Judg 6:8; 1 Kgs 9:9; Neh 9:17; Mic 6:4; Jer 24:13 ("Exodus in Romans 8:14–30," 42).

62. Schreiner, *Romans,* 424.

63. On the analogy between captivity to Sin and to the Mosaic law in Romans, see J. R. Daniel Kirk, *Unlocking Romans: Resurrection and the Justification of God* (Grand Rapids: Eerdmans, 2008), 106–31.

64. Ibid., 67. Cf. Edward Adams, *Constructing the World: A Study in Paul's Cosmological Language,* SNTW (Edinburgh: T&T Clark, 2000), 167–71.

65. *Pace* any who argue that Paul *reinterpreted* the Abrahamic promise and changed its original meaning (e.g., Adams, *Constructing the World,* 168). See, for example, Deut 1:7–8 where the borders of Israel's inheritance are enormous.

66. Adams, *Constructing the World,* 167–8.

67. On the inheritance as eschatological glory, see Donald L. Berry, *Glory in Romans and the Unified Purpose of God in Redemptive History* (Eugene, OR: Pickwick, 2016), 116–8.

68. Stephen G. Dempster, *Dominion and Dynasty: A Biblical Theology of the Hebrew Bible*, NSBT 15 (Leicester, England: Apollos; Downers Grove, IL: InterVarsity Press, 2003), 234.

69. Wagner, *Heralds of the Good News*, 51–6.

70. "Type" is defined as an analogical correspondence among persons, events, or institutions in Scripture which foreshadow future recapitulations (G. K. Beale, *Handbook on the New Testament Use of the Old Testament: Exegesis and Interpretation* [Grand Rapids: Baker Academic, 2012], 14).

71. Scott, *Adoption as Sons*, 96–117.

72. Ibid., 263. David B. Garner demurs only with Scott's position that 2 Sam 7:14 is the *primary* background but concurs with Scott that Paul's primary background is the Hebrew Bible of which 2 Sam 7:14 is a "vital dimension" (*Sons in the Son: The Riches and Reach of Adoption in Christ* [Phillipsburg: P&R, 2016], 47n39).

73. Brendan Byrne, *Romans*, ed. Daniel J. Harrington, SP 6 (Collegeville, MN: Liturgical Press, 1996), 249.

74. Scott, *Adoption as Sons,* 236.

75. Cf. Larry W. Hurtado, "Jesus' Divine Sonship in Paul's Epistle to the Romans," in *Romans and the People of God: Essays in Honor of Gordon D. Fee on the Occasion of His 65th Birthday* (Grand Rapids: Eerdmans, 1999), 228.

76. On a second exodus as the basis of future restoration, see J. Blenkinsopp, "The Scope and Depth of the Exodus Tradition in Deutero-Isaiah 40–55," in *The Dynamism of Biblical Tradition*, Concilium 20 (New York: Paulist Press, 1967), 41–50; Bernhard W. Anderson, "Exodus Typology in Second Isaiah," in *Israel's Prophetic Heritage: Essays in Honor of James Muilenburg* (New York: Harper, 1962), 177–95; Michael Fishbane, *Biblical Interpretation in Ancient Israel* (Oxford: Clarendon Press, 1988), 354–68; idem, *Biblical Text and Texture: A Literary Reading of Selected Texts* (Oxford: Oneworld, 1998), 124–40.

77. *Pace* N. T. Wright, who argues that "the story of the Exodus" is the overarching rubric through which to understand Paul's thought in Rom 3–8 ("New Exodus, New Inheritance," 26–35).

78. This point will be further discussed in the next section.

79. Adams, *Constructing the World,* 167–8; Dempster, *Dominion and Dynasty,* 234.

80. See Beale, *NTBT,* 52–7, under the subheading "The Differences between the Commission to Adam and What Was Passed on to His Descendants."

81. For descriptions of Canaan as Eden, cf. Gen 13:10; Isa 51:3; Ezek 36:35; 47:12; Joel 2:3.

82. This is an example of what Stephen Dempster calls the redemptive-historical movement from the universal to the particular and back to the universal (Dempster, *Dominion and Dynasty,* e.g., 30–5, 231).

83. Berry, *Glory in Romans,* 117.

84. Garner, *Sons in the Son*, 45.

85. Tyler Stewart, "The Cry of Victory: A Cruciform Reading of Psalm 44:22 in Romans 8:36," *JSPL* 3 (2013): 38–9.

86. "ὑπερνικάω," BDAG, BibleWorks 10, s.v.

87. Moo, *Romans,* 292–3.

88. Note the following parallels: ἀποκαλύπτω, ἀποκάλυψις (1:18//8:18–19); κτίσις (1:20, 25//8:19, 20, 21, 22); δόξα, δοξάζω (1:21, 23//8:18, 21); ματαιόω, ματαιότης (1:21//8:20); σῶμα (1:24//8:23); and εἰκών (1:23//8:29). These were adapted and expanded from Beverly Roberts Gaventa, *Our Mother Saint Paul* (Louisville: Westminster John Knox Press, 2007), 59.

89. Ibid. See chapter 3.

90. That is, according to the structure outlined by Horst Robert Balz, *Heilsvertrauen und Welterfahrung: Strukturen der paulinischen Eschatologie nach Römer 8, 18–39*, BEvT 59 (München: Kaiser, 1971), 35.

91. The cosmic scope of redemption is, perhaps, insinuated in Rom 5:12 when Paul describes sin entering τὸν κόσμον though Adam (Jonathan Moo, "Romans 8.19–22 and Isaiah's Cosmic Covenant," *NTS* 54 [2008]: 77–8), but Rom 8:19–22 clarifies more of what that entails.

92. There is no clear exegetical reason to distinguish the category of creation's suffering entirely from that of believers. The γάρ of Rom 8:18 clearly demonstrates the section is an explanation of the previous one and both 8:17 and 8:18 refer to suffering.

93. I will discuss the possible allusion to Gen 3:16 below.

94. Both the LXX and NT refer to κτίσις as "that which is created by God" but, in context, the specific reference can be much more narrow. Harry Alan Hahne notes that "apparently comprehensive expressions like 'all creation' (πᾶσα ἡ κτίσις) or the whole creation (ὅλη ἡ κτίσις) sometimes refer only to that part of creation in a certain class" (*The Corruption and Redemption of Creation: Nature in Romans 8:19–22 and Jewish Apocalyptic Literature*, LNTS 336 [London: T&T Clark, 2006], 177).

95. For a detailed survey of interpretations, see Olle Christoffersson, *The Earnest Expectation of the Creature: The Flood-Tradition as Matrix of Romans 8:18–27*, ConBNT 23 (Stockholm: Almqvist & Wiksell, 1990), 19–36.

96. For example, John Calvin, *Calvin's Commentaries: Acts 14–28, Romans 1–16*, trans. John Owen, vol. 19, 500th Anniversary Edition (Grand Rapids: Baker Books, 2009), 303–4; Frédéric Godet, *Commentary on the Epistle to the Romans*, trans. A. Cusin and Talbot W. Chambers (Grand Rapids: Zondervan, 1969), 314; Dunn, *Romans 1–8*, 469; Cranfield, *Romans*, 1:414; Fitzmyer, *Romans*, 506; Moo, *Romans*, 513–4; Murray, *Romans*, 303; Schreiner, *Romans*, 435; E. P. Sanders, *Paul and Palestinian Judaism: A Comparison of Patterns of Religion* (London: S.C.M, 1977), 473; Edward Adams, "Paul's Story of God and Creation: The Story of How God Fulfils His Purposes in Creation," in *Narrative Dynamics in Paul: A Critical Assessment* (Louisville: Westminster John Knox, 2002), 28.

97. For example, Käsemann, *Romans*, 233; Otto Michel, *Der Brief an Die Römer*, EKKNT 4 (Göttingen: Vandenhoeck & Ruprecht, 1978), 173; A. Viard, "Expectatio Creaturae (Rom 8:19–22)," *RB* 59 (1952): 337–54; Gaventa, *Our Mother Saint Paul*, 53–5; John G. Gibbs, "Pauline Cosmic Christology and Ecological Crisis," *JBL* 90 (1971): 466–79. More recent, neo-orthodox inspired readings have read the woes of creation to involve an anthropological-soteriological dimension. For example, John G. Gager acknowledges that creation originally referred to the whole of creation, but "in Paul, this cosmic dimension has been significantly limited to an anthropological category, and its primary reference has become the nonbelieving, human world" ("Functional Diversity in Paul's Use of End-Time Language," *JBL* 89 [1970]: 329). See also, John Henry Paul Reumann, *Creation and New Creation: The Past, Present, and Future of God's Creative Activity* (Minneapolis: Augsburg, 1973), for example, 329. Cf. John Bolt, "The Relation Between Creation and Redemption in Romans 8:18–27," *CTJ* 30 (1995): 35.

98. See *Mor. Eccl.* 13.23; *Fid. Symb.* 10.23; *Nupt.* 2.50. Augustine writes of "the humiliation which took place in Adam, in whom the whole human creature, as it were, being corrupted at the root, as it refused to be made subject to the truth, 'was made subject to vanity'" (*Enarrat. Ps.* 119:66). See Thomas E. Clarke, "St. Augustine and Cosmic Redemption," *Theological Studies* 19 (1958): 133–64. For a recent defense of κτίσις as only humanity, see Alberto Giglioli, *L'oumo o il Creato*?

s *in s. Paolo.* Stbib 21 (Bologna: EDB, 1994). But see also the critique by Settimio Cipriani, "ΚΤΙΣΙΣ: Creazione o genere Umano?" *RB* 44 (1996): 337–40.

99. See H. Paul Santmire, *The Travail of Nature: The Ambiguous Ecological Promise of Christian Theology* (Philadelphia: Fortress, 1985), 175–218, especially 202–10. Whereas the cosmic interpretation places humanity over nature in hierarchy, this view is distinct in the *complete* isolation of ecological interests from humanity.

100. Schreiner, *Romans,* 435.

101. Nicholas A. Meyer, *Adam's Dust and Adam's Glory in the Hodayot and the Letters of Paul: Rethinking Anthropogony and Theology*, NovTSup 168 (Leiden: Brill, 2016), 215.

102. James D. G. Dunn, *The Theology of Paul the Apostle* (Grand Rapids: Eerdmans, 1998), 83.

103. Andrzej Gieniusz, *Romans 8:18–30: "Suffering Does Not Thwart the Future Glory"* (Atlanta: Scholars Press, 1999), 146–7, convincingly demonstrates the link to Gen 3 and an analogous pattern of allusion in Second Temple literature. Cf. Cranfield, *Romans,* 1:413; Godet, *Romans,* 314; M. J. Lagrange, *Saint Paul: Épitre Aux Romains* (Paris: J. Gabalda, 1950), 208; Robin Scroggs, *The Last Adam: A Study in Pauline Anthropology* (Philadelphia: Fortress, 1966), 91; C. K. Barrett, *From First Adam to Last: A Study in Pauline Theology* (New York: Scribner's Sons, 1962), 9; John G. Gibbs, *Creation and Redemption: A Study in Pauline Theology,* NovTSup 26 (Leiden: Brill, 1971), 42.

104. Dunn, *Romans 1–8,* 470.

105. Gager, "Functional Diversity," 328.

106. Barrett, *From First Adam to Last,* 9.

107. Cranfield, *Romans,* 1:413.

108. For example, Dunn, *Romans 1–8,* 470; Moo, *Romans,* 584; Cranfield, *Romans,* 1:414; Schreiner, *Romans,* 435; Richard J. Dillon, "The Spirit as Taskmaster and Troublemaker in Romans 8," *CBQ* 60 (1998): 698n58.

109. For example, Christopher Bryan, *A Preface to Romans: Notes on the Epistle in Its Literary and Cultural Setting* (Oxford: Oxford University Press, 2000), 151; Byrne, *Romans*, 258, 260–1; idem, *Reckoning with Romans: A Contemporary Reading of Paul's Gospel*, GNS 18 (Wilmington, DE: Michael Glazier, 1986), 166–7; Balz, *Heilsvertrauen*, 41. For a survey of positions, see Gieniusz, *Romans 8:18–30*, 157–62.

110. John Chrysostom, *Homilies on the Epistle to the Romans 14* quoted in Gerald Lewis Bray, ed., *Romans*, ACCS 6 (Downers Grove, IL: InterVarsity Press, 1998), 216.

111. Dunn, *Romans 1–8,* 471.

112. See Cranfield, *Romans,* 1:413; Käsemann, *Romans,* 235; Murray, *Romans,* 303; C. H. Dodd, *The Epistle of Paul to the Romans*, Rev., MNTC 6 (London: Collins, 1959), 134; Lagrange, *Romains*, 208; Scroggs, *The Last Adam,* 91; Edmund Hill, "Construction of Three Passages from St Paul," *CBQ* 23 (1961): 296–9; Fitzmyer, *Romans,* 508.

113. It is rare, but not impossible. Διά + accusative can be used in the place of διά + genitive to denote the efficient cause of an action and translated with the English

preposition "by" ("διά," BDAG, Bible Works 10, s.v.). Cf. John 6:57; Rev 12:11; Ep. Arist 292; Sir 15:11; 3 Macc 6:36.

114. Dunn, *Romans 1–8*, 471.

115. Ibid.

116. Mark 7:34; Rom 8:23; 2 Cor. 5:2, 4; Heb 13:17; Jas 5:9; Job 9:27; 18:20; 24:12; 30:25; 31:38; Nah 3:7; Isa 19:8; 21:2; 24:7; 30:15; 46:8; 59:10; Jer 38:19; Lam 1:8, 21; Ezek 21:11–12; 26:15–16; Tob 3:1; 1 Macc 1:26; 4 Macc 9:21; Wis. 5:3; Sir. 30:20; 36:25.

117. For example, Schreiner, *Romans,* 437; Dunn, *Romans 1–8,* 472–3. See the discussion on messianic woes in chapter 4.

118. Notable exceptions are: Meyers, *Adam's Dust,* 217; D. T. Tsumura, "An OT Background to Rom 8:22," *NTS* 40 (1994): 620–1; J. Mark Lawson, "Romans 8:18–25—The Hope of Creation," *RevExp* 91 (1994): 562; Steve Moyise, "Intertextuality and the Study of the Old Testament in the New Testament," in *The Old Testament in the New Testament: Essays in Honour of J. L. North*, ed. Steve Moyise, JSNTSup 189 (Sheffield: Sheffield Academic, 2000), 24–5; Gieniusz, *Romans 8:18–30*, 146–7.

119. J. Schneider, "στενάζω, στεναγμός, συστενάζω," *TDNT* 7:600–3.

120. Balz identifies both verbs as describing the same ordeal (*Heilsvertrauen und Welterfahrung*, 53).

121. Laurie J. Braaten, "The Groaning Creation: The Biblical Background for Romans 8:22," *BR* 50 (2005): 22n9, 26–8.

122. For an argument toward a positive translation of ἀποκαραδοκία, see David R. Denton, "Ἀποκαραδοκία," *ZNW* 73 (1982): 138–40.

123. Cf. Paul's only other use of ἀποκαραδοκία in Phil 1:20, which also refers to eschatological hope for deliverance.

124. *Pace* Conrad H. Gempf, "Imagery of Birth Pangs," *TynBul* 45 (1994): 125–6.

125. This objection is raised, for example, by Braaten, "The Groaning Creation," 22–3.

126. Meyers convincingly argues that Braaten underestimates the effect of the curse on creation at large, noting that Adam, Eve, the ground, and the serpent were all affected, making "the created order" itself that which bears the curse: animal, humanity and earth (*Adam's Dust,* 216n124).

127. Brendan Byrne, *Sons of God, Seed of Abraham: A Study of the Idea of the Sonship of God of All Christians in Paul against the Jewish Background*, AnBib 83 (Rome: Biblical Institute, 1979), 105n100, observes that the notion of nature sharing in mankind's restoration has roots across the Hebrew Bible and later Judaism. He lists: Isa 11:6–9; Ezek 34:25–31; Hos 2:18; Zech 8:12; *1 En.* 45:4–5; 51:4–5; 2 Bar 29; *4 Ezra* 8:52; *Sib. Or.* 3:777–96.

128. Cranfield, *Romans,* 1:413; Byrne, *Sons of God,* 106.

129. This is consistent with the prior interpretation I gave of Rom 1:18–32, where mankind was meant to glorify God, but fails in that τέλος leading to futility, and frustrated purpose.

130. Gieniusz, *Romans 8:18–30*, 151.

131. Ibid.

132. Moyise, "Intertextuality," 19–25. Cf. idem, "The Catena of Romans 3:10-18," *ExpTim* 106 (1995): 367–70.

133. Bauernfeind"ματαιότης, ματαιόω, μάτην" *TDNT* 4:523. Cf. Gieniusz, *Romans 8:18–30*, 151–3; C. K. Barrett, *A Commentary on the Epistle to the Romans* (New York: Harper & Brothers, 1957), 166.

134. K. Seybold, "הֶבֶל," *TDOT* 3:318.

135. Ibid., 314.

136. Bauernfeind, *TDNT* 4:523.

137. The variant διότι has considerable support (א, $D^*$, F, G, 945), but a slightly stronger case exists for the ὅτι ($\mathfrak{P}^{46}$, A, B, C, $D^2$, K, L, P, Ψ, 0289, 33, 81, 104, 630, 1175, 1505, 1506, 1739, 1881, 2464, $\mathfrak{M}$).

138. Dunn, *Romans 1–8,* 471.

139. See, Berry, *Glory in Romans,* 133.

140. Ibid.

141. Peter T. O'Brien, "Romans 8:26, 27: A Revolutionary Approach to Prayer?," *RTR* 46 (1987): 69.

142. Some MSS read ταῖς ἀσθενείαις (K, L, P, 33, 1175, 1241). This reading is not well supported.

143. See Schreiner, *Romans,* 446; Cranfield, *Romans,* 1:425.

144. J. Moo, "Cosmic Covenant," 84.

145. Ibid.

146. Following a lengthy section of Isaiah's oracles regarding the foreign nations (Isa 13:1–23:18), the text of Isa 24:1–27:13 is a discrete section giving an eschatological oracle regarding Israel (24:1–27:13).

147. In the MT "land" is הָאָרֶץ and תֵּבֵל. 1QIsaa reads האדמה for Isa 24:1. The LXX uses τὴν οἰκουμένην and ἡ γῆ.

148. John D. W Watts, "Excursus: 'The Land,'" in *Isaiah 1-33*, WBC 24, ed. Bruce Metzger (Waco, TX: Word Books, 1985), 376–7.

149. As J. Moo notes, "Isaiah's Cosmic Covenant," 85n41, scholars are divided on the identity of this "eternal covenant." For a survey of interpretive options, see Donald C. Polaski, "Reflections on a Mosaic Covenant: The Eternal Covenant (Isaiah 24:5) and Intertextuality," *JSOT* 23 (1998): 55–73.

150. J. Moo, "Isaiah's Cosmic Covenant," 85.

151. Both instances use the verb אָבַל in the MT (ibid.).

152. Adjusting for the συν-prefix in Rom 8:22.

153. For example, ESV, KJV, NAS, RSV, NIV. Note, in particular, the NASB "we gave birth *as it were, only* to wind."

154. Whereas the LXX continues the phrase, the MT places the atnac under רוּחַ. Thus, the phrase ends with רוּחַ יָלַדְנוּ ("we birthed wind/spirit").

155. Dunn, *Romans 1–8,* 469.

156. J. Moo, "Isaiah's Cosmic Covenant," 88.

157. Dunn, *Romans 1–8,* 470.

158. Bryan, *A Preface to Romans*, 154.

159. Ibid.

## *Chapter 6*

# The Restoration of Adam and Israel in Romans 8:31–39

Scholars widely agree that, despite not concluding the letter itself, Rom 8:31–39 is Paul's conclusion of the argument thus far.[1] When Paul asks, "What shall we say to these things?" (8:31), he does so to signal his conclusion of both Rom 5–8, but also the letter up to that point.[2] It is not primarily didactic, but a celebration of the blessings God has granted to believers in Christ. The elevated style arises from Paul's enthusiasm for and boast in the gospel.[3] A future in glory is certain, as Paul made clear in Rom 8:29–30 as well as in Rom 5:1–5. Thus, Rom 5–8 both begins and ends with boasting in the hope of glory.

In this chapter, I will argue that Paul's boast provides more evidence that Paul sees Christians in an already-not yet condition of being spiritually restored from exile, but still awaiting the physical restoration. This conclusion is suggested in 8:32–34 when Paul alludes to Christ's work as Isaiah's servant. It is corroborated by his list of tribulations in Rom 8:35, which parallel Deuteronomic descriptions of exile. And it is substantiated by his explicit quotation of Ps 44:22 in Rom 8:36—a psalm of the righteous in exile.

## STRUCTURE OF ROMANS 8:31–39

Scholars have proposed various structures for Rom 8:31–39.[4] One clear structural indicator is Paul's use of four rhetorical questions which raise threats against Christian hope. Paul's answers restate gospel indicatives and affirm hope in glory.[5]

Paul's four answers echo several texts from the Hebrew Bible which shape his understanding of redemption and the Christian experience. As he proceeds through these questions and affirmations, his boast centers upon the

**Table 6.1 Rhetorical Questions in Romans 8:31–39**

| | *NA*[28] | *Translation* |
|---|---|---|
| 1. 8:31b–c | εἰ ὁ θεὸς ὑπὲρ ἡμῶν, τίς καθ' ἡμῶν... πῶς οὐχὶ καὶ σὺν αὐτῷ τὰ πάντα ἡμῖν χαρίσεται; | If God is for us, who can be against us . . . how will he not also with him grace all things to us? |
| 2. 8:33 | τίς ἐγκαλέσει κατὰ ἐκλεκτῶν θεοῦ; | Who will bring a charge against the elect ones of God? |
| 3. 8:34 | τίς ὁ κατακρινῶν; | Who will condemn? |
| 4. 8:35a | τίς ἡμᾶς χωρίσει ἀπὸ τῆς ἀγάπης τοῦ Χριστοῦ;[a] | Who will separate us from Christ's love? |

[a]Some MSS replace Χριστοῦ with θεοῦ (ℵ, 365, 1506). This is likely an attempt at harmonization with 8:39 (cf. Rom 5:5).

reality of union with Christ. The prevalence of σύν-prefixes throughout Rom 5–8 has insinuated this extensive participation.[6] Mark A. Seifrid writes, "As the structure of his argument shows, the gospel speaks especially to believers in their sufferings, which Paul stresses, are inescapable for those who belong to Christ (5:3–5; 8:17–18)."[7] That God did not spare his Son underscores his commitment to his adopted children.

The "all things" (τὰ πάντα) which God gives to his children with Christ is often interpreted as wholly positive.[8] However, in light of the implicit opposition in 8:32–36, the hardships that must be suffered with him (8:17), the "giving over" the Father did of Christ unto suffering, and the symmetry between the initial τὰ πάντα in 8:32 with Paul's conclusion in 8:37 that believers conquer ἐν τούτοις πᾶσιν ("in all these things"), it is more likely that τὰ πάντα includes present suffering as well as future inheritance.[9] The Son preserves the elect from *final* condemnation, not present suffering. Believers will be "with him" in "all things." The rhetorical questions that structure Paul's final boast demonstrate the reality of hardship, but also the impossibility that any ordeal can prevent believers from attaining glory.

## THE IRREVERSIBILITY OF JUSTIFICATION: ALLUSIONS TO ISAIAH IN ROMANS 8:31–34

It will be simplest to treat the first three rhetorical questions in one section. They share a legal motif and represent Paul's general boast in the finality of justification. Within that boast, scholars have detected echoes of Isaiah's third and fourth Servant Songs.[10] These allusions comport with the thesis I have argued throughout: Paul sees reconciliation to God through Christ to be the fulfillment of Isaiah's second exodus, the eschatological restoration of Israel.

Paul has already described God's people on a second exodus (Rom 8:14–17) and has shown that it was launched by the outpouring of the Spirit (Rom 5:5; 8:1–11, 14). As he concludes, Paul once again appeals to Isaiah to show the redemptive-historical background of redemption.

Paul's opening question, εἰ ὁ θεὸς ὑπὲρ ἡμῶν, τίς καθ' ἡμῶν; ("If God is for us, who can be against us?," 8:31b) is similar to Isa 50:9, κύριος βοηθεῖ μοι τίς κακώσει με ("The Lord helps me, who will do me evil"; cf. Isa 50:7). Paul's neglect to identify the adversary (τίς) is part of the point. The Isaianic context recalls the notion that the enemies of God's chosen ones are nothing, futile; they are less than human and pose no threat (cf. Isa 40:17; 41:24; 44:6–11; 45:21).[11] Then, in a clearer allusion to Isa 53:6b, and likely to Gen 22:12, 16 as well,[12] Paul clarifies: "he who did not spare his own Son, but handed him over for us all" (Rom 8:32).

There are clear lexical links to Isaiah, which are further corroborated by the similar contexts as well as the precedent Paul has already set for alluding to the final Servant Song. The probable allusion to the *'Aqedah* appeals to an important Jewish text, which is exemplary of a faithful Jew and the notion of a willing sacrifice.[13] Here, Paul employs it to demonstrate the faithfulness of God.[14] In defense of the allusion to the *'Aqedah*, Romano Penna observes that direct citation of Gen 22:12 was not an option because the verb φείδεσθαι refers to Abraham, not God.[15] He further notes that only Gen 22:12, 16 employ the negated verb οὐ φείδεσθαι and the noun υἱός together in all the LXX.[16] Penna concludes his defense of the allusion to Gen 22 by arguing that Paul's variation from Gen 22 is due to the second allusion to Isa 53, "The greatest novelty of Rom 8:32 over against Gen 22 stands . . . in the fact that the handing over of the Son by God has an expiatory value . . . the resonances of the Isaiah passage seem unquestionable to me in Rom 8:32b,

**Table 6.2 Allusion to Isaiah 53:6 and Genesis 22 in Romans 8:32**

| *Isaiah 53:6* | *Romans 8:32* | *Genesis 22:12* |
|---|---|---|
| πάντες ὡς πρόβατα ἐπλανήθημεν, ἄνθρωπος τῇ ὁδῷ αὐτοῦ ἐπλανήθη· καὶ κύριος παρέδωκεν αὐτὸν ταῖς ἁμαρτίαις ἡμῶν. | ὅς γε τοῦ ἰδίου υἱοῦ οὐκ ἐφείσατο ἀλλ' ὑπὲρ ἡμῶν πάντων παρέδωκεν αὐτόν, πῶς οὐχὶ καὶ σὺν αὐτῷ τὰ πάντα ἡμῖν χαρίσεται; | . . . καὶ οὐκ ἐφείσω τοῦ υἱοῦ σου τοῦ ἀγαπητοῦ δι' ἐμέ |
| We have all strayed like sheep; a man to his own way has strayed and the LORD has laid on him the iniquity of us all. | He who did not spare his own Son but gave him up for us all, how will he not also with him graciously give us all things? | . . . and you have not spared your beloved son for my sake. |

*Note:* The single underlined text reflects verbal parallel between Romans and Isaiah. The doubleunderlined text is verbal parallel between Romans and Genesis. The dotted underline is conceptual.

for thematic as well as lexical reasons."[17] Thus, we have two allusions carefully joined together. The juxtaposition of Gen 22:12 and Isa 53:6 indicates that the giving over of the beloved son was the means of atoning for Israel's sin and, consequently, enabling their restoration.[18]

The use of Isaiah, where the servant is offered in the place of Yahweh's wandering sheep, is noteworthy in light of Paul's upcoming citation of Ps 44:22, where it is God's people who are reckoned as sheep for slaughter.[19] There is no conflict, however. Christ bore the sins of his chosen ones in order to redeem them from their condemnation in Adam (Rom 4:25; 5:12–21). But, once raised, they participate in "all things" with Christ, including his suffering (cf. Rom 8:17, 32, 35, 36). The progression from Christ's individual, atoning suffering to the shared experience of suffering before glory reflects believers' participation in all things with Christ. This observation comports with the two categories of Paul's rhetorical questions. The opening three are legal, but the final question deals with the relational dimension of separation from God. In other words, the first three are Paul's boast in the finality of justification (8:32–34), but the final question (8:35a) is a boast that reconciliation can never be undone.

Paul's answer to the first rhetorical question (8:31b–c) demonstrates that God has delivered up his own Son for the curse of mankind. Thus, in light of the God's actions, he will certainly give all things along with him (σὺν αὐτῷ τὰ πάντα, 8:32). The return to the motif of participation in Christ (indicated by the preposition σύν) once again indicates this pattern of suffering than glory. Believers' participation begins in dying with Christ (Rom 6:8, ἀπεθάνομεν σὺν Χριστῷ; cf. Col 2:20), it continues throughout their lives in the Spirit before glory (Rom 8:17, συμπάσχομεν; cf. 2 Cor 13:4; Phil 3:10; Eph 2:6), and in glory (Rom 6:8, συζήσομεν αὐτῷ; 8:17, συνδοξασθῶμεν; cf. 1 Thess 4:17; 2 Tim 2:11–12).

Both the second and third questions focus upon condemnation. Two competing judges are in view: God is the final judge, but worldly opposition is also set up as a judge that would condemn the righteous until that time.[20] The second rhetorical question, "who shall bring a charge (ἐγκαλέσει)," again recalls Isa 50.[21] The third Servant Song also boasts that any accuser will fail because God, the justifier is near (Isa 50:8). The MT of Isa 50:8b, אִתִּי מִי־יָרִיב ("who will bring a legal case against me?"), is closer to Rom 8:33 than the LXX, τίς ὁ κρινόμενός μοι ("who is the one who judges me?"). Paul's answer that God is the one who justifies (θεὸς ὁ δικαιῶν) echoes Isa 50:8a: ἐγγίζει ὁ δικαιώσας με ("my justifier is near"). While the verbal links are not exact, they are close and there is clear conceptual correspondence. Hays writes, "In vocabulary, in sentence-rhythm, and in substance Paul's declaration of trust in God resonates deeply with Isaiah's. Without recourse to quotation or proof-texting, Paul has formulated his confession in language that wells up out of Israel's hope."[22] The scene envisaged by both passages is legal. Isaiah's servant is unjustly persecuted and killed (Isa 50:4–6), but is vindicated by God (Isa 50:7–11). Thus, there was an unjust judgment by the world but God vindicated his servant. Paul extends that notion beyond the individual servant to the people he redeems. His boast is that any sanction that could be raised against God's elect is overcome (cf. Rom 3:23).[23]

It may be significant that Paul calls the recipients of the attempted condemnation the "elect of God" (ἐκλεκτῶν θεοῦ, Rom 8:33). The use of ἐκλεκτός is rare in the Pauline corpus.[24] The exact phrase is only repeated in Tit 1:1. This appellation links believers with Christ, since they are chosen in him (8:28–29) and, perhaps, recalls the figure of the Isaianic servant who is singularly chosen (ὁ ἐκλεκτός μου, Isa 42:1).[25] G. Schrenk writes,

> Here [ἐκλεκτῶν θεοῦ] sums up emphatically all that has been said in [Rom] 8:14f. about the bearers of the Spirit, the υἱοὶ θεοῦ, the ἀγαπῶντες τὸν θεόν. In conclusion, then, the whole of the divine work, salvation, and new creation, from its pre-temporal origin (8:28–30) to the final glorification, is summed up in [ἐκλεκτῶν θεοῦ].[26]

I argued in chapters 4 and 5 that Paul has identified the NT community in Christ as eschatological Israel. Paul's use of the phrase ἐκλεκτῶν θεοῦ is consistent with that identification. Our particular interest in this phrase lies in its relationship to Isaianic restoration. The servant of Yahweh leads God's chosen people *out of their exile* (e.g., Isa 43:20; 45:4–13). The allusions to Isa 50 and 53 in Rom 8:31–34 and throughout Rom 5–8 are further evidence for interpreting ἐκλεκτῶν θεοῦ in light of Isaianic usage. Thus, describing NT believers as ἐκλεκτῶν θεοῦ corroborates other evidence that Paul considered NT believers to be participating in Isaiah's promised restoration.[27]

In the third rhetorical question, τίς ὁ κατακρινῶν ("Who is the one who condemns?," 8:34), Paul once again echoes Isa 50. The LXX of Isa 50:9 is similar, τίς κακώσει με ("Who will harm me"), but Paul's language is closer to the MT, מִי־הוּא יַרְשִׁיעֵנִי ("who will cause me to be condemned").[28] The apostle's answer demonstrates his internal logic. There is no one to condemn, because Christ Jesus died. He has already been condemned when he was "handed over" for the sins of the many (Rom 4:25; 8:32; cf. 1:24, 26, 28). Thus, the judgment has already been pronounced. Further, Paul continues, Christ is raised proving himself justified and everyone in union with him.

In sum, Paul's triumphant boast in justification draws upon Isaiah's third (Isa 50:7–11) and fourth Servant Songs (Isa 53:6, 8, 12). Like Paul in Rom 8:31–34, Isaiah uses a series of rhetorical questions to show the servant's adversaries that they cannot finally hold him guilty, because God alone justifies.[29] God's word to the servant in Isa 49:3 is fulfilled in the glory for which believers hope: εἶπέ μοι Δοῦλός μου εἶ σύ, Ισραηλ, καὶ ἐν σοὶ δοξασθήσομαι ("he said to me, 'You are my servant, Israel, and in you I will be glorified'").[30]

## THE IRREVERSIBILITY OF RECONCILIATION: ECHOES OF EXILE IN ROMANS 8:35–36

Paul's fourth rhetorical question shifts from the forensic sphere to the question of relational separation. He asks, τίς ἡμᾶς χωρίσει ἀπὸ τῆς ἀγάπης τοῦ Χριστοῦ; ("Who will separate us from Christ's love?," 8:35a). It is important to note that Paul's emphasis falls upon this final question as it both ends the series and is repeated in 8:39.[31] Mark Seifrid describes this fourth question as the *summa summarum,* which brings together, not only the ideas of the previous three questions, but the whole of the letter.[32] It seems that having demonstrated the impossibility of condemnation (i.e., undoing justification), Paul addresses the status of believers' relationship with God. He asks if reconciliation can ever be reversed.

The verb χωρίζω itself is often used to describe divorce. It denotes the undoing of legal union (cf. Matt 19:6; Mark 10:9; 1 Cor 7:10, 15 [2x]).[33] Thus, Paul inquires after the permanence of the *relationship*. Can God's chosen and justified children ever lose their reconciliation? We would expect an emphatic "No!" to the question. Instead, although the answer will ultimately come back negative, Paul spends the next two verses (8:35b–36) listing a series of hardships, which, Paul implies, ostensibly have the potential to separate believers from God (8:35b). I argue that these "dividers" are drawn from a theology of exile grounded in Deuteronomy. Paul's careful answer indicates that such sufferings will make it *seem* as if God has withdrawn from them as he did from Israel and from Adam. These sufferings suggest separation from God because they are the precise indicators from the previous redemptive-historical epoch that one *was* separated from God in exile. The reality, however, is that God has restored them in spirit, and will ultimately restore them in body. There is a reality of exilic condition that persists, but what has been undone in spirit and relationship will lead to a restoration of body as well.

The seven potential dividers are θλῖψις ("tribulation"), στενοχωρία ("distress"), διωγμὸς ("persecution"), λιμός ("famine"), γυμνότης ("nakedness"), κίνδυνος ("danger"), and μάχαιρα ("sword"). Most commentators do little with this *peristasis*[34] catalog beyond pointing to Paul's use of these terms elsewhere.[35] Alternatively, Wolfgang Schrage suggests Paul cobbled together the list from various sources in Second Temple Judaism.[36] Others have sought the catalog's meaning in Hellenistic traditions where suffering was meant to demonstrate the virtue of the sufferer.[37] However, in light of the previous context of Rom 5–8, Frank Thielman's suggestion that these hardships are adapted from "the portraits of the suffering of God's disobedient people painted in Deuteronomy 28 and Leviticus 26" is most convincing.[38] In other words, Paul uses terminology that previously functioned to demonstrate separation from God to show that nothing, not even these, can remove the certainty of believers' hope in glory. Just as Israel was delivered from Egypt but had to pass through the wilderness to reach the promised land, believers in the Christ-age are spiritually delivered from bondage to Sin, but will continue to experience the difficulties of separation from fully realized rest for the remainder of their earthly lives.

If it can be shown that this *peristasis* catalog is drawn from Israel's covenant curses, a series of questions follows. How do these hardships relate to τὰ παθήματα τοῦ νῦν καιροῦ in which creation, believers, and the Spirit participate (Rom 8:18, 19, 23, 26)? How could justified believers ever experience God's curse? Are these sufferings generally true, or do they specifically characterize the Christian's experience? Before answering these questions, we must consider other possible sources for Paul's *peristasis* catalog in Rom 8:35b. Then I will develop the case for Deuteronomy as the catalog's source. From there we will examine the context of Ps 44 and Paul's use of it in relation to the tribulation list. Then we will be situated to consider the nature of suffering in participation with Christ.

## Interpretations of the *Peristasis* Catalog

These seven tribulations are not Paul's only list of sufferings. The apostle enumerates a series of his hardships in ministry in 2 Cor 11:26–27 and 12:10, which includes all of the elements of the catalog from Rom 8:35 except for μάχαιρα. Most commentators simply remark upon Paul extrapolating from his own experiences. For example, Douglas Moo writes, "the list of difficulties that follows requires little comment, except to note that all of the items except the last are found also in 2 Cor. 11:26–27 and 12:10, where Paul lists some of those hazards he himself has encountered in his apostolic labors."[39]

Nevertheless, such catalogues are not unique to Paul in the first century. Bultmann has shown they were a rhetorical device in Hellenistic discourse.[40] Stoic philosophers would employ such lists to prove their ideological commitment. Patiently enduring hardships demonstrated their ability to transcend joy or pain.[41] Similarly, Robert Hodgson argues that the *religionsgeschichtliche* background should not be limited to Stoic (or Jewish apocalyptic) parallels, but must include the broader Hellenistic culture.[42] However, Hans Dieter Betz has shown that Paul does not employ his similar list of sufferings in 2 Corinthians for self-aggrandizement, but to demonstrate participation with Christ.[43] Robert Jewett also argues from the Greco-Roman background maintaining that "the key to understanding Rom 8:35, which contains nothing of the traditional claim of the virtuous sage, is that in Ephesus and Corinth, Paul's weaknesses, poverty, imprisonments, and other forms of adversity were used by opponents to show that he was not 'qualified' (2 Cor 2:7, 16; 3:5) to be an apostle."[44] He suggests that Paul employs the *peristasis* catalog and citation of Ps 44 to combat his hypothetical detractors who, Jewett avers, were citing Paul's suffering as evidence he was unworthy.[45] The logic is based upon the Deuteronomic principle that God would prosper the righteous, but bring disaster to the wicked.[46] I concur that Paul is employing a Deuteronomic theology. However, there is insufficient evidence to argue that Paul's *primary* purpose in Rom 8:35–6 is a defense of his apostolic qualifications.[47]

Alternatively, following Wolfgang Schrage, a cohort of scholars argue Paul cobbled together the list from various Jewish apocalyptic writings (e.g., *Jub.* 23:12–13; *1 En.* 103:9–15; *Pss. Sol.* 15:7) or the general milieu from which they arose.[48] The most frequently cited analogue is 2 *En.* 66:6, which combines virtuous qualities with eschatological sufferings and depicts both as expected prior to consummation:[49]

> Walk, my children, in long suffering, in meekness, in affliction, in distress, in faithfulness, in truth, in hope, in weakness, in derision, in assaults, in temptation, in deprivation, in nakedness, having love for one another, until you go out from this age of suffering, so that you may become inheritors of the never-ending age.[50]

The message is notably similar to Paul's, but *2 Enoch* should likely be dated later than Romans.[51] It is possible that both texts draw upon like traditions, but there is no direct case for dependence. Similarly, the texts cited above (*Jub.* 23:12–13, *1 En.* 103:9–15, and *Pss. Sol.* 15:7) each describe the last days and eschatological suffering. Admittedly, Jewish apocalyptic is nearer to Paul both in tradition and genre than Hellenistic philosophy. Paul may have been aware of such traditions, but the case for literary dependence simply lacks the evidence to convince.

Thus, neither the proposed backgrounds in Hellenistic or Second Temple Jewish traditions are fully persuasive. The similarity between Paul's hardships listed in 2 Corinthians 11:26–27, 12:10 and his list in Romans shows that there is a correspondence between the two lists, but I will argue in the following section that the *peristasis* catalog in Rom 8:35b is drawn from the descriptions of exile in Deut 28 and Lev 26. Indeed, a background in the Hebrew Bible should be the default expectation. Paul has demonstrated a significant dependence upon Isaiah, Deuteronomy and many other texts from the Jewish scriptures throughout Romans. The texts from *Jubilees* and *1 Enoch* I referenced previously describe suffering as a characteristic of ongoing exile, but these are not closer or clearer backgrounds than the Hebrew Bible. The likelihood of a background from the Jewish scriptures is strengthened by the concluding quotation from Psalm 44, which describes the plight of the righteous *in exile.* Indeed, Martin Ebner calls Ps 44 a "schriftgemäße Deutung des unmittelbar vorausgehended Peristasenkatalogs."[52] According to Ebner's reading, the quotation marks Paul's implicit use of the full context of Ps 44 and sums up the message of the *peristasis* catalog.

I concur with Ebner that the Ps 44:22 in Rom 8:36 is an interpretation of the *peristasis* catalog. Both reflect a background of Israel's experience of exile. The list of hardships is not meant to demonstrate Paul's (or any other Christian's) virtue, but to show the ongoing futility that persists even in the Christ-age. Jesus underwent a unique experience of futility because he was completely righteous, belonged to the age to come, and, hence, experienced the hatred of the world (John 15:18; cf. 1 John 3:13–14). Paul has been explaining in Rom 5–8 that believers are now united to Christ and must participate in his sufferings (Rom 8:17). They will experience the frustration of continuing to live in a world ruled by Sin and their ongoing *physical* separation from God.

## The *Peristasis* Catalog as Deuteronomic Curse

I will begin this investigation by stating the obvious: this list is nowhere mirrored in the Scripture in its full form. Paul is not explicitly quoting any unbroken pericope. He is, however, using terminology that can be found elsewhere in the Pauline corpus as well as the Hebrew Bible.[53] Paul may be alluding to one specific passage, to several passages, using familiar language, or he may be repeating himself. Some of the terms are uncommon, but many are not.[54] My method has been to identify any instance of two or more of the terms from the *peristasis* catalog to be used in close context in the Hebrew Bible. I expanded the search based upon common Septuagintal renderings of an underlying Hebrew term. For instance, the Heb. word חֶרֶב ("sword") is translated with either μάχαιρα or ῥομφαία.[55] I have also included the notion of "pestilence" (Gk. θάνατος) in the search because of the frequency it occurs in combination with the notions of "sword" and "famine."[56] Whereas a number of instances in the MT mention sword (חֶרֶב), famine (רָעָב), *and pestilence* (דֶּבֶר), the LXX frequently omits pestilence or translates it with θάνατος. Such a tendency in the Septuagintal tradition may account for the absence of the term in Paul's list.

Results show isolated instances in 2 Chronicles. More terminology from Paul's list occurs in the prophetic corpus. But the most complete collection of these terms comes from the covenant curses passage, Deut 28:15–68.[57]

The words κίνδυνος and διωγμός did not reveal any significant pattern of use, but I will return to their underlying concepts after considering the word groupings that do occur.

**Table 6.3 *Peristasis* Catalog Terminology in the OT**

| *Word Grouping* | *Concept* | *Texts* |
|---|---|---|
| θλῖψις and στενοχωρία | Affliction and distress | Deut 28:53, 55, 57; Isa 8:22–23; 30:6. |
| Μάχαιρα/ῥομφαία and λιμός | Sword and famine | Job 5:17–20; Jer 5:12; 14:15; 15:2; 18:21; 21:9; 32:36 (39:36 LXX). |
| Μάχαιρα/ῥομφαία and λιμός (where LXX lacks θάνατος, but MT has דֶּבֶר or a cognate). | Sword, famine (and pestilence) | Deut 31:24–25 (MT); Jer 21:9; 27:8 (34:8 LXX); 32:36 (39:36 LXX); 38:2 (45:2 LXX); 42:22 (49:22 LXX). |
| Μάχαιρα/ῥομφαία and λιμός, and θάνατος | Sword, famine, and pestilence | Lev 26:25–26; Jer 14:12; 16:4; 21:7; 24:10; 27:13; 29:18; 34:17 (41:17 LXX); 42:16–17 (49:16–17 LXX); 51:12, 13, 18, 27; Ezek 6:11–12; 7:15; 12:16; cf. 5:12; 14:12–21. |
| θλῖψις, λιμός, ῥομφαία, θάνατος | Affliction, famine, sword, and pestilence | 2 Chron 20:9. |
| θλῖψις, λιμός, and θάνατος | Affliction, Famine, and pestilence | 2 Chron 32:11 |
| λιμός and γυμνότης[a] | Famine and nakedness | Deut 28:48 |

[a]"Nakedness" may refer not only to Deut 28:48 but also to Gen 3:10–11 and the shame of the fall of man.

### *θλῖψις and στενοχωρία in the Hebrew Bible*

There are only two potential sources for the θλῖψις and στενοχωρία word group in the Hebrew Bibles: Isaiah or Deuteronomy.[58] The word στενοχωρία exclusively occurs in conjunction with θλῖψις.[59] Canonically speaking, the earliest context in which θλῖψις and στενοχωρία occur is the promise of covenant curse for disobedience in Deut 28:15–68. The word pair appears three times in short succession (28:53, 55, 57) to describe the misery that will come upon Israel at the hands of an oppressive foreign nation leading to exile (Deut 28:64–68).

In Isaiah, the pair occurs in two contexts: 8:22–23 and 30:6. The instance in 30:6 comes in a lament over rebellious Israel depending upon Egypt (30:1–18).[60] The land is called a place of θλῖψις and στενοχωρία to express its disfavor within a broader curse against Yahweh's idolatrous children.[61] The instance in Isa 8:22–23 comes in a pericope that contrasts the way of rebellion and darkness with the way of obedience and light (8:11–9:7 [9:6 LXX]). The salient point is the use of θλῖψις and στενοχωρία to depict the misery of the way of darkness that comes from turning away from Yahweh.[62] Both of these texts reflect the inevitable consequences of idolatry. In sum, everywhere in the Hebrew Bible (and in Rom 2:9) this phrase functions as a formula for divine wrath.[63]

## "Sword," "Famine," and "Pestilence" in the Hebrew Bible[64]

The threefold judgment of sword (μάχαιρα or ῥομφαία), famine (λιμός), and pestilence (θάνατος) conveys the notion of comprehensive judgment.[65] As table 6.3 indicates, there are three groupings of these terms: the earliest is pentateuchal passages warning of the consequences of breaking the covenant (Lev 26:14–45; Deut 28:15–68; 32:1–43). The second is Ezekiel and Jeremiah's prophetic description of Yahweh's discipline. Finally, there are two instances in 2 Chronicles. Ezekiel and especially Jeremiah use the phrase "sword, famine, and pestilence" as a formula for discipline.[66] The trio occurs so frequently that Walther Zimmerli describes it as "customary" for Jeremiah and Ezekiel.[67] However, it is unlikely that the terminology is an innovation of either prophet. Jack R. Lundbom argues that Jeremiah coined the formulaic combination of these three based upon Deut 28 and 32.[68] They warn of impending calamity and interpret that calamity in terms of the covenant curses of Leviticus and Deuteronomy in particular.[69] We will test Lundbom's view by examining the instances in Leviticus and Deuteronomy before moving to representative passages from Jeremiah and Ezekiel. All three notions appear in the section of Leviticus that enumerates the covenant curses which would come upon Israel if the people turned from Yahweh (Lev 26:14–45).[70] Leviticus 26:25 incorporates both sword and pestilence: "And I will bring upon you an avenging sword (μάχαιραν) which will execute the penalty of the covenant, and you will flee to your cities and I will send pestilence (θάνατον) among you and you will be handed over (παραδοθήσεσθε) into your enemies hands." Famine is conceptually present in the next verse, 26:26, "When you are afflicted (θλῖψις) for lack of bread . . . you will eat and never be satisfied."

The parallel curse in Deuteronomy mentions pestilence and although the LXX and Vulgate omit it, the MT also mentions sword:

> May the Lord cause pestilence (τὸν θάνατον) to cling to you until it utterly destroys you from the land which you are entering there to inherit it. 22 May the Lord strike you with difficulty and fever and cold and irritation and killing and with blight and paleness, and they will pursue (καταδιώξονταί) you until they destroy you. (Deut 28:21–22 LXX)

Verse 22a of the MT reads:

> Yahweh will strike you with consumption and with fever and with inflammation and with the heat of fever *and with the sword* (וּבַחֶרֶב) (Deut 28:22a, my emphasis)

Within the explicit context of covenant cursing, God threatens an array of sicknesses, pestilence, and sword. He clarifies in Deut 28:59–62 that the pestilence he brings is the precise plague he inflicted upon Egypt, but more severe. The point is that Israel's sin would betray the covenant, forfeit its special relationship with Yahweh, and render the people effectively to become like Gentiles. The Song of Moses also contains curses against idolatry which link sword, famine, and plague in Deut 32:24–25. Both the MT and LXX describe Israel being wasted by famine (מְזֵי רָעָב /τηκόμενοι λιμῷ, 32:24) and bereaved of children by the sword (תְּשַׁכֶּל־חֶרֶב/ἀτεκνώσει αὐτοὺς μάχαιρα, 32:25), but the MT mentions Israel's affliction by plague (רֶשֶׁף וּלְחֻמֵי, 32:24).[71] Thus, Lev 26 and Deut 28 represent the earliest canonical use of the terms sword, famine, and pestilence to describe the curse. In both books, the curse culminates in exile from the land and God's presence (Lev 26:32–35, 43; Deut 28:63–8).

Turning now to the prophets, we see sword, famine, and pestilence used in precisely the same manner. Both Ezekiel and Jeremiah use the terminology to demonstrate the covenantal background of Israel's hardships. Jeremiah's message generally deals with the problem of Israel's covenant disobedience and exile,[72] but Jer 15:1b–2 makes the connection explicit. The immediate context (14:17–15:4) is a national lament in which Israel first recites the description of their sorrows and asks God for deliverance (14:17–22).[73] But Yahweh responds that even if Moses and Samuel were pleading for them he would not relent (15:1a). He passes the following judgment:

> Send them away from my presence and let them go! And it shall be that when they say to you, "Where should we go?" then you are to tell them, "Thus says the LORD: 'As many as for death (θάνατον), to death (θάνατον);[74] And as many as for the sword (μάχαιραν), to the sword (μάχαιραν); and as many as for famine (λιμόν), to famine (λιμόν); And as many as for captivity (αἰχμαλωσίαν), to captivity (αἰχμαλωσίαν).'" (Jer 15:1b–2)

This passage is significant in its combination of "sword" and "famine" with "captivity."[75] Sword and famine describe aspects of God's covenant discipline which resulted in Israel's captivity. Likewise, Jer 24:10 is clear about the purpose for which the Lord sent sword, famine, and pestilence against his people. Its context is a vision given to Jeremiah regarding the people's false hope during Zedekiah's reign.[76] The vision concludes, "And I will send upon them famine (τὸν λιμόν), and pestilence (τὸν θάνατον), and the sword (τὴν μάχαιραν) *until they die out from the land which I gave to them*" (Jer 24:10, my emphasis). The two passages just discussed are representative for Jeremiah's consistent use of sword, famine, and pestilence to describe Yahweh's covenant discipline which leads to exile.

Ezekiel exhibits a similar pattern. All of Ezek 6–7 is taken up with the theme of God's wrath against the inhabitants of Judah.[77] In Ezek 6:1–14,

Yahweh appears and calls Ezekiel to prophesy against the mountains of Israel (ἐπὶ τὰ ὄρη Ισραηλ καὶ προφήτευσον ἐπ᾽ αὐτὰ, 6:2). His message is one of calamity and misery leading to Israel's scattering among the nations (6:8): "For all the abominations of the house of Israel they will fall by sword (ἐν ῥομφαίᾳ) and by pestilence (ἐν θανάτῳ), and by famine (ἐν λιμῷ, 6:11)." The abominations and idolatry of Israel resulted in exile. But Israel's physical removal from its land was only the tip of the iceberg of the assortment of woes which accompanied Yahweh's judgment. The trend continues in Ezek 7:1–27. Yahweh announces that he will finally judge the entire land of Israel and the whole world in the "Day of the Lord" (7:2–3).[78] The terms appear in Ezek 7:15, where the day is described as a one of war and judgment: "War by the sword is without and famine and pestilence are within" (ὁ πόλεμος ἐν ῥομφαίᾳ ἔξωθεν καὶ ὁ λιμὸς καὶ ὁ θάνατος ἔσωθεν). Sword, famine, and pestilence are instances of the array of curses that culminate in exile. Just after announcing sword without and famine and pestilence within, Yahweh clarifies that he will give their possessions to "foreigners" (ἀλλότριοι, Ezek 7:21) and that Yahweh will turn his face from Israel (ἀποστρέψω τὸ πρόσωπόν μου ἀπ᾽ αὐτῶν, 7:22).

Ezekiel 12:16 also uses this terminology to describe the coming exile. The context is Ezekiel's announcement of the deportation of Jerusalem (Ezek 12:1–16).[79] As a prophetic sign-act, he prepares his own "baggage of captivity" (σκεύη αἰχμαλωσίας) and symbolically carries it into exile in front of the people of Jerusalem (6:7). The interpretation is Ezek 12:10–16. Ezekiel's declares, "As I have done, so shall it be for them; they shall go in exile and in captivity" (ὃν τρόπον πεποίηκα οὕτως ἔσται αὐτοῖς ἐν μετοικεσίᾳ καὶ ἐν αἰχμαλωσίᾳ πορεύσονται, 12:11). The interpretation concludes:

> And I will spare a number of men from among them from sword (ἐκ ῥομφαίας) and from famine (ἐκ λιμοῦ) and from pestilence (ἐκ θανάτου), so that they might tell of all their lawless acts among the nations where they enter, and they will know that I am the Lord. (Ezek 12:16)

Once again, sword, famine, and pestilence characterize Yahweh's covenant discipline. Those who survive them endure exile. Likewise, Ezek 14:12–21 describes Yahweh's judgment in stages beginning with famine (14:13), then sword (14:17), and finally pestilence (14:17). So also, 2 Chronicles uses the terminology in the context of exile and deportation. The first instance appears in Jehoshaphat's prayer for deliverance from being driven out of their inheritance, God had given them (2 Chr 20:11). He prays that in the threat of "evil, sword, judgment, pestilence, [or] famine" (κακά, ῥομφαία, κρίσις, θάνατος, λιμός) they will be faithful (2 Chr 20:9). Similarly, when the Assyrian army was encamped against Hezekiah at Jerusalem, the Assyrian commander taunts the people suggesting Hezekiah's rebellion would lead "to death, famine, and thirst" (εἰς θάνατον καὶ εἰς λιμὸν καὶ εἰς δίψαν, 2 Chr 32:11). The end of the threat was deportation and exile, just as the Assyrians had done to the Northern Kingdom.

In sum, these hardships consistently describe the experience of covenant curse. Moreover, the indicators of Deuteronomic influence in Ezekiel and Jeremiah strongly suggest that Lev 26 and Deut 28 are the original source. Wenham argues this point in his commentary on Lev 26:25–26, "Frequently the prophets Jeremiah and Ezekiel refer to sword and plague as heaven-sent judgments, on occasions clearly quoting from Leviticus."[80] There is a pattern established by Moses and continued in the prophets in which this terminology indicates God's discipline leading to separation from him and the land.

### *"Famine" and "Nakedness" in the Hebrew Bible*

After sword and disease is threatened in Deut 28:22, famine (λιμός) is also threatened along with nakedness (γυμνότης) and a general "lack of all things" in Deut 28:48. This is the only passage in the Hebrew Bible where γυμνότης occurs with *any* of Paul's other terms from Rom 8:35b. The addition of the rare word γυμνότης narrows the field considerably.[81] It occurs only here in the LXX. Not even the parallel in Leviticus refers to nakedness as an element of covenant curse.[82] However, "nakedness" (γυμνός) can be found with "captivity" (αἰχμαλωσία) in Isa 20:4, also discussing the misery of the exilic experience.

### *Deuteronomy 28 as the Background*

At this point, in light of the pattern of these various word groups and the absence of γυμνότης elsewhere, Deut 28 is the most likely candidate for Paul's source material. Five out of seven of the troubles Paul lists in Rom 8:35 have verbal parallels in the description of the covenant curse in Deut 28:15–68:

**Table 6.4 Parallels between Romans 8:35 and Deuteronomy 28**

| *Romans 8:35* | *Deuteronomy 28 LXX* |
|---|---|
| θλῖψις | Deut 28:53, 55, 57; 31:17 |
| στενοχωρία | Deut 28:53, 55, 57 |
| διωγμός | Conceptual parallel: Deut 28:22, 45 (רדף). Cf. Lev 26:17 |
| λιμός | Deut 28:48; 32:24 |
| γυμνότης | Deut 28:48 |
| κίνδυνος | – |
| μάχαιρα | Deut 28:22 (MT only); 32:25, 41–42. Cf. Lev 26:25, 33. |

As noted above, the investigation did not reveal a pattern for the words διωγμός or κίνδυνος and they do not appear in Deut 28. However, their concepts may be there. Although, διωγμός ("persecution") does not have a precise verbal parallel, it is both conceptually present in the atrocities the enemy nation commits against Israel and there is an etymological link.[83] The verb καταδιώκω is etymologically related to διωγμός. Both are derived from the basic verb form, διώκω, referring to pursuit or persecution.[84] Deuteronomy 28:45 summarizes the totality of the curse, "So all these curses shall come on you and pursue (καταδιώκω) you and overtake you until you are destroyed" (cf. 28:15, 22). The parallel passage Lev 26:17 uses the verb διώκω to communicate the same notion. The underlying Heb. in Deut 28:22, 45 and Lev 26:17 is רָדַף "pursue." There is some flexibility in translation for the term.[85] In one instance, the LXX translators render the verb רָדַף with the noun διωγμός (cf. Prov 11:19). Therefore, despite lacking a direct verbal parallel, the concept and an etymological link are present. As a reader of Hebrew, Aramaic, and Greek, Paul was likely aware of connection between רָדַף and the noun διωγμός. If this argument is granted, six out of the seven terms have a textual link to Deuteronomy 28.

The only remaining term is the relatively rare word κίνδυνος ("danger"). This word is the biggest obstacle to my case that Paul derives his list of tribulations from the Pentateuchal descriptions of covenant curse. There is no direct lexical parallel with Deut 28 or Lev 26. Nevertheless, there should be little doubt that the concept of danger is present in the siege described in Deut 28:49–57.[86] The militaristic tone of Deut 28 further points to a conceptual overlap since κίνδυνος is sometimes used to connote danger *in battle* (e.g., Polyb. 1.87.10).[87] We should also recognize that κίνδυνος is a relatively new word in the Greek lexicon. It is not attested prior to the sixth century BC.[88] It is possible that Septuagintal translators were reticent to use such a novel term in the translation of ancient texts. Of the twelve instances κίνδυνος occurs in the LXX,[89] only one, Ps 116:3 (114:3 LXX), is paralleled in the MT.[90] By the final four centuries BC, it was an accepted term for danger. The Maccabean writings, for example, regularly employ it for the military threats of foreign powers against the Jewish people. Thus, while Deut 28 does not specifically use κίνδυνος, there are plausible reasons to see that Paul could have drawn this seventh term from his understanding of covenant discipline.

Finally, Paul's specific choice of seven tribulations may suggest a background of covenant discipline. There are seven afflictions of pestilence in Deut 28:21–22 and seven more in Deut 28:27–29. Similarly, Lev 26 describes the covenant curses as coming in sevens on four occasions (Lev 26:18, 21, 24, 28). Wenham comments, "Seven seems to be a round number for repeated punishments (cf. Ps. 79:12; Prov. 24:26; Isa. 4:1). It is an appropriate and evocative number in view of the importance of the seventh in Israelite religion, and *it serves as a reminder that these punishments are for breach of the heart of this religion, the covenant* (cf. [Lev 26:]25)."[91] The Book of Job also describes divine discipline in terms of seven woes (Job 5:17–27). This list of tribulations includes famine (λιμός) and sword (χειρὸς σιδήρου; MT: חֶרֶב). In light of this pattern of sevens, particularly those in Deut 28 and Lev 26, Paul's choice of seven elements may reflect the continuation of covenant discipline in the context of Rom 8.

## Conclusion of *Peristasis* Catalog as Based upon Deuteronomy 28

In sum, we have seen an instructive pattern of word usage. Paul was likely aware of Jeremiah, Ezekiel, and Isaiah's use of this language, but the passage that incorporates the most elements—as well as likely generating the later uses—is Deut 28.[92] Six out of seven Pauline troubles have a parallel in the covenant curses of Deut 28:15–68. In light of the high correspondence between these two passages of Deut 28:15–28 and Rom 8:35b, I argue that Paul's list of seven hardships which are perceived as "dividers" between Christ's love and believers are shaped by covenant curses. Paul's intent to invoke the reality of the miseries of exile is strengthened by Jeremiah's, Isaiah's, and Ezekiel's use of the same terminology. From one perspective, the presence of the prophetic use of this terminology may seem to blur the likelihood of an allusion to Deuteronomy. However, this need not be the case. Rather, the lexical correspondence focuses the allusion to Deut 28, but further use by the prophets of groupings of curses amplifies the likelihood that they are themselves based on Deuteronomy and that Paul both knew that this list of tribulations was exilic and chose it for that very reason.

The list of earthly troubles that threaten to separate believers from Christ's love are the very things which Israel experienced as a sign of separation from God. These "dividers" include the willful acts of evil men against God's people and the destructive forces of a still-fallen cosmos. The peace with God which Christ brings is, for the time being, only in the Spirit (Rom 8:9–10). Believers continue to live in the present age (Rom 8:18). As such, they will continue to experience futility (Rom 8:20; cf. 1:21). Mark Seifrid links the sorrows of Rom 8:35b to the "birth pangs" of creation, calling them the "convulsions of the creation-rendered-futile."[93] However, a key difference between these sufferings as Deuteronomy portrays them and as Paul portrays them in Romans is their cause. Israel was exiled because of unfaithfulness to God's covenant. Exile, sword, famine, and other hardships were his chastening. That is, in addition to humankind's separation from God through Adam, Israel underwent an additional and typological exile. Likewise, NT believers undergo the sufferings of exile themselves in Adam, just as all humankind does. However, as a function of their faith and participation in Christ, believers additionally experience a new sense of exile. But, this renewed sense is not a function of covenant discipline, as with Israel, but of belonging to the kingdom of heaven.[94] Whereas, all humanity persists in its separation from God in Eden, believers no longer belong there. The guilt of sin, the obstacle of return, was removed. So, unlike the unbeliever, Christians experience the conditions of exile in their righteousness (Rom 5:1–2; 8:1). Hence, Paul's next hermeneutical choice is to quote Psalm 44:22, which depicts the experience of the righteous in exile.

## Psalm 44:22 in Romans 8:36

Immediately following the Rom 8:35b list of seven troubles believers will undergo as they experience "the sufferings of the present time" (Rom 8:18) and co-suffer with Christ (Rom 8:17), Paul quotes Ps 44:22 (Ps 43:23 LXX; Ps 44:23 MT),[95] which describes the tribulations of the righteous in exile. As Jewett and others have noted, there is a formal link between the seven tribulations and the quotation indicated by the quotation formula, "as it is written," and the repeated possibility of capital punishment: "sword" (8:35) and "slaughter" (8:36).[96]

As the comparison above demonstrates, with the exception of the preposition ἕνεκεν/ἕνεκα, Paul employs the exact wording of the LXX. He introduces the quote with the deictic formula καθὼς γέγραπται and follows with what is either the exact wording of the recension he used,[97] or his modernization of it,[98] or, less likely, his own translation which happens to coincide. In any case, Paul has now broken the long drought in Romans of formal quotations since 4:23–5. However, his specific reasons for citing the psalm are not immediately apparent. At the least, it seems to be an affirmation from Jewish scripture that the righteous will suffer. Yet several competing interpretations have arisen.

One simple interpretation is Cranfield's, who argues "[t]he main effect of the quotation of Ps 44.22 is to show that the tribulations which face Christians

**Table 6.5 Psalm 44:22 in Romans 8:36**

| *Ps 44:22 (44:23 MT; 43:23 LXX)* | *Rom 8:36* |
|---|---|
| | καθὼς γέγραπται ὅτι[a] |
| ὅτι ἕνεκα σοῦ θανατούμεθα ὅλην τὴν ἡμέραν ἐλογίσθημεν ὡς πρόβατα σφαγῆς | ἕνεκεν σοῦ θανατούμεθα ὅλην τὴν ἡμέραν, ἐλογίσθημεν ὡς πρόβατα σφαγῆς |

*Note*: Solid underlines indicate direct parallels.

[a]Commentators disagree on whether this ὅτι introduces the quotation or is itself the first word of the quotation. Notably Cranfield argues that it is not part of the quotation (*Romans*, 1:440) whereas Sanday and Headlam argue that it is—in the previous edition of the same commentary (*A Critical and Exegetical Commentary on the Epistle to the Romans*, ICC [Edinburgh: T&T Clark, 1902], 221). Based upon the text of Rom 8:31–39, and the flow of thought, it seems most likely that Cranfield is correct and ὅτι introduces the quotation rather than serving as the first word of it.

are nothing new or unexpected, but have all along been characteristic of the life of God's people."[99] The problem with this identification, however, is its failure to reckon with redemptive-historical advancement accomplished by Christ. The specific problem of the Psalm is that the righteous are experiencing curse despite their innocence. They have not "been false to the covenant" (Ps 44:17), yet they experience the woes of exile. They are "like sheep for slaughter" and are "scattered among the nations" (44:11). Yahweh "hides his face" from them (44:24). While it is true that God's people have experienced futility since Adam, the recognition that woes of the psalm are *exilic* suffering raises questions that Cranfield does not address.

Alternatively, Robert Jewett argues that the hermeneutical key is found in the conflict between Christian factions Rome, between the "weak" (i.e., returned Jewish-Christian exiles from the Edict of Claudius)[100] and the "strong" (cf. 2 Cor 2:6, 16; 3:5 ).[101] According to this view, the psalm citation is the culmination of the *peristasis* catalog. Jewett argues, "The strong were attempting to disqualify the weak for their suffering and vulnerability as a sign of their standing under a divine curse."[102] The argument presumes a strict Deuteronomic understanding of blessing and curse among the "strong" in Rome.[103] If a believer experiences any of the tribulations of Rom 8:35b, that could be taken as evidence of God's curse against them. According to Jewett's reconstruction, "the strong" were taking the reality of persecution and suffering as evidence that "the weak" were not true disciples. He points to Paul's conflict with the Corinthians super-apostles, who interpreted his affliction as disqualification for his office.[104] It is noteworthy that Jewett also identifies the sufferings of Rom 8:35 as depicting those who appear to be under curse. The problem, however, is there has been little evidence of inter-faith conflict in Romans. Paul is clear that there will be suffering, but it is consistently portrayed as the futility of the world and the persecution that comes through the reign of Sin over the present evil age. Paul's focus is cosmic, not quotidian.

Richard Hays offers a third interpretation. He argues that Paul interprets Ps 44 to be a "prophetic prefiguration of the experience of the Christian church," which describes the experience of God's people during the "eschatological interval between Christ's resurrection and the ultimate redemption of the world."[105] Further, Hays views the quotation—in context with the previously discussed allusions to Isaiah—to be Paul's deliberate overlapping of Isaiah's description of the servant's ordeal with the psalm's prophecy of the hardships of the eschatological people of God. It should not be doubted, Hays reasons, that having depended upon Isaiah throughout the epistle thus far, clearly alluding to the fourth Servant Song several times before (e.g., Rom 4:24–25; [5:1, 6, 8,] 15–19; [8:32;] cf. 10:16; 15:21),[106] Paul would have been aware of the similarity between Ps 44:22 and Isa 53:7.[107] Whereas it is the righteous in exile who are ὡς πρόβατα σφαγῆς ("like sheep to be slaughtered") in Ps 44, in Isa 53 it is the singular servant who is ὡς πρόβατον ἐπὶ σφαγὴν ἤχθη ("like a sheep led to slaughter"). Hays concludes, "those who have ears to hear will hear and understand that the people of God, reckoned as sheep to be slaughtered, are suffering with Christ (Rom. 8:17: συμπάσχομεν) and thus living out the vocation prophesied for them in the Scriptures."[108] Thus, for Hays, the quotation of Ps 44 integrates with and completes the previous allusions to Isaiah.

However, Hays overinterprets the parallel. He concludes with the dramatic, but flawed statement: "Upon them [i.e., NT believers] is the chastisement that makes others whole, and with their stripes creation is healed."[109] In a charitable reading, Hays is claiming a participation between Christ's sufferings and that of believers akin to Paul's statement in, say, Col 1:24 when Paul rejoices in his sufferings and claims to "fill up" in his flesh what was lacking from Christ's afflictions. However, it cannot be said that Christian participation in Christ's suffering brings healing *to creation*. Paul is reticent to make such an identification for a reason. Christ is the servant of Isaiah who suffers and brings redemption. In the overlap of the ages, believers will suffer in union him, but their suffering is not redemptive. Rather it is the continued enmity between flesh and Spirit which will continue until their exile is fully ended through the resurrection of the body.

A final, and more recent, interpretation is that of Tyler A. Stewart, who argues that the theme of participation in Christ throughout Rom 5–8 should be applied to the interpretation of Rom 8:35b–36.[110] The bulk of Stewart's argument shows the nature of participation in Christ as a transfer from a position in Adam by dying with Christ to the law (Rom 6:4, 6; 7:6) and being raised in participation with Christ's resurrection life.[111] Thus, believers exist in an overlap between two ages, which Stewart calls an "apocalyptic dualism" where suffering precedes glory.[112] Based upon this interpretation of Rom 5–8, Stewart concludes, "Paul read Ps 44 as an anguished prophetic announcement of participation in the crucified Messiah."[113] The quotation is Paul's summary of suffering-in-Christ assumed throughout Rom 5–8 beginning with θλῖψις in Rom 5:3. The present study is largely in agreement with Stewart. Nevertheless, Stewart has missed the full significance of Paul's allusions to Isaiah 50 and 53. He also fails to acknowledge fully the nature of the hardships in 8:35 as Deuteronomic descriptions, which Jewett rightly notes.

I argue that the *peristasis* catalog and psalm citation stand together, as Jewett and Stewart also acknowledge.[114] Each refers to divine curse, which in the previous redemptive-historical epoch was evidence of separation from God. The list of tribulations draws from the threat of exile in the law, as well as subsequent prophetic portrayals of its experience. Psalm 44, likewise, describes the experience of curse. Following Hays, I argue that Paul's allusions to Isaiah join with his later reference to exile to accomplish a singular purpose in Rom 8:31–39, namely, to boast in the assurance of glory. Paul uses exilic terminology in Rom 8:35b–36 in order to show that even vestiges of the curse cannot prevent final redemption. Deuteronomy 28 and Ps 44 both typologically point to the already-not yet experience of believers with Christ, and indicate the eschatological reversal of the curse. In order to make the case, we will now examine the broader context of Ps 44.

### *The Context of Psalm 44*[115]

Work on the editing of the Psalter indicates Psalms 42–44 should be viewed as guidance for the post-exilic community in coping with the "disorienting reality of exile."[116] Psalm 44 is a unique communal lament. While there are some individual laments that claim the righteousness of the psalmist (e.g., Ps 7:3–9; 17:3–5; 18:20–24; 26:1–12; 59:4–5), only this psalm claims the entire lamenting community is righteous.[117] The basic structure is as follows:

44:1–8 Affirmation of God's former deliverance
9–16 *Lament:* Description current suffering and shame
17–22 *Lament:* Affirmation of righteousness
23–27 Call for God to arise and deliver

Verses 1–8 affirms God's previous blessing, yet this only serves to highlight the contrast with the community's present experience. The first lament (44:9–16) describes a series of misfortunes which are doubly modeled after God's treatment of the Canaanites during the conquest (cf. 44:2–3) and Deuteronomic descriptions of covenant curse. The people mourn defeat in battle (44:9), which is directly due to God's absence (44:10–11). This would be understandable if God's people had sinned, but it is inexplicable to them because they had not (Ps 44:17–18, 20–21).

The second lament (44:17–22) shifts to the question of why God has allowed such suffering when the people did *not* violate his covenant.[118] The psalmist writes "All these things came upon us and we did not forget you and we did no iniquity against your covenant" (ταῦτα πάντα ἦλθεν ἐφ' ἡμᾶς καὶ οὐκ ἐπελαθόμεθά σου καὶ οὐκ ἠδικήσαμεν ἐν διαθήκῃ σου, 44:17 [43:18 LXX]). The context of Psalm 44, then, is disillusionment due to separation from God's blessing. The experience of curse has so clouded the congregation's eyes that all the blessings repeated in 44:1–8 are obscured. The interplay between the phrase ὅλην τὴν ἡμέραν ("all the day") in 44:8 (43:9 LXX) and again in 44:15 (43:16 LXX) suggests that the congregation's shame has wholly overshadowed the memory of their former deliverance.[119] Whereas, in 44:8a the community's boast is in God "all the day," in 44:15 it is disgrace (ἡ ἐντροπή) that is always before it. Moreover, the disgrace is related to God "turning his face away"—a typical Deuteronomic expression of exile (44:24; cf. Deut 31:17; Ps 104:29).

Paul's quotation is drawn from 44:22, but the notion of being "sheep for slaughter" first occurs as a description of military defeat in 44:11. When Ps 44:11 is compared to 44:22, a number of comparisons can be made:

Ps 44:11a ἔδωκας ἡμᾶς ὡς πρόβατα βρώσεως
11b καὶ ἐν τοῖς ἔθνεσιν διέσπειρας ἡμᾶς
22a ὅτι ἕνεκα σοῦ θανατούμεθα ὅλην τὴν ἡμέραν
22b ἐλογίσθημεν ὡς πρόβατα σφαγῆς

The terminology both verses share is "sheep for slaughter/eating."[120] The first colon of verse 11 opens with the verb "you gave"; the last colon concludes with the verb "you scattered." Similarly, "sheep for eating" is parallel with "among the nations." It follows that that 44:11b "you scattered us among the nations" is closely related to 44:22a "for your sake we are put to death all the day." At the least, it should be clearly understood that the location of the slaughter is ἐν τοῖς ἔθνεσιν. Although perhaps not exactly identical, being "given over like sheep" is a description of exile, just as being scattered among the nations is. This scattering is the exact description of the divine response to covenant disobedience (cf. Lev 26:33; Deut 28:64).

The problem of the psalm is God's agency in afflicting his own righteous people. The nations may scorn them (44:13–14), but the actual activities of crushing (44:19), of covering with darkness (44:19), of rejecting (44:9), of humiliating and scattering them among the nations (44:11, 13) are all done by God himself. God has turned his face from them and they cannot see why (44:24). God's people lament because they know they are in exile. Yet there is no mention of covenant infidelity of any kind.

### *The Use of Psalm 44:22 in Jewish Literature*

The earliest usage of Ps 44:22 in the literature still belongs to later Judaism.[121] Other than Rom 8:36, the first reference I have found is an allusion in 4 Ezra 15:10 which uses Ps 44:22 as a reference to righteous martyrdom: "'I will surely avenge them,' says the Lord, 'and will receive to myself all the innocent blood from among them. Behold, *my people is [sic] led like a flock to the slaughter.*'"[122] The remainder of Jewish references to Ps 44:22 belong to the Talmudim and Midrashim. Psalm 44:22 is typically employed as an indirect prophecy that is fulfilled in the martyrdom of a righteous individual or group.[123]

One rabbinic usage that bears upon our interpretation is a midrash of Num 13:2, which describes Yahweh's future meeting with the righteous in glory:

> In the hereafter the Holy One, blessed be He, will prepare a feast for the righteous in the Garden of Eden . . . The Holy One, blessed be He, enters the Garden of Eden. Hence it is written, *I am come into my garden, my sister (*ahothi*), my bride*—Kallah, etc. (Song 5:1). *'My Sister'* because they have become joined to Me in exile. *'Kallah,'* because they were consumed (*nithkallu*) in exile, as is borne out by the text, *But for Thy sake are we killed all the day,* etc. (Ps 44:22). (*Num. Rab.* 12:3)[124]

According to this passage, "being killed all the day" describes an exile that will end when God's people reenter Eden. It can be concluded that in some sections of Judaism during the rabbinic period it was believed that restoration from exile—perhaps particularly restoration from the exile in view in Ps 44:22—would not merely involve a return to Palestine, but to Eden.

In sum, while none of these later Jewish references could have influenced Paul's writing of Romans, it is helpful to note that, in at least one case, there was an early rabbinic interpretation which viewed Ps 44:22 as describing the righteous in an exile which would end with restoration to Eden.

## Paul's Use of the *Peristasis* Catalog and Psalm 44

Having now examined the context of Ps 44 and determined the background of Paul's *peristasis* catalog as a description of Deuteronomic curse, I can now address Paul's use of the Hebrew Bible in Rom 8:35b–36. I argued above that Paul's final rhetorical question, "Who will separate us from Christ's love?" (Rom 8:35a), is not only the most significant of the four questions, but encapsulates his argument from all Rom 5–8. Although we might have expected a simple denial that believers could be separated from Christ, Paul instead lists a series of seven Deuteronomic sufferings. Under a simple Deuteronomic framework where obedience leads to blessing and disobedience to curse, these sufferings indicate divine disfavor.[125] However, Paul goes on to cite Ps 44:22 to show that the hardships of the righteous community in exile would not be due to sin, but for Christ's sake. Christ's suffering on his people's behalf is now repeated in believers' earthly lives, yet with atonement having been fully accomplished. The experience of exile does not indicate God's disfavor, but participation in Christ. Paul uses these scriptural descriptions of exile to provide a theologically and redemptive-historically situated interpretation of the "sufferings of the present time" he had predicted in Rom 8:18.

Paul's purpose throughout Rom 5–8 has been to describe life in the Spirit. He has painstakingly demonstrated that participation in Christ will involve suffering then glory (cf. 5:3–5; 8:14–17; 8:23–30). The character of that suffering is now clearly defined as the experience of curse. The relationship between Israel and Yahweh where rest and peace in the land were contingent upon faithfulness to the covenant is, in fact, an instance of the broader principle. Adam's rest, peace, and flourishing in the land were also contingent upon obedience. All the scriptural descriptions of covenant curse which accurately reflect Israel's experience of exile, *mutatis mutandis,* may also be ascribed to humanity's exile in Adam. Christ inaugurated the end of that exile, but full restoration remains in the future.

This raises the question: Why must participation in Christ involve the experience of exile? The answer is found in Paul's Adamic Christology. Although the Israel motif in Rom 5–8 can identify the experience as exile, it does not answer why it must continue. It does not explain why the righteous would experience curse. We should recall, however, that Israel was in Adam. Even before Israel and Judah experienced the Assyrian or Babylonian exiles (which were a recapitulation of Adam's expulsion from Eden), they already lived in the cosmic exile by virtue of their position in Adam. The exile of Israel was a picture of Adam's curse. Jesus Christ, however, reverses both the small-scale, typological curse of Israel's exile and the cosmic curse against Adam. Yet, until all of God's people enter glory and receive their inheritance, the Adamic exile will continue.

Reconciliation to God in Christ is the end of the exile *spiritually,* but Paul has carefully demonstrated that redemption will not be consummated until the resurrection *of the body* (Rom 8:10–11, 23). The physical side remains unfulfilled. Thus, even believers in Christ will continue to experience some consequences of exile until the resurrection. While the same may be said of the rest of creation, participation in Christ also results in an added exilic experience. The redeemed belong to the kingdom of God and are not ruled by Sin and Death any longer. Union with Christ results in the exchange of their former belonging to this world and gaining a yet-unrealized heavenly inheritance. Until the redemption of the body (Rom 8:23), they will continue to live, as it were, outside of Eden. Much of the misery of exile is due to the enmity of a still-futile world against the children of God. As Käsemann notes, the present age is opposed to the age-to-come:

> Reconciliation with God necessarily means enmity with the world according to the law of the apocalyptic. If this is not understood, it is hard to see that [Rom 8:]19–27 belong with this passage [i.e., Rom 8:36] as its reverse side. The solidarity of believers with the world is more than a mere understanding of fellow human beings and readiness for them, for it is always linked to the cross.[126]

Thus, Paul concludes this portion of Romans by boasting in the assurance of glory.[127] However, that boast is not limited to the future. Every believer may presently boast ἐν ταῖς θλίψεσιν (5:3) because these afflictions indicate participation in Christ. Likewise, in Rom 8:35, he triumphantly boasts that not even the ongoing afflictions exile can separate the believer from God.

## CONCLUSION

Paul concludes the argument of Rom 5–8 precisely how he began it. He began by demonstrating the renewed, peaceful relationship believers have with God through Christ's atoning work as Isaiah's servant (Rom 4:25; 5:1). He concludes boasting that justification (8:32–34) and reconciliation (8:35–36) can never be reversed (8:37–39). Nevertheless, despite the certainty of Paul's boast in Rom 8:31–39, it is given while fully acknowledging hostility. The opposition is unnamed (τίς, 8:31, 33, 34, 35), but always present. The threats that lie behind Paul's boast represent instances of the "sufferings of the present time" (8:18). While they will one day be replaced by glory (8:18) and the redemption of the body (8:23), until then, they embody the futility of the present age.

I have argued that there have been indicators of restoration from exile throughout Rom 5–8. The eschatological outpouring of the Spirit (5:5; 8:1–11), the repeated allusions to the restoration prophecy of Ezek 36–37, the launch of Isaiah's second exodus (8:14–17), and the imminent reception of the Abrahamic inheritance (4:13; 8:17) indicate the inauguration of restoration. I argued for each of these by implication on the basis of Paul's allusions to Jewish scripture. However, Paul's answer to his final question in Rom 8:35a, "Who will separate us from Christ's love?," explicitly points to exile. Whereas we might expect an emphatic negative answer to the question, Paul's answer is cautious. He is cognizant of the reality that there will be no glory apart from suffering (8:17). Indeed, the very nature of the suffering will suggest at times that God has rejected his people. It will *feel* like exile because it is. But, it is an exile that is coming to an end. That feeling of exile arises from the twofold reality for the NT Christian that (1) all humanity is still undergoing the exile of Adam and (2) believers participate in Christ's suffering. Thus, while the feeling of exile is common to humanity, it is heightened for believers who, by virtue of union with Christ, no longer find their home in fallen creation.

Thus, there is a key difference. Whereas Adam and Israel experienced exile because of their covenant disobedience, Christ suffered ὑπὲρ ἡμῶν (Rom 5:6, 8; 8:32). Believers will now experience the sufferings of the present time in union with Christ. Forthwith, it is believers who suffer ἕνεκεν θεοῦ. Yet they are not experiencing God's wrath, but the ongoing futility of the world, the evil of the present age. The exile they experience is not due to disobedience, but to the incomplete status of their restoration. As citizens of the kingdom of heaven, they live in a foreign realm outside of the paradise God has prepared for them. Their exile will continue until God makes all things new.

## NOTES

1. For example, A. H. Snyman, "Style and the Rhetorical Situation of Romans 8:31–39," *NTS* 34 (1988): 227–8; Robert Jewett and Roy David Kotansky, *Romans: A Commentary,* Hermeneia (Minneapolis: Fortress, 2007), 535.

2. Paul regularly uses rhetorical questions to conclude a section (e.g., 3:1; 4:1). Because the first rhetorical question centers on God being ὑπὲρ ἡμῶν, which recalls Rom 5:6 where Paul argued that Christ died ὑπὲρ ἀσεβῶν while *we* (ἡμῶν) were weak. Indeed, the argument of 8:32 parallels with 5:8–9 and also echoes Isa 53 such that Rom 5–8 seems to be the focus of his conclusion. With that said, there seem to be allusions in 8:31–39 to the earlier portion of Romans such that the whole of Paul's argument should not be excluded from view despite a relative emphasis upon 5–8. See C. E. B. Cranfield, *A Critical and Exegetical Commentary on the Epistle to the Romans,* 2 vols., ICC (Edinburgh: T&T Clark, 1975), 1:434; Peter Stuhlmacher, *Paul's Letter to the Romans: A Commentary*, trans. Scott J. Hafemann, 1st ed. (Louisville, KY: Westminster/John Knox Press, 1994), 138.

3. It is unlikely that the style arises from Paul's assimilation of hymnic material. On this debate, see Peter von der Osten-Sacken, *Römer 8 als Beispiel paulinischer Soteriologie*, FRLANT 112 (Göttingen: Vandenhoeck und Ruprecht, 1975), 20–47; Gottfried Schille, "Die Liebe Gottes in Christus: Beobachtungen zu Rm 8:31–39," *ZNW* 59 (1968): 233–5; Douglas J. Moo, *The Epistle to the Romans,* NICNT (Grand Rapids: Eerdmans, 1996), 538; James D. G. Dunn, *Romans 1–8,* WBC 38A (Dallas: Word Books, 1988), 499.

4. For example, Moo proposes two basic divisions of 8:31–34, 35–49 (*Romans,* 538). Käsemann lists three: 8:31–32, 33–34, 35–39 (Ernst Käsemann, *Commentary on Romans*, trans. G. W. Bromiley [Grand Rapids: Eerdmans, 1980], 246). Cranfield lists four divisions: 8:31–32, 33–34, 35–37, 38–39 (Cranfield, *Romans,* 1:434). The disagreement stems, in part, from different punctuation patterns (see Moo, *Romans,* 541n27). I follow the punctuation choices of the NA[28].

5. I take Paul's opening question Τί οὖν ἐροῦμεν πρὸς ταῦτα; ("What then shall we say to these things," 8:31) as transitional. The four subsequent questions function as the substance of the pericope rather than its introduction.

6. Dunn notes that Rom 8:32 "gather[s] up the σύν-compounds of v 17, in particular" (*Romans 1–8,* 499), but the pattern is much broader. See the following instances of the σύν preposition or prefix with reference to participation in Christ in Rom 5–8: Rom 6:4 (συνθάπτω), 5 (συνθάπτω), 6 (συσταυρόω), 8 (σὺν Χριστῷ and συζάω); 8:16 (συμμαρτυρέω), 17 (συμμαρτυρέω, συμπάσχω, συνδοξάζω), 22 (συνδοξάζω, συνωδίνω), 26 (συναντιλαμβάνομαι), and 32 (σὺν αὐτῷ). For an

exegetical and theological analysis of σύν in Romans and other Pauline literature, see Murray J. Harris, *Prepositions and Theology in the Greek New Testament: An Essential Reference Resource for Exegesis* (Grand Rapids: Zondervan, 2012), 200–5.

7. Mark A. Seifrid, "Romans," in *Commentary on the New Testament Use of the Old Testament*, ed. G. K. Beale and D. A. Carson (Grand Rapids: Baker Academic, 2007), 633.

8. For example, Moo implies an exclusively positive reading (*Romans,* 541).

9. Seifrid, "Romans," 633.

10. For example, Richard B. Hays, *Echoes of Scripture in the Letters of Paul* (New Haven: Yale University Press, 1989), 57–63; Seifrid, "Romans," 633–7; Shiu-Lun Shum, *Paul's Use of Isaiah in Romans: A Comparative Study of Paul's Letter to the Romans and the Sibylline and Qumran Sectarian Texts*, WUNT 2/156 (Tübingen: Mohr Siebeck, 2002), 200–2.

11. Seifrid, "Romans," 634.

12. Several commentators recognize both allusions: Cranfield, *Romans,* 1:436; C. K. Barrett, *A Commentary on the Epistle to the Romans* (New York: Harper & Brothers, 1957), 172; Ulrich Wilckens, *Der Brief an die Römer*, 3 vols., EKKNT 6 (Zürich: Benziger; Neukirchen-Vluyn: Neukirchener Verlag, 1980), 2:173. See also, Romano Penna, "The Motif of the '*Aqedah* Against the Background of Romans 8:32," in *Paul the Apostle: A Theological and Exegetical Study*, trans. Thomas P. Wahl, vol. 1, 2 vols. (Collegeville, MN: Liturgical Press, 1996), 158–68; Shum, *Isaiah in Romans*, 200–1; Hans Joachim Schoeps, "The Sacrifice of Isaac in Paul's Theology," *JBL* 65 (1946): 385–92; Daniel R. Schwartz, "Two Pauline Allusions to the Redemptive Mechanism of the Crucifixion," *JBL* 102 (1983): 263–5. Nevertheless, scholars are mixed on the likelihood of the allusion to Gen 22. For example, Robert J. Daly calls it "certain" ("Soteriological Significance of the Sacrifice of Isaac," *CBQ* 39 [1977]: 66–7). Alternatively, Marie-Louise Gubler argues more conservatively that typology of Isaac in the NT should be divided into explicit and implicit categories with Rom 8:32 belonging to the latter (*Die frühesten Deutungen des Todes Jesu: eine motivgeschichtliche Darstellung aufgrund der neueren exegetischen Forschung* [Göttingen: Vandenhoeck & Ruprecht, 1977], 336–75).

13. Dunn, *Romans 1–8*, 501. Cf. Leroy Huizenga, *The New Isaac: Tradition and Intertextuality in the Gospel of Matthew*, NovTSup 131 (Leiden: Brill, 2009), for example, 74–7.

14. Ibid.

15. Penna, "The '*Aqedah*," 163.

16. Ibid., 163–4.

17. Ibid., 164–5.

18. Thus, there is a theological connection between atonement and restoration. Following the mention of Abraham in Rom 4:25, the next verse, Rom 5:1, announces reconciliation.

19. Hays notes the parallel (*Echoes of Scripture in the Letters of Paul,* 63). I interact with his view below.

20. G. K. Beale, *A New Testament Biblical Theology: The Unfolding of the Old Testament in the New* (Grand Rapids: Baker Academic, 2011), 502–3.

21. Florian Wilk, *Die Bedeutung Des Jesajabuches Für Paulus*, FRLANT 179 (Göttingen: Vandenhoeck & Ruprecht, 1998), 280–4, argues Paul intentionally recapitulates the language of Isa 50:8–9. Cf. Osten-Sacken, *Römer 8*, 43–5; Otto Michel, *Der Brief an Die Römer*, EKKNT 4 (Göttingen: Vandenhoeck & Ruprecht, 1978), 281.

22. *Echoes of Scripture in the Letters of Paul,* 60.

23. Wilk, *Die Bedeutung Des Jesajabuches Für Paulus*, 283.

24. Elsewhere only Rom 16:13; Col. 3:12; 1 Tim 5:21; 2 Tim 2:10; Tit 1:1.

25. For the corporate aspect of the servant, see Isa 43:10; 49:1–13. Cf. Isa 14:1–2.

26. G. Schrenk, "ἐκλεκτός," *TDNT* 4:191.

27. What is implicit in Paul is explicit in 1 Peter where the "chosen" are further defined as "exiles and sojourners of the dispersion" (ἐκλεκτοῖς παρεπιδήμοις διασπορᾶς, 1:1) and a "chosen race . . . strangers and exiles" (γένος ἐκλεκτόν . . . παροίκους καὶ παρεπιδήμους, 2:9, 11).

28. Seifrid, "Romans," 635. In the hiphil stem, רשׁע can refer to either a judicial announcement, "declare guilty," or to the act itself, "cause to be condemned" ("רשׁע," *HALOT,* Bible Works 10, s.v.).

29. Shum, *Isaiah in Romans,* 201–2.

30. This restoration promise is surrounded by second exodus imagery (cf. Isa 48:20–22; 49:9–12; cf. Exod 15:27; 16:4ff.; 17:6). Isaiah 48:20 begins with the command, "Go out from Babylon." After the song (49:1–6), Isaiah speaks of the upcoming restoration when the land will be redistributed (49:8; cf. Num 32:33). Zion will believe that the Lord has forsaken it (49:14), but Yahweh assures them that he will not forget them (49:15) and that the Gentiles will be restored to a newly inhabited land with them (49:19, 22) (G. P. Hugenberger, "The Servant of the Lord in the 'Servant Songs' of Isaiah: A Second Moses Figure," in *The Lord's Anointed: Interpretation of Old Testament Messianic Texts*, ed. P. E. Satterthwaite, R. S. Hess, and G. J. Wenham, TynHS [Grand Rapids: Baker, 1995], 127).

31. Tyler Stewart, "The Cry of Victory: A Cruciform Reading of Psalm 44:22 in Romans 8:36," *JSPL* 3 (2013): 43.

32. Seifrid, "Romans," 636.

33. "χωρίζω," *NIDNTTE* 4:713–7.

34. From Gk. περίστασις ("danger," or "circumstances"). For a discussion on the origin and use of περίστασις, see J. T. Fitzgerald, *Cracks in an Earthen Vessel: An Examination of the Catalogues of Hardships in the Corinthian Correspondence*, SBLDS 99 (Atlanta: Scholars Press, 1988), 33–46.

35. See below.

36. Wolfgang Schrage, "Leid, Kreuz und Eschaton: die Peristasenkataloge als Merkmale paulinischer Theologia Crucis und Eschatologie," *EvT* 34 (1974): 141–75. Cf. Stuhlmacher, *Romans*, 138; Seifrid, "Romans," 636; Dunn, *Romans 1–8,* 505.

37. See Fitzgerald, *Cracks*, which develops the classic study by Rudolf Bultmann, *Der Stil der paulinischen Predigt und die kynisch-stoische Diatribe* (Gottingen: Vandenhoeck & Ruprecht, 1910), 71–2; Robert Hodgson, "Paul the Apostle and First Century Tribulation Lists," *ZNW* 74 (1983): 59–80.

38. Frank Thielman, "The Story of Israel and the Theology of Romans 5–8," *Society of Biblical Literature 1993 Seminar Papers,* SBLSP 32 (Atlanta: Society of Biblical Literature, 1993), 239. Similarly, Gerhard Münderlein argues for Paul's literary dependence upon Deut 28:48, 53–7 ("Interpretation einer Tradition, Bemerkungen zu Röm 8:35f," *KD* 11 (1965): 136–42. I was first introduced to the notion of Rom 8:35 as exilic suffering by Dr. G. K. Beale, who was himself alerted to it by a former student. I am grateful to them both for the fascinating idea which has been the genesis of this entire project.

39. Moo, *Romans,* 543. See also, Michel, *Römer*, 283; Richard N. Longenecker, *The Epistle to the Romans*, NIGTC (Grand Rapids: Eerdmans, 2016), 757; Cranfield, *Romans,* 1:440; Joseph A. Fitzmyer, *Romans: A New Translation with Introduction and Commentary*, AB 33 (New York: Doubleday, 1993), 534.

40. Bultmann introduced the comparison of NT *Peristasenkatalogen* with those of the Stoics (*Der Stil der paulinischen Predigt*, esp. 71–2). J. T. Fitzgerald later developed them (*Cracks*, 7–31, 207). Indeed, Fitzgerald notes a variety of types of catalog functioning in the first century (*Cracks,* 47–51).

41. See Fitzgerald, *Cracks*, 107: "the suffering sage is clearly worthy of the highest praise."

42. Hodgson, "First Century Tribulation Lists," 59–80.

43. Hans Dieter Betz, *Der Apostel Paulus und die sokratische Tradition: eine exegetische Untersuchung zu seiner Apologie 2 Korinther 10–13*, BHT 45 (Tübingen: Mohr Siebeck, 1972), 74–89.

44. Jewett, *Romans,* 545. He develops this argument more fully in idem, "Impeaching God's Elect: Romans 8.33–37 in Its Rhetorical Situation," in P*aul, Luke and the Graeco-Roman World: Essays in Honour of Alexander J.M. Wedderburn*, LNTS 217 (Sheffield: Sheffield Academic, 2002), 37–58.

45. Ibid.

46. Ibid.

47. See Stewart's similar critique of Jewett, "The Cry of Victory," 33.

48. Schrage, "Leid," 141–75. Cf. Stuhlmacher, *Romans*, 138; Seifrid, "Romans," 636; Dunn, *Romans 1–8,* 505.

49. For example, *2 Enoch* is listed by Schrage ("Leid," 143), Hodgson ("First Century Tribulation Lists," 68–9), and Dunn (*Romans 1–8,* 505).

50. Translation by F. I. Andersen, "2 (Slavonic Apocalypse of) Enoch (Late First Century A.D.)," *OTP* 2.

51. Ibid., 94–7. While the date of 2 Enoch is unclear, its possible dates range from late first century AD to the medieval period. It is unlikely that it would have been an influence upon Paul (F. I. Andersen, "2 [Slavonic Apocalypse of] Enoch: Late First Century A.D.): A New Translation and Introduction," *OTP* 1:94–7).

52. Martin Ebner, *Leidenslisten und Apostelbrief: Untersuchungen zu Form, Motivik und Funktion der Peristasenkataloge bei Paulus*, FZB 66 (Würzburg: Echter Verlag, 1991), 375.

53. There are similar lists elsewhere in Pauline literature (cf. 1 Cor 4:10–13; 2 Cor 6:4–10; 11:23–29; 12:10; Phil 4:12) and Second Temple literature (e.g., *Jub.* 23:12–3; *1 En.* 103:9–15; 2 *En.* 66:6; and *Pss. Sol.* 15:7).

54. For example, a search on the lemma θλῖψις in the Hebrew Bible yields more than 100 results.

55. Münderlein, "Interpretation einer Tradition," 138n13. Ezekiel 5:12 is a good illustration of this interchangeability: "a third of you will die by pestilence or be consumed by famine among you, one third will fall by the *sword* (חֶרֶב /ῥομφαία) surrounding you, and one third I will scatter to every wind, and I will unsheathe a *sword* (חֶרֶב /μάχαιρα) behind them."

56. See below. The Heb. דֶּבֶר ("pestilence") is frequently translated as θάνατος (cf. 2 Sam 24:13, 15; 1 Kgs 8:37; 1 Chron 21:12, 14; 2 Chron 6:28; 7:13; 20:9; Ps 77:50; Amos 4:10; Jer 14:12; 21:6, 7; 24:10; 34:17 [41:17 LXX]; 44:13 [51:13 LXX]; Ezek 5:12, 17; 6:11, 12; 7:15 [2x]; 12:16; 14:19, 21; 28:23; 33:27; 38:22) which can mean death as well as pestilence leading to death ("θάνατος," *BDAG*, BibleWorks 10, s.v., definition 3). The use of θάνατος to refer to some form of plague or disease is not directly mirrored in Rom 8:35, though διωγμός may be understood in this way. The plagues "pursued" and "persecuted" Israel (Deut 28:22, 45).

57. Münderlein reaches the same conclusion: ("Interpretation einer Tradition," 139).

58. Esther 1 LXX has an instance of the pair in the extended verse 1, but it does not appear in the MT.

59. "στενοχωρία," *NIDNTTE* 4:368.

60. John N. Oswalt, *The Book of Isaiah, Chapters 1–39*, NICOT (Grand Rapids: Eerdmans, 1986), 464.

61. John D. W. Watts, *Isaiah 1–33*, rev. ed., WBC 24 (Nashville, TN: Thomas Nelson, 1985), 464.

62. Oswalt, *Isaiah, 1–39*, 238.

63. Jewett, "Impeaching God's Elect," 50.

64. Although only "sword" and "famine" appear in Rom 8:35b, I have chosen to treat all three because of the frequency with which they appear together and the presence of the concept of pestilence in Deuteronomy (cf. Deut 28:21; 32:24).

65. Walther Zimmerli, *Ezekiel 1: A Commentary on the Book of the Prophet Ezekiel, Chapters 1–24,* ed. Frank Moore Cross and Klaus Baltzer, trans. Ronald E. Clements, Hermeneia (Philadelphia: Fortress, 1979), 191.

66. Ibid.

67. Ibid., 208.

68. Jack R. Lundbom, *Deuteronomy: A Commentary* (Grand Rapids: Eerdmans, 2013), 769.

69. Preston M. Sprinkle, *Paul and Judaism Revisited: A Study of Divine and Human Agency in Salvation* (Downers Grove, IL: IVP Academic, 2013), 49–60, identifies Isaiah and Jeremiah's deliberate use of Deuteronomy in their depictions of restoration. Sprinkle rightly identifies the Deuteronomic background, but wrongly argues that the prophets' emphasis upon God's monergistic work to restore is a deliberate contradiction of the Deuteronomic requirement of Israel's repentance.

70. Gordon J. Wenham, *The Book of Leviticus*, NICOT (Grand Rapids: Eerdmans, 1979), 327, 331–2.

71. The Heb. term רֶשֶׁף is the name of an Ugaritic deity associated with fire or flame. This notion led to its metaphorical use in Heb. for a devastating, feverish disease identified as the pestilence which comes for apostasy (Jackie A. Naudé/ R. K. Harrison, "רֶשֶׁף," *NIDOTTE* 3:1205).

72. See J. A. Thompson, *The Book of Jeremiah,* NICOT (Grand Rapids: Eerdmans, 1979), 107–17, under the heading "The Message of Jeremiah."

73. Thompson, *Jeremiah*, 384–5. I follow Thompson's structure and exegesis throughout this section.

74. Although θάνατος is present, the underlying Hebrew is מָוֶת "death" not דֶּבֶר "pestilence."

75. For a discussion of αἰχμαλωσία and its cognates as Septuagintal language depicting exile, see Robert J. V. Hiebert, "Exile and Restoration Terminology in the Septuagint and New Testament," in *Exile: A Conversation with N. T. Wright*, ed. James M. Scott (Downers Grove, IL: IVP Academic, 2017), 98–110.

76. Thompson, *Jeremiah*, 507.

77. The curses described also point to God's final judgment against the whole world. Derek Thomas (*God Strengthens: Ezekiel Simply Explained* [Darlington: Evangelical Press, 1993], 55–65) lists both Ezek 6 and 7 under the heading "The Day of the LORD," arguing that Deut 28–32 is the literary background for specific judgments enumerated in Ezek 4–10 (p. 67).

78. Citing parallels (Isa 11:2; Rev 7:1; cf. Isa 24:16; Job 37:3; 38:13) Zimmerli argues that the "four corners of the earth (הָאָרֶץ)" would have been understood as a universal reference, not a local one (*Ezekiel 1,* 203).

79. Zimmerli, *Ezekiel 1,* 267.

80. Wenham, *Leviticus*, 331–2.

81. Vaticanus lacks this term, but it is well attested in other traditions including the MT.

82. This may be an allusion to Adam's separation from God and his shameful nakedness (γυμνός, Gen 3:10–11).

83. "διωγμός," *BDAG*, BibleWorks 10, s.v.

84. Pierre Chantraine, "διώκω," *DELG* 1:289.

85. According to T. Muraoka, ἀποδιώκω, διωγμός, ἐπιδιώκω, and καταδιώκω are among the renderings of Heb. רָדַף (T. Muraoka, "רדף," "Appendix 4: Hebrew/Aramaic Index to the Septuagint," in Edwin Hatch and Henry A. Redpath, *A Concordance to the Septuagint and the other Greek Versions of the Old Testament: (Including the Apocryphal Books)*, 2nd ed. [Grand Rapids: Baker Book House, 1998], 343).

86. Isaiah 28:13 uses the verb form κινδυνεύω along with θλῖψις and ἁλίσκομαι "to be taken captive." Hence, there is a Hebrew Bible passage which links the experience of captivity with this root. But, this is a tenuous connection.

87. As noted in Silva, "κίνδυνος, κινδυνεύω," *NIDNTTE* 2:682.

88. Ibid.

89. The other occurrences of κίνδυνος in the LXX are: Add Esth 4:17 (12); Tob 4:4; 1 Macc 11:23; 14:29; 2 Macc 1:11; *3 Macc.* 6:26; *4 Macc.* 3:15; 13:15; Wis 18:9; Sir 3:26; 43:24.

90. Psalm 116:3 uses κίνδυνος as the translation for the rare Heb. noun מֵצַר ("distress," cf. Ps 118:5; Lam 1:3). It is noteworthy that Lam 1:3 uses מֵצַר to describe the "distress" of Judah's exile.

91. Wenham, *Leviticus*, 331. My emphasis. Perhaps in the same vein Jesus pronounces seven woes against the Pharisees in Matt 23:13–29. Likewise, in Revelation, the seals (6:1–8:5), trumpets (8:6–11:19), and bowls (15:5–16:21) come in groups of seven.

92. As it stands in parallel with Lev 26.

93. Seifrid, "Romans," 636.

94. Thanks to Dr. Richard B. Gaffin Jr. for this particular formulation.

95. Unless specified otherwise, I will follow English versification throughout this chapter.

96. Jewett, "Impeaching God's Elect," 53–4. Cf. Dietrich-Alex Koch, *Die Schrift als Zeuge des Evangeliums,* BHT 69 (Tübingen: Mohr Siebeck, 1986), 264; Ebner, *Leidenslisten*, 375.

97. Codices Sinaiticus and Alexandrinus have ἕνεκεν whereas Vaticanus has ἕνεκα.

98. Bauer and Danker report that around the third century BC the classical spelling ἕνεκα morphed into ἕνεκεν and this became the dominant spelling in nearly all instances ("ἕνεκα," *BDAG,* BibleWorks 10, s.v.).

99. Cranfield, *Romans,* 1:440.

100. Jewett, "Impeaching God's Elect," 49.

101. Ibid., 37–58. Cf. idem, *Romans,* 548.

102. Ibid., 37.

103. I use the term "Deuteronomic" narrowly, here, to express the rigid belief that obedience leads to blessing and disobedience to curse. Job's so-called friends illustrate the over-simplicity of this position.

104. Ibid., 50. He follows the reconstruction of the Corinthian conflict by Dieter Georgi, *The Opponents of Paul in Second Corinthians: A Study of Religious Propaganda in Late Antiquity* (Philadelphia: Fortress, 1986).

105. Hays, *Echoes of Scripture in the Letters of Paul,* 58.

106. The list is Hays's. My additions are in brackets.

107. Ibid., 62–3.

108. Ibid., 63.

109. Ibid.

110. Stewart, "The Cry of Victory," 25–45.

111. Ibid., 33–44.

112. Ibid., 36.

113. Ibid., 44.

114. Jewett, "Impeaching God's Elect," 53; Stewart, "The Cry of Victory," 32. Cf. Koch, *Die Schrift als Zeuge*, 164; Ebner, *Leidenslisten*, 375.

115. This section follows English versification unless specified otherwise.

116. J. Clinton McCann Jr., "Books I-III and the Editorial Purpose of the Hebrew Psalter," in *The Shape and Shaping of the Psalter*, JSOTSup 159 (Sheffield: JSOT

Press, 1993), 95. Cf. O. Palmer Robertson, *The Flow of the Psalms: Discovering Their Structure and Theology* (Phillipsburg, NJ: P&R, 2015), 86–8.

117. Stewart, "The Cry of Victory," 28n10.

118. Hays, *Echoes of Scripture in the Letters of Paul,* 59.

119. Gert Kwakkel, *According to My Righteousness: Upright Behaviour as Grounds for Deliverance in Psalms 7, 17, 18, 26, and 44*, OtSt 41 (Leiden: Brill, 2002), 201.

120. The minor difference between σφαγή, "slaughter," and βρῶσις, "eating," does not substantially change the meaning.

121. There are several fragments of Ps 44 among the DSS (1QPs[c] frgs. 1-7, 11). 1QPs[c] frg. 5 contains v. 23 (v. 22 EVV).

122. Translation by Bruce M. Metzger, "The Fourth Book of Ezra (Late First Century A. D.)," *OTP* 1. Although 4 Ezra is fictionally set 30 years after the destruction of the first temple in 587 BC, its actual date is likely c. AD 100, 30 years after the Roman destruction of Jerusalem (George W. E. Nickelsburg, *Jewish Literature between the Bible and the Mishnah: A Historical and Literary Introduction* [Minneapolis: Fortress, 1981], 270–1).

123. For example, *Lam. Rab.* 1:16:45, 50.

124. Translation by Judah Slotki, *Midrash Rabbah*, Vol. 2, 3rd ed. (New York: Soncino Press, 1983), 500–1. Emphasis original.

125. Jewett, *Romans,* 545.

126. Käsemann, *Romans,* 249.

127. Moo, *Romans,* 294–5.

# *Chapter 7*

# Conclusion

This study began with two related questions: Would Paul hold to a view of continuing exile and how should "exile" be understood? I have argued that previous discussions regarding the duration of exile, which presume that the *event* of Israel's historical exiles will control the subsequent *idea*, obscure an important aspect of Paul's theology. Paul's view of exile is not a reconstruction of Second Temple theologians, but it is derived from God's covenant, particularly as it is portrayed in Deuteronomy and Leviticus. In other words, the theological idea precedes the event. Death resulting from covenant disobedience should be understood in terms of spiritual and physical separation from God's presence. Just as obedience to God's covenant led to blessing in the land he provided, disobedience resulted in the loss of land and peace with God.

This investigation of Paul's use of the Hebrew Bible in Rom 5 and 8 has revealed a consistent pattern of allusions to Adam and Israel which indicate both the duration of the exile and its theological characterization. While the concentration of allusions is found in Rom 5, 8, they begin with Rom 1:18–32, where man's unrighteousness is framed as a recapitulation of Adam and Israel's idolatry. Likewise, Paul's concluding exhortation that Satan will soon be crushed under believers' feet also alludes to Adam (Rom 16:20). Hence, I argued that references to Adam "bookend" Romans. Hence, it is no surprise to find more allusions to Adam within the body of the letter. The Adam-tradition is clearly employed in Rom 5, 8, where Paul interweaves allusions to Israel's restoration with assurances that Jesus has reversed the curse of Adam. At times the Israel motif rises to prominence (e.g., Paul's depiction of the new exodus in 8:14–17), at others Paul speaks more directly about Adam (e.g., Rom 5:12–21). Yet, I have argued that he is not telling separate stories, but working out his conviction that Jesus is the last Adam (Rom 5:14) and the true Israel. Paul alludes to failed sons to demonstrate Christ the Son's redemption of the children of God.

Romans 5–8 is written in a chiastic structure. Paul introduces themes in Rom 5 which he resumes and expands in Rom 8. I have argued that this ring structure enables an exceptional possibility for confirmation. For example, Paul announces the outpouring of the Spirit upon justified humanity in Rom 5:5, but develops the Spirit's indwelling in Rom 8:1–11. I argued that Paul portrays the coming of the Spirit in Rom 5:5 as the prophesied end of Israel's exile, but admitted that evidence could be stronger. But, when Paul resumes the theme in 8:1–11, he does so with clear allusions to Ezek 36–37 which corroborates Israel's restoration. Yet the entire structure is framed with flesh versus Spirit terminology grounded in Rom 5:12–21 which indicates the reversal of *Adam's* curse. As was previously noted, the dichotomies of flesh versus Spirit and life versus death employed in Romans 5–8 are grounded upon the Adam-Christ typology laid out in Rom 5:12–21. Thus, Rom 5–8 is particularly well suited to study Paul's view of the reversal of the curse. Both at the beginning and end of the section, Paul affirms that justification irreversibly leads to glory (5:1–2; 8:28–30, 31–39).

The implication in Rom 5 that restoration from exile has begun is corroborated by Rom 8:14–17 where Paul uses the image of a new exodus to describe life in the Spirit before glory. It is the fulfillment of Isaiah's promised second exodus that marks the end of Israel's exile, the ingathering of the Gentiles, and a new era of peace. I argued that the leading of the Spirit is the antitype of the *Shekinah* glory-cloud leading Israel in the wilderness. Once again, Yahweh delivered his people from slavery and was leading them toward a land of rest and blessing. However, the slavery in question is not to a human tyrant—the kings of Egypt or Babylon—but to the reign of Sin and Death (cf. 5:14; 8:1–3). They are usurpers of Adam's rule that were put in place by Adam's sin. Thus, this exodus is greater than Israel's because it marks the end of estrangement from God. The inheritance toward which believers journey was previously defined as the "world" (Rom 4:13). I argued that, in the context of Rom 8:18–23, this inheritance is renewed creation, released from the Adamic curse.

I have shown a pattern of allusions to the figures of both Adam and Israel throughout Rom 5, 8 which supports the conclusion that Jesus inaugurated the end of exile. Restoration to God begins in spirit, but will be consummated in body. Thus, believers exist in an already-not yet condition of spiritual restoration to God's presence, but continuing to live outside of their inheritance of the renewed creation before glory. Paul's interweaving of allusions to Israel's restoration and the reverse of Adam's curse indicates this restoration, but the clearest evidence is Paul's quotation of Ps 44:22 in Rom 8:36. As he concludes his presentation of life in the Spirit, Paul boasts that neither justification (8:32–34) nor reconciliation (8:35–6) can be undone. Yet he does so in a qualified way. In Rom 8:35 he asks, "What can separate us from the love of Christ," and offers seven potential "dividers" which we have seen arise from the Deuteronomic descriptions of exile. He then quotes Ps 44:22—which describes the sufferings of the righteous community in exile—as the culminating description of suffering before glory. Paul's point is that the sufferings that precede glory are exilic sufferings. The afflictions will suggest that the believer is separated from God and not loved. But Paul is emphatic that separation from God cannot happen because Christ is raised. Rather, believers experience the conditions of exile because of the incomplete status of their restoration and their exchange of this world for the next, not because of any estrangement from God. Nevertheless, it will sometimes feel like they are. As believers continue to follow the Spirit in faith before the redemption of the body, they will suffer for Christ's sake (Rom 8:36). But unlike the previous redemptive-historical epoch, their exile does not indicate curse, but blessing.[1] For this reason Paul explains:

> καυχώμεθα ἐν ταῖς θλίψεσιν, εἰδότες ὅτι ἡ θλῖψις ὑπομονὴν κατεργάζεται,4 ἡ δὲ ὑπομονὴ δοκιμήν, ἡ δὲ δοκιμὴ ἐλπίδα. 5 ἡ δὲ ἐλπὶς οὐ καταισχύνει, ὅτι ἡ ἀγάπη τοῦ θεοῦ ἐκκέχυται ἐν ταῖς καρδίαις ἡμῶν διὰ πνεύματος ἁγίου τοῦ δοθέντος ἡμῖν. (Rom 5:3–5)

In conclusion, Paul does hold to a theology of continuing exile. Humankind was separated from God due to Adam's transgression in the archetypal exile. God later presented many of the Adamic commands to Abraham in promise form. Abraham's descendants are later treated as a corporate entity and called God's son (Exod 4:22–23). That sonship is the basis of redemption from Egypt. God blessed the people of Israel and made a covenant with them in which he promised to be their God and to give them the promised land if they kept his covenant. But Israel the son failed, just as Adam the son did. Both Adam and Israel were exiled on the basis of the same principle: the blessing of God's presence can only be enjoyed by the righteous. Thus, Paul's theology of exile holds that when Christ died and was raised "for our justification" (διὰ τὴν δικαίωσιν ἡμῶν, Rom 4:25) the true restoration could begin.[2] Jesus, the Son of God, renders the many righteous, begins their restoration, and offers them glory. Before glory, however, God calls his children to suffer with Christ, follow the Spirit, and cry "Abba, Father."

## NOTES

1. Psalm 44 indicates that a righteous remnant experienced exile even prior to Christ. However, this was not the norm that came to be established in the NT.

2. Thus, Paul's transition to address the exile and restoration of ethnic Israel in Rom 9–11 is not nearly so stark as some have thought. It naturally arises from Rom 5–8.

# Bibliography

Abegg, Martin G. "Exile in the Dead Sea Scrolls." Pages 111–25 in *Exile: Old Testament, Jewish, and Christian Conceptions*. Edited by James M. Scott. JSJsup 56. Leiden: Brill, 1997.

Ackroyd, Peter R. *Exile and Restoration: A Study of Hebrew Thought of the Sixth Century B.C.* Philadelphia: Westminster John Knox, 1968.

Adams, Edward. *Constructing the World: A Study in Paul's Cosmological Language*. SNTW. Edinburgh: T&T Clark, 2000.

———. "Paul's Story of God and Creation: The Story of How God Fulfils His Purposes in Creation." Pages 19–43 in *Narrative Dynamics in Paul: A Critical Assessment*. Louisville: Westminster John Knox, 2002.

Allen, David M. *Deuteronomy and Exhortation in Hebrews: A Study in Narrative Re-Presentation*. WUNT 2/238. Tübingen: Mohr Siebeck, 2008.

Anderson, Bernhard W. "Exodus Typology in Second Isaiah." Pages 177–95 in *Israel's Prophetic Heritage: Essays in Honor of James Muilenburg*. New York: Harper & Brothers, 1962.

Anderson, Gary M. "Celibacy or Consummation in the Garden: Reflections on Early Jewish and Christian Interpretations of the Garden of Eden." *HTR* 82 (1989): 121–48.

Balz, Horst Robert. *Heilsvertrauen und Welterfahrung: Strukturen der paulinischen Eschatologie nach Römer 8, 18-39*. BEvT 59. München: Kaiser, 1971.

Balz, Horst Robert, Gerhard Krause, and Gerhard Müller, eds. *Theologische Realenzyklopädie*. 10 vols. Berlin: de Gruyter, 1977.

Barclay, John M. G. *Jews in the Mediterranean Diaspora: From Alexander to Trajan (323 BCE – 117 CE)*. Edinburgh: T&T Clark, 1996.

Barrett, C. K. *A Commentary on the Epistle to the Romans*. New York: Harper & Brothers, 1957.

———. *From First Adam to Last: A Study in Pauline Theology*. New York: Scribner's Sons, 1962.

Bauckham, Richard. *Jude, 2 Peter*. WBC 50. Waco, TX: Word Books, 1983.

———. *God Crucified: Monotheism and Christoloy in the New Testament*. Grand Rapids [etc.: William B. Eerdmans, 1998.

Beale, G. K. "The Old Testament Background of Reconciliation in 2 Corinthians 5-7 and Its Bearing on the Literary Problem of 2 Corinthians 6:14-7:1." *NTS* 35 (1989): 550–81.

———. *The Temple and the Church's Mission: A Biblical Theology of the Dwelling Place of God*. NSBT 17. Leicester, England; Downers Grove, IL: Apollos; Inter-Varsity Press, 2004.

———. *We Become What We Worship: A Biblical Theology of Idolatry*. Downers Grove, IL: IVP Academic, 2008.

———. *A New Testament Biblical Theology: The Unfolding of the Old Testament in the New*. Grand Rapids: Baker Academic, 2011.

———. *Handbook on the New Testament Use of the Old Testament: Exegesis and Interpretation*. Grand Rapids: Baker Academic, 2012.

Beale, G. K., and D. A. Carson, eds. *Commentary on the New Testament Use of the Old Testament*. Grand Rapids; Nottingham, England: Baker Academic; Apollos, 2007.

Beetham, Christopher A. *Echoes of Scripture in the Letter of Paul to the Colossians*. BibInt 96. Leiden: Brill, 2008.

Beker, J. Christiaan. *Paul the Apostle: The Triumph of God in Life and Thought*. Philadelphia: Fortress, 1980.

———. "The Relationship Between Sin and Death in Romans." Pages 55–61 in *Conversation Continues: Studies in Paul & John in Honor of J Louis Martyn*. Nashville: Abingdon Pr, 1990.

Bentzen, Aage. "On the Ideas of 'the Old' and 'the New' in Deutero-Isaiah." *ST* 1 (1947): 183–87.

Bergey, Ronald. "The Song of Moses (Deuteronomy 32.1-43) and Isaianic Prophecies: A Case of Early Intertextuality?" *JSOT* 28 (2003): 33–54.

Berkouwer, G. C. *Man: The Image of God*. Grand Rapids: Eerdmans, 1962.

Berry, Donald L. *Glory in Romans and the Unified Purpose of God in Redemptive History*. Eugene, OR: Pickwick, 2016.

Bertone, John A. "The Function of the Spirit in the Dialectic Between God's Soteriological Plan Enacted But Not Yet Culminated: Romans 8.1-27." *JPT* 7 (1999): 75–97.

Best, Ernest. *The Temptation and the Passion: The Markan Soteriology*. 2nd ed. SNTSMS 2. Cambridge: Cambridge University Press, 1990.

Betz, Hans Dieter. *Der Apostel Paulus Und Die Sokratische Tradition: Eine Exegetische Untersuchung Zu Seiner Apologie 2 Korinther 10-13*. BHT 45. Tübingen: Mohr, 1972.

Betz, Otto. "Die Proselytentaufe Der Qumransekte Und Die Taufe Im Neuen Testament." *Revue de Qumran* 1.2 (1958): 213–34.

———. *Offenbarung und Schriftforschung in der Qumransekte*. WUNT 6. Tübingen: Mohr, 1960.

———. "Fleischliche und 'Geistliche' Christuserkenntnis nach 2. Korinther 5:16." Pages 114–28 in *Jesus, der Herr der Kirche: Aufsätze zur biblischen Theologie II*. Tübingen: Mohr Siebeck, 1990.

Beuken, W. M. "Servant and Herald of Good Tidings: Isaiah 61 as an Interpretation of Isaiah 40-55." Pages 411–42 in *Book of Isaiah-Le Livre d'Isaïe. les oracles et leurs relectures. unité et complexité de l'ouvragee*. Edited by J. Vermeylen. BETL 81. Leuven: Leuven Universit Press, 1989.

Bigg, Charles. *A Critical and Exegetical Commentary on the Epistles of St. Peter and St. Jude*. ICC. Edinburgh: T&T Clark, 1902.

Bird, Michael F. "Jesus and the Continuing Exile of Israel in the Writings of N.T. Wright." *JSHJ* 13 (2015): 209–31.

Black, C. Clifton. "Pauline Perspectives on Death in Romans 5-8." *JBL* 103 (1984): 413–33.

Black, Matthew. *The Scrolls and Christian Origins: Studies in the Jewish Background of the New Testament*. New York: Scribner's Sons, 1961.

Blackwell, Benjamin C. "Immortal Glory and the Problem of Death in Romans 3.23." *JSNT* 32 (2010): 285–308.

Blenkinsopp, Joseph. "The Scope and Depth of the Exodus Tradition in Deutero-Isaiah 40-55." Pages 41–50 in *The Dynamism of Biblical Tradition*. Concilium 20. New York: Paulist Press, 1967.

———. *Ezra-Nehemiah: A Commentary*. OTL. Philadelphia: Westminster Press, 1988.

Block, Daniel I. "Gog and the Pouring out of the Spirit: Reflections on Ezekiel 39:21-29." *VT* 37 (1987): 257–70.

———. *The Gods of the Nations: Studies in Ancient Near Eastern National Theology*. ETSStud 2. Grand Rapids: Baker Academic, 2000.

Bolt, John. "The Relation Between Creation and Redemption in Romans 8:18-27." *Calvin Theological Journal* 30.1 (1995): 34–51.

Botterweck, G. Johannes, and Helmer Ringgren, eds. *Theological Dictionary of the Old Testament*. Translated by John T. Willis, G. W. Bromiley, and David E. Green. 15 vols. Grand Rapids: Eerdmans, 1978.

Bovell, Carlos. "Genesis 3:21: The History of Israel in a Nutshell?" *ExpTim* 115 (2004): 361–66.

Braaten, Laurie J. "The Groaning Creation: The Biblical Background for Romans 8:22." *BR* 50 (2005): 19–39.

Brandenburger, Egon. *Adam und Christus: Exegetisch-religions-geschichtliche Untersuchung zu Röm. 5 12-21 (1.Kor. 15)*. WMANT 7. Neukirchen: Neukirchener Verlag, 1962.

Bray, Gerald Lewis, ed. *Romans*. ACCS 6. Downers Grove, IL: InterVarsity Press, 1998.

Breytenbach, Cilliers. *Versöhnung: Eine Studie zur paulinischen Soteriologie*. WMANT 60. Neukirchen-Vluyn: Neukirchener Verlag, 1989.

Brown, Raymond Edward, Joseph A. Fitzmyer, and Ronald E. Murphy, eds. *The New Jerome Biblical Commentary*. Reissue, Subsequent edition. Englewood Cliffs, NJ: Pearson, 1990.

Bruce, F. F. *Paul: Apostle of the Heart Set Free*. Grand Rapids: Eerdmans, 1977.

Brunson, Andrew C. *Psalm 118 in the Gospel of John: An Intertextual Study on the New Exodus Pattern in the Theology of John*. WUNT 2/158. Tübingen: Mohr Siebeck, 2003.

Bryan, Christopher. *A Preface to Romans: Notes on the Epistle in Its Literary and Cultural Setting*. Oxford: Oxford University Press, 2000.

Bryan, Steven M. *Jesus and Israel's Traditions of Judgement and Restoration*. SNTSMS 117. Cambridge: Cambridge University Press, 2002.

Bultmann, Rudolf K. *Der Stil Der Paulinischen Predigt Und Die Kynisch-Stoische Diatribe*. Gottingen: Vandenhoeck & Ruprecht, 1910.

Byrne, Brendan. *Sons of God, Seed of Abraham: A Study of the Idea of the Sonship of God of All Christians in Paul against the Jewish Background*. AnBib 83. Rome: Biblical Institute, 1979.

———. *Reckoning with Romans: A Contemporary Reading of Paul's Gospel*. GNS 18. Wilmington, DE: Michael Glazier, 1986.

———. *Romans*. SP 6. Collegeville, MN: Liturgical Press, 1996.

Byron, John. *Slavery Metaphors in Early Judaism and Pauline Christianity: A Traditio-Historical and Exegetical Examination*. WUNT 2/162. Tübingen: Mohr Siebeck, 2003.

Byrskog, Samuel. "Christology and Identity in an Intertextual Perspective: The Glory of Adam in the Narrative Substructure of Paul's Letter to the Romans." Pages 1–18 in *Identity Formation in the New Testament*. Tübingen: Mohr Siebeck, 2008.

Calvin, John. *Commentaries on the Epistle of Paul the Apostle to the Romans*. Translated by John Owen. Grand Rapids: Baker, 2003.

———. *Commentaries on the Books of Acts 14-28 and Romans 1-16*. Translated by Henry Beveridge. Vol. 19. 23 vols. 500th Anniversary ed. Calvin's Commentaries. Grand Rapids: Baker, 2009.

Campbell, Douglas A. *The Rhetoric of Righteousness in Romans 3.21-26*. JSNTSup 65. Sheffield: JSOT Press, 1992.

Campbell, J. G. "Essene-Qumran Origins in the Exile: A Scriptural Basis?" *JJS* 46 (1995): 143–56.

Carrez, Maurice. *De La Souffrance à La Gloire: De La Δοξα Dans La Pensée Paulinienne*. Bibliothèque Théologique. Neuchatel, Switzerland: Delachaux & Niestle, 1964.

Carson, D. A. "Summaries and Conclusions." Pages 505–48 in *The Complexities of Second Temple Judaism*. Edited by D. A. Carson, Peter T. O'Brien, and Mark A. Seifrid. Vol. 1 of *Justification and Variegated Nomism*. Edited by D. A. Carson, Peter T. O'Brien, and Mark A. Seifrid. Tübingen: Mohr Siebeck; Grand Rapids: Baker Academic, 2001.

Carroll, Robert P. "Exile! What Exile? Deportation and the Discourses of Diaspora." Pages 62–79 in *Leading Captivity Captive: "The Exile" as History and Ideology*. Edited by Lester L. Grabbe. JSOTsup 278. Sheffield: Sheffield Academic, 1998.

Casey, Maurice. "Where Wright Is Wrong: A Critical Review of N.T. Wright's Jesus and the Victory of God." *JSNT* 69 (1998): 95–103.

Ceresko, Anthony R. "The Rhetorical Strategy of the Fourth Servant Song (Isaiah 52:13-53:12): Poetry and the Exodus-New Exodus." *CBQ* 56 (1994): 42–55.

Chantraine, Pierre. *Dictionnaire étymologique de la langue Grecque: Histoire des Mots*. 4 vols. Paris: Klincksieck, 1968.

Charles, Robert Henry. *The Book of Jubilees, or the Little Genesis*. London: SPCK, 1917.

Charlesworth, James H., ed. *The Old Testament Pseudepigrapha*. 2 vols. Hendrickson, 2010.

Christensen, Duane L. *Deuteronomy. 21:10-34:12*. WBC 6b. Nashville: Thomas Nelson, 2002.

Christoffersson, Olle. *The Earnest Expectation of the Creature: The Flood-Tradition as Matrix of Romans 8:18-27*. ConBNT 23. Stockholm: Almqvist & Wiksell, 1990.

Ciampa, Roy. "Genesis 1-3 and Paul's Theology of Adam's Dominion in Romans 5-6." Pages 103–22 in *From Creation to New Creation: Biblical Theology and Exegesis*. Peabody, MA: Hendrickson, 2013.

Cipriani, Settimio. "ΚΤΙΣΙΣ: Creazione O Genere Umano?" *RB* 44 (1996): 337–40.

Clarke, Thomas E. "St. Augustine and Cosmic Redemption." *TS* 19 (1958): 133–64.

Clements, Ronald E. "The Unity of the Book of Isaiah." *Int* 36 (1982): 117–29.

Clifford, Richard J. "Isaiah 40-66." *HBC*. Edited by James Luther Mays. San Francisco: Harper & Row, 1988.

Clines, D. J. A. "The Image of God in Man." *TynBul* 19 (1968): 53–103.

Collins, John J. "Interpretations of the Creation of Humanity in the Dead Sea Scrolls." Pages 29–43 in *Biblical Interpretation at Qumran*. Edited by Matthias Henze. StDSSRL. Grand Rapids: Eerdmans, 2005.

Constantineanu, Corneliu. *The Social Significance of Reconciliation in Paul's Theology: Narrative Readings in Romans*. LNTS 421. London; New York: T&T Clark, 2010.

Conzelmann, Hans. *1 Corinthians: A Commentary on the First Epistle to the Corinthians*. Hermeneia. Philadelphia: Fortress, 1975.

Cranfield, C. E. B. *A Critical and Exegetical Commentary on the Epistle to the Romans*. 2 vols. ICC. Edinburgh: T&T Clark, 1975.

Crouser, Wesley. "Satan, the Serpent, and Witchcraft Accusations: Reading Romans 16:17-20a in Light of Allusions and Anthropology." *JSPL* 4 (2014): 215–33.

Crowe, Brandon D. *The Obedient Son: Deuteronomy and Christology in the Gospel of Matthew*. BZNW 188. Berlin: De Gruyter, 2012.

———. *The Last Adam: A Theology of the Obedient Life of Jesus in the Gospels*. Grand Rapids: Baker Academic, 2017.

Cullmann, Oscar. *The Christology of the New Testament*. Translated by Shirley C. Guthrie and Charles A. M. Hall. Philadephia: Westminster Press, 1963.

Dahl, Nils Alstrup. "Two Notes on Romans 5." *ST* 5 (1952): 37–48.

Daly, Robert J. "Soteriological Significance of the Sacrifice of Isaac." *CBQ* 39 (1977): 45–75.

Davenport, Gene L. *The Eschatology of the Book of Jubilees*. StPB 20. Leiden: Brill, 1971.

Davids, Peter H. *The First Epistle of Peter*. NICNT. Grand Rapids: Eerdmans, 1990.

Davies, Philip R. *The Damascus Covenant: An Interpretation of the "Damascus Document."* JSOTsup 25. Sheffield: JSOT Press, 1983.

———. "The Birthplace of the Essenes: Where Is 'Damascus'?" *RevQ* 14 (1990): 503–19.

Davies, W. D. *Paul and Rabbinic Judaism: Some Rabbinic Elements in Pauline Theology*. 4th ed. Philadelphia: Fortress, 1980.

de Boer, Martinus. *The Defeat of Death: Apocalyptic Eschatology in 1 Corinthians 15 and Romans 5*. JSNTSup 22. Sheffield: JSOT Press, 1988.

Dempster, Stephen G. *Dominion and Dynasty: A Biblical Theology of the Hebrew Bible*. NSBT 15. Leicester, England: Apollos; Downers Grove, IL: InterVarsity Press, 2003.

Dennis, John A. *Jesus' Death and the Gathering of True Israel: The Johannine Appropriation of Restoration Theology in the Light of John 11:47-52*. WUNT 2/217. Tübingen: Mohr Siebeck, 2006.

Denton, David R. "Ἀποκαραδοκία." *ZNW* 73 (1982): 138–40.

Di Lella, Alexander A. "The Deuteronomic Background of the Farewell Discourse in Tob 14:3–11." *CBQ* 41.3 (1979): 380–89.

Dillon, Richard J. "The Spirit as Taskmaster and Troublemaker in Romans 8." *CBQ* 60 (1998): 682–702.

Dittmann, Wilhelm. *Die Auslegung der Urgeschichte (Genesis 1-3) im Neuen Testament*. Göttingen: Vandenhoeck & Ruprecht, 1953.

Dochhorn, Jan. "Paulus und die polyglotte Schriftgelehrsamkeit seiner Zeit: Eine Studie zu den exegetischen Hintergründen von Röm 16,20a." *ZNW* 98 (2007): 189–212.

Dodd, C. H. *The Epistle of Paul to the Romans*. MNTC. New York: Harper & Brothers, 1932.

Doran, Robert. *2 Maccabees: A Critical Commentary*. Hermeneia. Minneapolis: Fortress, 2012.

Dubis, Mark. *1 Peter: A Handbook on the Greek Text*. Waco, TX: Baylor University Press, 2010.

Dumbrell, William J. "Genesis 2:1–17: A Foreshadowing of the New Creation." In *Biblical Theology: Retrospect and Prospect*. Edited by Scott J. Hafemann. Downers Grove, IL: InterVarsity Press, 2002.

Dunn, James D. G. *Romans 1–8*. WBC 38A. Dallas, TX: Word Books, 1988.

———. *Romans 9-16*. WBC 38B. Dallas, TX: Word Books, 1988.

———. *Christology in the Making: A New Testament Inquiry into the Origins of the Doctrine of the Incarnation*. 2nd ed. Grand Rapids: Eerdmans, 1996.

———, ed. *Paul and the Mosaic Law: The Third Durham-Tübingen Research Symposium on Earliest Christianity and Judaism, Durham, September, 1994*. WUNT 89. Tübingen: Mohr Siebeck, 1996.

———. *The Theology of Paul the Apostle*. Grand Rapids: Eerdmans, 1998.

———. *Jesus Remembered*. Grand Rapids: Eerdmans, 2003.

Dunning, Benjamin. "The Intersection of Alien Status and Cultic Discourse in the Epistle to the Hebrews." Pages 179–98 in *Hebrews: Contemporary Methods—New Insights*. Edited by G. Gelardini. Leiden: Brill, 2005.

Ebner, Martin. *Leidenslisten und Apostelbrief: Untersuchungen zu Form, Motivik und Funktion der Peristasenkataloge bei Paulus*. FZB 66. Würzburg: Echter Verlag, 1991.

Elliott, Mark Adam. *The Survivors of Israel: A Reconsideration of the Theology of Pre-Christian Judaism*. Grand Rapids: Eerdmans, 2000.

Elliott, Neil. *The Rhetoric of Romans: Argumentative Constraint and Strategy and Paul's Dialogue with Judaism.* JSNTSup 45. Sheffield, England: JSOT Press, 1990.

Enderlein, Steven E. "To Fall Short or Lack the Glory of God?: The Translation and Implications of Romans 3:23." *JSPL* 1 (2011): 213–23.

———. "The Faithfulness of the Second Adam in Romans 3:21-26: A Response to Porter and Cirafesi." *JSPL* 3 (2013): 11–24.

Eskola, Timo. *A Narrative Theology of the New Testament: Exploring the Metanarrative of Exile and Restoration.* WUNT 350. Tübingen: Mohr Siebeck, 2015.

Fee, Gordon D. *Pauline Christology: An Exegetical-Theological Study.* Peabody, MA: Hendrickson, 2007.

Feldman, Louis H. "The Concept of Exile in Josephus." Pages 145–72 in *Exile: Old Testament, Jewish, and Christian Conceptions.* Edited by James M. Scott. JSJsup 56. Leiden: Brill, 1997.

Feuillet, A. "Le règne de la mort et le règne de la vie." *RB* 77 (1970): 481–521.

Fishbane, Michael. *Biblical Interpretation in Ancient Israel.* Oxford: Clarendon Press, 1988.

———. *Biblical Text and Texture: A Literary Reading of Selected Texts.* Oxford: Oneworld, 1998.

Fitzgerald, John T. *Cracks in an Earthen Vessel: An Examination of the Catalogues of Hardships in the Corinthian Correspondence.* SBLDS 99. Atlanta: Scholars Press, 1988.

Fitzmyer, Joseph A. *Romans: A New Translation with Introduction and Commentary.* AB 33. New York: Doubleday, 1993.

———. "The Consecutive Meaning of ἐφ' ᾧ in Romans 5:12." *NTS* 39 (1993): 321–39.

Fletcher-Louis, Crispin H. T. *All the Glory of Adam: Liturgical Anthropology in the Dead Sea Scrolls.* STDJ 42. Leiden: Brill, 2002.

Fuller, Michael E. *The Restoration of Israel: Israel's Re-Gathering and the Fate of the Nations in Early Jewish Literature and Luke-Acts.* BZNW 138. Berlin: De Gruyter, 2006.

Furnish, Victor Paul. "Elect Sojourners in Christ: An Approach to the Theology of 1 Pewter." *PSTJ* 28 (1975): 1–11.

Gaffin, Richard B., Jr. "The Obedience of Faith: Some Reflections on the Rationale for Romans." Pages 71–85 in *Israel and the Church: Essays in Honour of Allan Macdonald Harman on His 65th Birthday and Retirement.* Edited by Allan M. Harman and Douglas J. W. Milne. Melbourne, Victoria: Theological Education Committee, Presbyterian Church of Victoria, 2001.

———. *"By Faith, Not by Sight": Paul and the Order of Salvation.* Bletchley, Bucks, [U.K.]; Waynesboro, GA: Paternoster, 2006.

Gager, John G. "Functional Diversity in Paul's Use of End-Time Language." *JBL* 89 (1970): 325–37.

García Martínez, Florentino, and Eibert J. C. Tigchelaar, eds. *The Dead Sea Scrolls Study Edition.* 2 vols. Leiden: Brill, 1997.

Garlington, Don B. *Faith, Obedience, and Perseverance: Aspects of Paul's Letter to the Romans*. WUNT 79. Tübingen: Mohr Siebeck, 1994.

———. *The Obedience of Faith: A Pauline Phrase in Historical Context*. WUNT 2/38. Eugene: Wipf & Stock Pub, 2009.

Garner, David B. *Sons in the Son: The Riches and Reach of Adoption in Christ*. Phillipsburg: P&R, 2016.

Gathercole, Simon J. *Where Is Boasting?: Early Jewish Soteriology and Paul's Response in Romans 1-5*. Grand Rapids: Eerdmans, 2002.

Gaventa, Beverly Roberts. *Our Mother Saint Paul*. Louisville: Westminster John Knox Press, 2007.

Geldenhuys, Norval. *Commentary on the Gospel of Luke*. NICNT. Grand Rapids: Eerdmans, 1951.

Gempf, Conrad H. "The Imagery of Birth Pangs in the New Testament." *TynBul* 45 (1994): 119–35.

Georgi, Dieter. *The Opponents of Paul in Second Corinthians: A Study of Religious Propaganda in Late Antiquity*. Philadelphia: Fortress, 1986.

Gibbs, John G. *Creation and Redemption: A Study in Pauline Theology*. NovTSup 26. Leiden: Brill, 1971.

———. "Pauline Cosmic Christology and Ecological Crisis." *JBL* 90 (1971): 466–79.

Gignilliat, Mark. "A Servant Follower of the Servant: Paul's Eschatological Reading of Isaiah 40-66 in 2 Corinthians 5:14-6:10." *HBT* 26 (2004): 98–124.

———. *Paul and Isaiah's Servants Paul's Theological Reading of Isaiah 40-66 in 2 Corinthians 5:14-6:10*. LNTS 330. London: T&T Clark, 2007.

Gieniusz, Andrzej. *Romans 8:18–30: "Suffering Does Not Thwart the Future Glory."* Atlanta: Scholars Press, 1999.

Giglioli, Alberto. *L'uomo o il creato?* Κτίσις *in s. Paolo*. StBib 21. Bologna: DHB, 1994.

Gile, Daniel. "Ezekiel 16 and the Song of Moses: A Prophetic Transformation?" *JBL* 130 (2011): 87–108.

Gile, Jason. "Deuteronomy and Ezekiel's Theology of Exile." Pages 287–306 in *For Our Good Always: Studies on the Message and Influence of Deuteronomy in Honor of Daniel I. Block*. Winona Lake, IN: Eisenbrauns, 2013.

Ginzberg, Louis. *The Legends of the Jews*. Translated by Henrietta Szold. 7 vols. 2nd ed. Philadelphia: The Jewish Publication Society of America, 1909.

Gladd, Benjamin L. "The Last Adam as the 'Life-Giving Spirit' Revisited: A Possible Old Testament Background of One of Paul's Most Perplexing Phrases." *WTJ* 71 (2009): 297–309.

Godet, Frédéric. *Commentary on the Epistle to the Romans*. Translated by A. Cusin and Talbot W. Chambers. Grand Rapids: Zondervan, 1969.

Goldstein, Jonathan A. *I Maccabees: A New Translation, with Introduction and Commentary*. AB 41. Garden City, NY: Doubleday, 1976.

———. *II Maccabees*. AB 41A. Garden City, NY: Doubleday, 1983.

Gosse, Bernard. "L'année de grâce du Seigneur selon Is 61,1-2a et sa citation en Lc 4,18-19." *Science et Esprit* 69 (2017): 91–106.

Grappe, Christian. “Qui me délivrera de ce corps de mort?: L’esprit de vie! Romains 7,24 et 8,2 comme éléments de typologie Adamique.” *Bib* 83 (2002): 472–92.

Green, Joel B. *The Gospel of Luke*. NICNT. Grand Rapids: Eerdmans, 1997.

Green, Joel B., and Lee Martin McDonald, eds. *The World of the New Testament: Cultural, Social, and Historical Contexts*. Grand Rapids: Baker Academic, 2013.

Gubler, Marie-Louise. *Die frühesten Deutungen des Todes Jesu: eine motivgeschichtliche Darstellung aufgrund der neueren exegetischen Forschung*. Vandenhoeck & Ruprecht, 1977.

Gunkel, Hermann. *Schöpfung und Chaos in Urzeit und Endzeit: Eine religionsgeschichtliche Untersuchung über Gen 1 und Ap Joh 12*. Göttingen: Vandenhoeck & Ruprecht, 1895.

Hahne, Harry Alan. *The Corruption and Redemption of Creation: Nature in Romans 8:19-22 and Jewish Apocalyptic Literature*. LNTS 336. London: T&T Clark, 2006.

Hahn, Scott, and John S. Bergsma. “What Laws Were ‘Not Good’?: A Canonical Approach to the Theological Problem of Ezekiel 20:25-26.” *JBL* 123 (2004): 201–18.

Halpern-Amaru, Betsy. *Rewriting the Bible: Land and Covenant in Post-Biblical Jewish Literature*. Valley Forge, PA: Trinity Press International, 1994.

Halvorson-Taylor, Martien A. *Enduring Exile: The Metaphorization of Exile in the Hebrew Bible*. VTSup 141. Leiden: Brill, 2011.

Hamerton-Kelly, Robert G. “Sacred Violence and Sinful Desire: Paul’s Interpretation of Adam’s Sin in the Letter to the Romans.” Pages 35–54 in *Conversation Continues: Studies in Paul and John in Honor of J. Louis Martyn*. Nashville: Abingdon, 1990.

Hamilton, James. “The Skull Crushing Seed of the Woman: Inner-Biblical Interpretation of Genesis 3:15.” *SBTJ* 10 (2006): 30–54.

Harris, Murray J. *Prepositions and Theology in the Greek New Testament: An Essential Reference Resource for Exegesis*. Grand Rapids: Zondervan, 2012.

Harvey, John D. *Romans*. EGGNT. Nashville, TN: B&H Academic, 2017.

Hatch, Edwin, and Henry A. Redpath. *A Concordance to the Septuagint and the Other Greek Versions of the Old Testament: (Including the Apocryphal Books)*. 2nd ed. Grand Rapids: Baker Book House, 1998.

Hawthorne, Gerald F., Ralph P. Martin, and Daniel G. Reid, eds. *Dictionary of Paul and His Letters: A Compendium of Contemporary Biblical Scholarship*. Downers Grove, IL: InterVarsity, 1993.

Hays, Richard B. *Echoes of Scripture in the Letters of Paul*. New Haven: Yale University Press, 1989.

———. *The Conversion of the Imagination: Paul as Interpreter of Israel’s Scripture*. Grand Rapids: Eerdmans, 2005.

———. “‘Who Has Believed Our Message?’ Paul’s Reading of Isaiah.” Page 1:205-225 in *Society of Biblical Literature 1998 Seminar Papers*. 2 vols. SBLSP 37. Atlanta: Society of Biblical Literature, 1998.

Head, Peter M. “The Curse of Covenant Reversal: Deuteronomy 28:58-68 and Israel’s Exile.” *Churchman* 111 (1997): 218–26.

Helyer, Larry R. “Luke and the Restoration of Israel.” *JETS* 36.3 (1993): 317–29.

Herold, Gerhart. *Zorn und Gerechtigkeit Gottes bei Paulus: Eine Untersuchung zu Röm. 1, 16-18*. EH 14. Bern: Peter Lang, 1973.

Hiebert, Robert J. V. "Exile and Restoration Terminology in the Septuagint and New Testament." Pages 93–118 in *Exile: A Conversation with N. T. Wright*. Edited by James M. Scott. Downers Grove, IL: IVP Academic, 2017.

Hill, Edmund. "Construction of Three Passages from St Paul." *CBQ* 23 (1961): 296–301.

Hodgson, Robert. "Paul the Apostle and First Century Tribulation Lists." *ZNW* 74 (1983): 59–80.

Hofius, Otfried. "Erwägungen zur Gestalt und Herkunft des paulinischen Versöhnungsgedankens." *ZTK* 77 (1980): 186–99.

———. "Die Adam-Christus-Antithese und das Gesetz: Erwägungen zu Röm 5,12-21." Pages 165–206 in *Paul and the Mosaic Law: The Third Durham-Tübingen Research Symposium on Earliest Christianity and Judaism, Durham, September, 1994*. Tubingen: Mohr Siebeck, 1996.

Hooker, Morna D. "Adam in Romans 1." *NTS* 6 (1960): 297–306.

———. "Further Note on Romans 1." *NTS* 13 (1967): 181–83.

———. "*Adam Redivivus*: Philippians 2 Once More." Pages 220–24 in *The Old Testament in the New Testament: Essays in Honour of J. L. North*. Edited by Steve Moyise and J. L. North. JSNTSup 189. Sheffield: Sheffield Academic, 2000.

Hübner, Hans. *Die Theologie des Paulus und ihre neutestamentliche Wirkungsgeschichte*. 2 vols. Göttingen: Vandenhoeck & Ruprecht, 1990.

Hugenberger, G.P. "The Servant of the Lord in the 'Servant Songs' of Isaiah: A Second Moses Figure." Pages 105–40 in *The Lord's Anointed: Interpretation of Old Testament Messianic Texts*. Edited by P. E. Satterthwaite, R. S. Hess, and G. J. Wenham. TynHS. Grand Rapids: Baker, 1995.

Huizenga, Leroy. *The New Isaac: Tradition and Intertextuality in the Gospel of Matthew*. NovTSup 131. Leiden: Brill, 2009.

Hultgren, Arland J. *Paul's Letter to the Romans: A Commentary*. Grand Rapids: Eerdmans, 2011.

Hultgren, Stephen J. "The Origin of Paul's Doctrine of the Two Adams in 1 Corinthians 15.45-49." *JSNT* 25 (2003): 343–70.

Hurtado, Larry W. "Jesus' Divine Sonship in Paul's Epistle to the Romans." Pages 217–33 in *Romans and the People of God: Essays in Honor of Gordon D. Fee on the Occasion of His 65th Birthday*. Grand Rapids: Eerdmans, 1999.

Hyldahl, Niels. "Reminiscence of the Old Testament at Romans 1:23." *NTS* (1956): 285–88.

Jervell, Jacob. *Imago Dei: Gen 1, 26f. im Spätjudentum, in der Gnosis und in den paulinischen Briefen*. FRLANT 76. Göttingen: Vandenhoeck & Ruprecht, 1960.

Jewett, Robert. "Impeaching God's Elect: Romans 8.33-37 in Its Rhetorical Situation." Pages 37–58 in *Paul, Luke and the Graeco-Roman World: Essays in Honour of Alexander J.M. Wedderburn*. LNTS 217. Sheffield: Sheffield Academic, 2002.

Jewett, Robert, and Roy David Kotansky. *Romans: A Commentary*. Hermeneia. Minneapolis: Fortress, 2007.

Käsemann, Ernst. *Commentary on Romans*. Translated by G. W. Bromiley. Grand Rapids: Eerdmans, 1980.

———. *The Wandering People of God: An Investigation of the Letter to the Hebrews*. Translated by R. A. Harrisville and I. L. Sundberg. Minneapolis: Augsburg, 1984.

Keener, Craig S. *Romans: A New Covenant Commentary*. NCCS 6. Eugene, OR: Cascade, 2009.

Keesmaat, Sylvia C. "Exodus and the Intertextual Transformation of Tradition in Romans 8:14-30." *JSNT* 54 (1994): 29–56.

———. *Paul and His Story: (Re)-Interpreting the Exodus Tradition*. JSNTSup 181. Sheffield: Sheffield Academic, 1999.

Keiser, Thomas A. "The Song of Moses a Basis for Isaiah's Prophecy." *VT* 55 (2005): 486–500.

Kidner, Derek. *Genesis: An Introduction and Commentary*. TOTC 1. Chicago: InterVarsity Press, 1967.

Kidwell, Brian. "The Adamic Backdrop of Romans." *CTR* 11 (2013): 103–20.

Kiefer, Jörn. *Exil und Diaspora: Begrifflichkeit und Deutungen im antiken Judentum und in der hebräischen Bibel*. ABG 19. Leipzig: Evangelische Verlagsanstalt, 2005.

Kim, Seyoon. *The Origin of Paul's Gospel*. WUNT 2/4. Tübingen: Mohr Siebeck, 1984.

Kirk, J. R. Daniel. *Unlocking Romans: Resurrection and the Justification of God*. Grand Rapids: Eerdmans, 2008.

Kittel, Gerhard, ed. *Theological Dictionary of the New Testament*. Translated by G. W. Bromiley. 10 vols. Grand Rapids: Eerdmans, 1964.

Knibb, Michael A. "Exile in the Literature of the Intertestamental Period." *HeyJ* 17 (1976): 253–72.

Klauck, Hans-Josef. *Vorspiel im Himmel?: Erzähltechnik und Theologie im Markusprolog*. BibTS 32. Neukirchen-Vluyn: Neukirchener, 1997.

Kline, Meredith G. *Images of the Spirit*. Eugene, OR: Wipf & Stock, 1980.

———. *Kingdom Prologue: Genesis Foundations for a Covenantal Worldview*. Eugene, OR: Wipf & Stock, 2000.

Koch, Dietrich-Alex. *Die Schrift als Zeuge des Evangeliums: Untersuchungen zur Verwendung und zum Verständnis der Schrift bei Paulus*. BHT 69. Tübingen: Mohr Siebeck, 1986.

Kreitzer, L. Joseph. "Christ and Second Adam in Paul." *CV* 32 (1989): 55–101.

Kwakkel, Gert. *According to My Righteousness: Upright Behaviour as Grounds for Deliverance in Psalms 7, 17, 18, 26, and 44*. OtSt 41. Leiden: Brill, 2002.

Lagrange, M. J. *Saint Paul: Épitre aux Romains*. Paris: Gabalda, 1950.

Lawson, J Mark. "Romans 8:18-25--The Hope of Creation." *RevExp* 91.4 (1994): 559–65.

Leaney, A. R. C., ed. *The Rule of Qumran and Its Meaning: Introduction Translation, and Commentary*. NTL. Philadelphia: Westminster Press, 1966.

Lee, Yongbom. *The Son of Man as the Last Adam: The Early Church Tradition as a Source of Paul's Adam Christology*. Eugene, OR: Pickwick, 2012.

Leithart, Peter. "Adam, Moses, and Jesus: A Reading of Romans 5:12-14." *CTJ* 43 (2008): 257–73.

Lénart, J. De Regt. "Language, Structure, and Strategy in Isaiah 53:1-6: אָכֵן, Word Order, and the Translator." Pages 417–36 in *Tradition and Innovation in Biblical Interpretation: Studies Presented to Professor Eep Talstra on the Occasion of His Sixty-Fifth Birthday*. Edited by E. Talstra, W. Th van Peursen, and J. W. Dyk. Leiden: Brill, 2011.

Leslie, Allen C. "The Old Testament in Romans I-VIII." *VE* 3 (1964): 6–41.

———. *Psalms 101-150*. WBC 21. Waco, TX: Word Books, 1983.

———. "Structure, Tradition, and Redaction in Ezekiel's Death Valley Vision." Pages 127–42 in *Among the Prophets: Language, Image, and Structure in the Prophetic Writings*. Edited by Philip R. Davies and David J. A. Clines. JSOTSup 144. Sheffield: Sheffield Academic, 1993.

Levison, John R. "Is Eve to Blame? A Contextual Analysis of Sirach 25:24." *CBQ* 47 (1985): 617–23.

———. *Portraits of Adam in Early Judaism: From Sirach to 2 Baruch*. JSPSup 1. Sheffield: Sheffield Academic, 1988.

Levitt Kohn, Risa. *A New Heart and a New Soul: Ezekiel, the Exile and the Torah*. JSOTSup 358. London: Sheffield Academic, 2002.

Lim, Timothy H. *The Formation of the Jewish Canon*. New Haven: Yale University Press, 2013.

———. "Qumran Scholarship and the Study of the Old Testament in the New Testament." *JSNT* 38 (2015): 68–80.

Linebaugh, Jonathan A. "Announcing the Human: Rethinking the Relationship between Wisdom of Solomon 13-15 and Romans 1.18-2.11." *NTS* 57 (2011): 214–37.

Litwa, Matthew David. "Behold Adam: A Reading of John 19:5." *HBT* 32 (2010): 129–43.

Longenecker, Richard N. *Introducing Romans: Critical Issues in Paul's Most Famous Letter*. Grand Rapids: Eerdmans, 2011.

———. *The Epistle to the Romans*. NIGTC. Grand Rapids: Eerdmans, 2016.

Lucas, Alec J. *Evocations of the Calf?: Romans 1:18–2:11 and the Substructure of Psalm 106 (105)*. BZNW 201. Berlin: De Gruyter, 2015.

Lührmann, Dieter. *Das Markusevangelium*. HNT 3. Tübingen: Mohr Siebeck, 1987.

Lust, J. "The Final Text and Textual Criticism: Ez 39,28." Pages 48–54 in *Ezekiel and His Book: Textual and Literary Criticism and Their Interrelation*. Leuven: Uitgeverij Peeters, 1986.

Luz, Ulrich. "Zum Aufbau von Röm 1–8." *TZ* 25 (1969): 161–81.

Lyons, Michael A. *From Law to Prophecy: Ezekiel's Use of the Holiness Code*. LHBOTS 507. New York: T&T Clark, 2009.

Malina, B. J. "Some Observations on the Origin of Sin in Judaism and St Paul." *CBQ* 31 (1969): 18–34.

Marcus, Joel. "Son of Man as Son of Adam." *RB* 110 (2003): 38–61.

———. "Son of Man as Son of Adam: Part II: Exegesis." *RB* 110 (2003): 370–86.

Marsh, Clive. "Theological History? N. T. Wright's Jesus and the Victory of God." *JSNT* 69 (1998): 77–94.

Marshall, I. Howard. "The Meaning of 'Reconciliation.'" Pages 117–32 in *Unity and Diversity in New Testament Theology: Essays in Honor of George E. Ladd*. Grand Rapids: Eerdmans, 1978.

Martin, Oren R. *Bound for the Promised Land: The Land Promise in God's Redemptive Plan*. NSBT 34. Downers Grove, IL: InterVarsity Press, 2015.

Martin, Ralph P. *Reconciliation: A Study of Paul's Theology*. Grand Rapids: Zondervan, 1989.

Mason, Steve. "N. T. Wright on Paul the Pharisee and Ancient Jews in Exile." *SJT* 69 (2016): 432–52.

Matera, Frank J. *Romans*. Paideia. Grand Rapids: Baker Academic, 2010.

May, David M. "The Straightened Woman (Luke 13:10-17): Paradise Lost and Regained." *PRst* 24 (1997): 245–58.

McCann Jr., J. Clinton. "Books I-III and the Editorial Purpose of the Hebrew Psalter." Pages 93–107 in *The Shape and Shaping of the Psalter*. JSOTSup 159, 1993.

McCartney, Dan G. "Ecce Homo: The Coming of the Kingdom as the Restoration of Human Vicegerency." *WTJ* 56 (1994): 1–21.

Mccomiskey, Douglas S. "Exile and the Purpose of Jesus' Parables (Mark 4:10-12; Matt 13:10-17; Luke 8:9-10)." *JETS* 51 (2008): 59–85.

McConville, J. G. "Ezra-Nehemiah and the Fulfillment of Prophecy." *VT* 36 (1986): 205–24.

———. *Grace in the End: A Study of Deuteronomic Theology*. Grand Rapids: Zondervan, 1993.

McDonald, Patricia. "Romans 5:1–11 as a Rhetorical Bridge." *JSNT* 40 (1990): 81–96.

Mendenhall, George E. "Covenant Forms in Israelite Tradition." *BA* 17 (1954): 50–76.

———. *Law and Covenant in Israel and the Ancient Near East*. Pittsburgh: Biblical Colloquium, 1955.

Meyer, Nicholas A. *Adam's Dust and Adam's Glory in the Hodayot and the Letters of Paul: Rethinking Anthropogony and Theology*. NovTSup 168. Leiden: Brill, 2016.

Michaels, J. Ramsey. *1 Peter*. WBC 49. Waco, TX: Word Books, 2015.

Michel, Otto. *Der Brief an Die Römer*. EKKNT 4. Göttingen: Vandenhoeck & Ruprecht, 1978.

Milne, Douglas J. W. "Genesis 3 in the Letter to the Romans." *RTR* 39 (1980): 10–18.

Moo, Douglas J. *The Epistle to the Romans*. NICNT. Grand Rapids: Eerdmans, 1996.

———. "Israel and the Law in Romans 5–11: Interaction with the New Perspective." Pages 185–216 in *The Paradoxes of Paul*. Edited by D. A. Carson, Peter T. O'Brien, and Mark A. Seifrid. Vol. 2 of *Justification and Variegated Nomism*. Edited by D. A. Carson, Peter T. O'Brien, and Mark A. Seifrid. Tübingen: Mohr Siebeck; Grand Rapids: Baker Academic, 2001.

Moo, Jonathan. "Romans 8.19–22 and Isaiah's Cosmic Covenant." *NTS* 54 (2008): 74–89.

Moore, Carey A. *Tobit: A New Translation with Introduction and Commentary*. AB 40A. New York: Doubleday, 1996.

Morris, Leon. *The Apostolic Preaching of the Cross*. Grand Rapids: Eerdmans, 1955.

Morris, Paul. "Exiled from Eden: Jewish Interpretations of Genesis." Pages 117–68 in *A Walk in the Garden: Biblical, Iconographical and Literary Images of Eden*. Edited by Paul Morris and Deborah Sawyer. JSOTSup 136. Sheffield: JSOT Press, 1992.

Moyise, Steve. "The Catena of Romans 3:10-18." *ExpTim* 106 (1995): 367–70.

———. "Intertextuality and the Study of the Old Testament in the New Testament." *The Old Testament in the New Testament: Essays in Honour of J. L. North*. Edited by Steve Moyise. JSNTSup 189. Sheffield: Sheffield Academic, 2000.

Münderlein, Gerhard. "Interpretation einer Tradition, Bemerkungen zu Röm 8:35f." *KD* 11 (1965): 136–42.

Murray, John. *The Epistle to the Romans: The English Text with Introduction, Exposition, and Notes*. NICNT. Grand Rapids: Eerdmans, 1959.

———. *The Imputation of Adam's Sin*. Grand Rapids: Eerdmans, 1959.

Nanos, Mark D. *The Mystery of Romans: The Jewish Context of Paul's Letter*. Minneapolis: Fortress, 1996.

Newman, Carey C. *Paul's Glory-Christology: Tradition and Rhetoric*. NovTSup 69. Leiden: Brill, 1992.

Newman, Carey C., and Craig A. Evans, eds. *Jesus and the Restoration of Israel: A Critical Assessment of N.T. Wright's Jesus and the Victory of God*. Downers Grove, IL: InterVarsity Press, 1999.

Neusner, Jacob. *Self-Fulfilling Prophecy: Exile and Return in the History of Judaism*. SFSHJ 2. Atlanta: Scholars Press, 1990.

Nickelsburg, George W. E. *Jewish Literature between the Bible and the Mishnah: A Historical and Literary Introduction*. Minneapolis: Fortress, 1981.

———. *1 Enoch: A Commentary on the Book of 1 Enoch*. Hermeneia. Minneapolis: Fortress, 2001.

Noth, Martin. *A History of Pentateuchal Traditions*. Translated by Bernard W. Anderson. Englewood Cliffs, NJ: Prentice-Hall, 1971.

Nygren, Anders. *Commentary on Romans*. Translated by Carl C. Rasmussen. Minneapolis: Fortress, 1983.

O'Brien, Peter T. "Romans 8:26, 27: A Revolutionary Approach to Prayer?" *RTR* 46 (1987): 65–73.

Ollenburger, Ben C. "Isaiah's Creation Theology." *ExAud* 3 (1987): 54–71.

Olson, Robert C. *The Gospel as the Revelation of God's Righteousness: Paul's Use of Isaiah in Romans 1:1-3:26*. WUNT 2/428. Tübingen: Mohr Siebeck, 2016.

Oropeza, B. J. "Echoes of Isaiah in the Rhetoric of Paul: New Exodus, Wisdom, and the Humility of the Cross in Utopian-Apocalyptic Expectations." Pages 87–112 in *Intertexture of Apocalyptic Discourse in the New Testament*. Atlanta: Society of Biblical Literature, 2002.

Osten-Sacken, Peter von der. *Römer 8 als Beispiel paulinischer Soteriologie*. FRLANT 112. Göttingen: Vandenhoeck & Ruprecht, 1975.

Pao, David W. *Acts and the Isaianic New Exodus*. WUNT 2/130. Tübingen: Mohr Siebeck, 2000.

Parkman, Joel William. "Adam Christological Motifs in the Synoptic Traditions." PhD diss., Baylor University, 1994.

Pate, C. Marvin. *Adam Christology as the Exegetical and Theological Substructure of 2 Corinthians 4:7-5:21*. Lanham, MD: University Press of America, 1991.

———. *The Glory of Adam and the Afflictions of the Righteous: Pauline Suffering in Context*. Lewiston: Mellen, 1993.

———. *The Reverse of the Curse: Paul, Wisdom, and the Law*. WUNT 2/114. Tübingen: Mohr Siebeck, 2000.

Pate, C. Marvin, J. Scott Duvall, J. Daniel Hays, E. Randolph Richards, W. Dennis Tucker Jr., and Preben Vang. *The Story of Israel: A Biblical Theology*. Downers Grove, IL : Leicester, England: InterVarsity Press; Apollos, 2004.

Penna, Romano. "The Motif of the *'Aqedah* Against the Background of Romans 8:32." Pages 142–68 in *Paul the Apostle: A Theological and Exegetical Study*. Translated by Thomas P. Wahl. Vol. 1. 2 vols. Collegeville, MN: Liturgical Press, 1996.

Philo. *Works*. Translated by F. H. Colson. 10 vols. LCL. Cambridge: Harvard University Press, 1939.

Piotrowski, Nicholas G. "'I Will Save My People from Their Sins': The Influence of Ezekiel 36:28b-29a; 37:23b on Matthew 1:21." *TynBul* 64 (2013): 33–54.

———. "'After the Deportation': Observations in Matthew's Apocalyptic Genealogy." *BBR* 25 (2015): 189–203.

———. *Matthew's New David at the End of Exile: A Socio-Rhetorical Study of Scriptural Quotations*. NovTSup 170. Leiden: Brill, 2016.

———. "The Concept of Exile in Late Second Temple Judaism: A Review of Recent Scholarship." *CBR* 15 (2017): 214–47.

Pitre, Brant. *Jesus, the Tribulation, and the End of the Exile: Restoration Eschatology and the Origin of the Atonement*. WUNT 2/204. Tübingen: Mohr Siebeck, 2005.

Plöger, Otto. *Theocracy and Eschatology*. Translated by S. Rudman. Richmond: John Knox Press, 1968.

Polaski, Donald C. "Reflections on a Mosaic Covenant: The Eternal Covenant (Isaiah 24:5) and Intertextuality." *JSOT* 23 (1998): 55–73.

Potterie, Ignace de la. "Le chrétien conduit par l'esprit dans son cheminement eschatologique (Rom 8,14)." Pages 209–41 in *The Law of the Spirit in Rom 7 and 8*. Edited by Lorenzo de Lorenzi. Rome: St. Paul's Abbey, 1976.

Porter, Stanley E. καταλλάσσω *in Ancient Greek Literature: With Reference to the Pauline Writings*. EFN 5. Cordoba: Ediciones el Almendro, 1994.

———. "The Use of the Old Testament in the New Testament: A Brief Comment on Method and Terminology." Pages 79–96 in *Early Christian Interpretation of the Scriptures of Israel: Investigations and Proposals*. Sheffield: Sheffield Academic, 1997.

Porter, Stanley E., and Wally V. Cirafesi. "ὑστερέω and πίστις Χριστοῦ in Romans 3:23: A Response to Steven Enderlein." *JSPL* 3 (2013): 1–9.

Postell, Seth D. *Adam as Israel: Genesis 1-3 as the Introduction to the Torah and Tanakh*. Eugene, OR: Pickwick, 2011.

Rensburg, J. J. J. van. "The Children of God in Romans 8." *Neot* (1981): 139–61.

Reumann, John Henry Paul. *Creation and New Creation: The Past, Present, and Future of God's Creative Activity*. Minneapolis: Augsburg, 1973.

Ridderbos, Herman. *Paul: An Outline of His Theology*. Translated by John Richard De Witt. Grand Rapids: Eerdmans, 1997.

Robertson, A. T. *A Grammar of the Greek New Testament in the Light of Historical Research*. Nashville: Broadman, 1934.

Robertson, O. Palmer. *The Christ of the Prophets*. Phillipsburg, NJ: P&R, 2004.

———. *The Flow of the Psalms: Discovering Their Structure and Theology*. Phillipsburg, NJ: P&R, 2015.

Rom-Shiloni, Dalit. "Deuteronomic Concepts of Exile Interpreted in Jeremiah and Ezekiel." Pages 101–23 in vol. 1 of *Birkat Shalom*. Edited by Chaim Cohen and Shalom M. Paul. Winona Lake, IN: Eisenbrauns, 2008.

Ryken, Leland, James C. Wilhoit, and Tremper Longman III, eds. *Dictionary of Biblical Imagery*. Downers Grove, IL: InverVarsity, 1998.

Sahlin, Harald. "The New Exodus of Salvation according to Paul." Pages 81–95 in *The Root of the Vine: Essays in Biblical Theology*. Edited by Anton Friedrich et al. London: Dacre, 1953.

Sanday, W., and Arthur C. Headlam. *A Critical and Exegetical Commentary on the Epistle to the Romans*. ICC. Edinburgh: T&T Clark, 1902.

Sanders, E. P. *Paul and Palestinian Judaism: A Comparison of Patterns of Religion*. London: S.C.M, 1977.

Santmire, H. Paul. *The Travail of Nature: The Ambiguous Ecological Promise of Christian Theology*. Philadelphia: Fortress, 1985.

Scaer, Peter J. "Lukan Christology: Jesus as Beautiful Savior." *CTQ* 69 (2005): 63–74.

Schiffman, Lawrence H. "The Concept of Restoration in the Dead Sea Scrolls." Pages 203–22 in *Restoration: Old Testament, Jewish, and Christian Perspectives*. Edited by James M. Scott. JSJSup 72. Leiden: Brill, 2001.

Schille, Gottfried. "Die Liebe Gottes in Christus: Beobachtungen zu Rm 8:31-39." *ZNW* 59 (1968): 230–44.

Schlatter, Adolf. *Romans: The Righteousness of God*. Translated by Siegfried Schatzmann. Peabody, MA: Hendrickson, 1995.

Schmitt, John J. "Israel as Son of God in Torah." *BTB* 34 (2004): 69–79.

Schoeps, Hans Joachim. "The Sacrifice of Isaac in Paul's Theology." *JBL* 65 (1946): 385–92.

Schrage, Wolfgang. "Leid, Kreuz und Eschaton: Die Peristasenkataloge als Merkmale paulinischer Theologia Crucis und Eschatologie." *EvT* 34 (1974): 141–75.

Schreiner, Thomas R. *Romans*. BECNT. Grand Rapids: Baker Books, 1998.

———. *Commentary on Hebrews*. BTCP. Nashville, TN: Holman Reference, 2015.

Schultz, Richard L. "Intertextuality, Canon, and 'Undecidability': Understanding Isaiah's 'New Heavens and New Earth' (Isaiah 65:17-25)." *BBR* 20 (2010): 19–38.

Schwartz, Daniel R. "Two Pauline Allusions to the Redemptive Mechanism of the Crucifixion." *JBL* 102 (1983): 259–68.

Scott, James M. *Adoption as Sons of God: An Exegetical Investigation into the Background of υἱοθεσία in the Pauline Corpus*. WUNT 2/48. Tubingen: Mohr Siebeck, 1992.

———. "'For as Many as Are of Works of the Law Are under a Curse' (Galatians 3:10)." Pages 187–221 in *Paul and the Scriptures of Israel*. Edited by James A. Sanders and Craig A. Evans. JSNTSup 83. Sheffield: Sheffield Academic, 1993.

———. "Paul's Use of Deuteronomic Tradition." *JBL* 112 (1993): 645–65.

———. "Philo and the Restoration of Israel." Pages 553–75 in *Society of Biblical Literature 1995 Seminar Papers*, SBLSP 34. Atlanta: Scholars Press, 1995.

———, ed. *Exile: Old Testament, Jewish, and Christian Conceptions*. JSJSup 56. Leiden: Brill, 1997.

———, ed. *Restoration: Old Testament, Jewish, and Christian Perspectives*. JSJSup 72. Leiden: Brill, 2001.

———. *On Earth as in Heaven: The Restoration of Sacred Time and Sacred Space in the Book of Jubilees*. Leiden: Brill, 2005.

———, ed. *Exile: A Conversation with N. T. Wright*. Downers Grove: IVP Academic, 2017.

Scroggs, Robin. *The Last Adam: A Study in Pauline Anthropology*. Philadelphia: Fortress, 1966.

Seifrid, Mark A. "Blind Alleys in the Controversy over the Paul of History." *TynBul* 45 (1994): 73–95.

Seitz, Christopher R. "Isaiah 1–66: Making Sense of the Whole." Pages 105–26 in *Reading and Preaching the Book of Isaiah*. Philadelphia: Fortress, 1988.

*Septuaginta: Vetus Testamentum Graecum Auctoritate Academiae Scientarum Gottingensis editum*. 20 vols. Göttingen: Vandenhoeck & Ruprecht, 1931–.

Sharp, Carolyn J. "The Trope of 'Exile' and the Displacement of Old Testament Theology." *PRSt* 31 (2004): 153–69.

Sharpe, John L. "Second Adam in the Apocalypse of Moses." *CBQ* 35 (1973): 35–46.

Shum, Shiu-Lun. *Paul's Use of Isaiah in Romans: A Comparative Study of Paul's Letter to the Romans and the Sibylline and Qumran Sectarian Texts*. WUNT 2/156. Tübingen: Mohr Siebeck, 2002.

Silva, Moisés, ed. *New International Dictionary of New Testament Theology and Exegesis*. 5 vols. 2nd ed. Grand Rapids: Zondervan, 2014.

Skehan, Patrick W., and Alexander A. Di Lella. *The Wisdom of Ben Sira: A New Translation with Notes, Introduction, and Commentary*. AB 39. New York: Doubleday, 1987.

Snyman, A. H. "Style and the Rhetorical Situation of Romans 8:31-39." *NTS* 34 (1988): 218–31.

Sommer, Benjamin D. *A Prophet Reads Scripture: Allusion in Isaiah 40-66*. Stanford, CA: Stanford University, 1998.

Sprinkle, Preston M. "The Afterlife in Romans: Understanding Paul's Glory Motif in Light of the Apocalypse of Moses and 2 Baruch." Pages 201–33 in *Lebendige Hoffnungewiger Tod?!: Jenseitsvorstellungen km Hellenismus, Judentum, und Christentum*. Edited by Michael Labahn and Manfred Lang. Leipzig: Evangelische Verlagsanstalt, 2007.

———. *Paul and Judaism Revisited: A Study of Divine and Human Agency in Salvation*. Downers Grove, IL: IVP Academic, 2013.

Starling, David. *Not My People: Gentiles as Exiles in Pauline Hermeneutics*. BZNW 184. Berlin: De Gruyter, 2011.

Steck, Odil H. *Israel Und Das Gewaltsame Geschick Der Propheten. Untersuchungen Zur Überlieferung Des Deuteronomistischen Geschichtsbildes Im Alten Testament, Spätjudentum Und Urchristentum*. WMANT 23. Neukirchen-Vluyn: Neukirchener Verlag, 1967.

———. "Das Problem theologischer Strömungen in nachexilischer Zeit." *EvT* 28 (1968): 445–58.

———. *Das apokryphe Baruchbuch: Studien zu Rezeption und Konzentration "kanonischer" Überlieferung*. FRLANT 160. Göttingen: Vandenhoeck & Ruprecht, 1993.

Stendahl, Krister. *Paul among Jews and Gentiles: And Other Essays*. Philadelphia: Fortress Press, 1976.

Stewart, Tyler. "The Cry of Victory: A Cruciform Reading of Psalm 44:22 in Romans 8:36." *JSPL* 3 (2013): 25–45.

Stone, Michael E. "Satan and the Serpent in the Armenian Tradition." Pages 141–86 in *Beyond Eden: The Biblical Story of Paradise (Genesis 2-3) and Its Reception History*. Tübingen: Mohr Siebeck, 2008.

Stowers, Stanley. *A Rereading of Romans: Justice, Jews, and Gentiles*. New Haven: Yale University Press, 1994.

Strack, Hermann Leberecht, and Paul Billerbeck. *Kommentar zum Neuen Testament aus Talmud und Midrasch*. 6 vols. München: Beck, 1922.

Stuhlmacher, Peter. "The Gospel of Reconciliation in Christ: Basic Features and Issues of a Biblical Theology of the New Testament." Translated by George R. Edwards. *Horizons in Biblical Theology* 1 (1979): 161–90.

———. *Paul's Letter to the Romans: A Commentary*. Translated by Scott J. Hafemann. Louisville, KY: Westminster/John Knox Press, 1994.

Sweeney, Marvin A. "The Book of Isaiah in Recent Research." *CurBS* 1 (1993): 141–62.

Talmon, Shemaryahu. "Waiting for the Messiah: The Spiritual Universe of the Qumran Covenanters." Pages 111–38 in *Judaisms and Their Messiahs at the Turn of the Christian Era*. Edited by Jacob Neusner, William Scott Green, and Ernest S. Frerichs. Cambridge: Cambridge University Press, 1988.

Tiller, Patrick A. *A Commentary on the Animal Apocalypse of I Enoch*. EJL 4. Atlanta: Scholars Press, 1993.

Thielman, Frank. "The Story of Israel and the Theology of Romans 5-8." Pages 227–49 in *Society of Biblical Literature 1993 Seminar Papers*. SBLSP 32. Atlanta: Society of Biblical Literature, 1993.

Thiselton, Anthony C. *The First Epistle to the Corinthians: A Commentary on the Greek Text*. NIGTC. Grand Rapids: Eerdmans, 2000.

Thomas, Derek. *God Strengthens: Ezekiel Simply Explained*. Darlington: Evangelical Press, 1993.

Thompson, J. A. *The Book of Jeremiah*. NICOT. Grand Rapids: Eerdmans, 1979.

Thompson, Michael B. *Clothed with Christ: The Example and Teaching of Jesus in Romans 12.1–15.13*. JSNTSup 59. Sheffield: JSOT Press, 1991.

Tannehill, Robert C. *Dying and Rising in Christ: A Study in Pauline Theology*. BZNW. Berlin: Töpelmann, 1967.

Tobin, Thomas H. *Paul's Rhetoric in Its Contexts: The Argument of Romans*. Peabody, MA: Hendrickson, 2004.

Torrey, Charles C. *The Composition and Historical Value of Ezra-Nehemiah*. BZAW 2. Giessen: J. Ricker, 1896.

Tromp, Johannes. "Literary and Exegetical Issues in the Story of Adam's Death and Burial (GLAE 31-42)." Pages 25–42 in *The Book of Genesis in Jewish and Oriental Christian Interpretation: A Collection of Essays*. Edited by Judith Frishman and Lucas van Rompay. TEG 5. Lovanii: Peeters, 1997.

Tsumura, D. T. "An OT Background to Rom 8:22." *NTS* 40 (1994): 620–21.

Turner, Kenneth J. *The Death of Deaths in the Death of Israel: Deuteronomy's Theology of Exile*. Eugene, OR: Wipf & Stock, 2011.

———. "Deuteronomy's Theology of Exile." Pages 189–220 in *For Our Good Always: Studies on the Message and Influence of Deuteronomy in Honor of Daniel I. Block*. Edited by Jason S. DeRouchie, Jason Gile, and Kenneth J. Turner. Winona Lake, IN: Eisenbrauns, 2013.

Turner, Max. *Power from on High: The Spirit in Israel's Restoration and Witness in Luke-Acts*. Sheffield: Sheffield Academic, 1996.

Unnik, W. C. van. *Das Selbstverständnis der jüdischen Diaspora in der hellenistisch-römischen Zeit*. AGJU 17. Leiden: Brill, 1993.

VanderKam, James C. "Exile in Jewish Apocalyptic Literature." Pages 89–109 in *Exile: Old Testament, Jewish, and Christian Conceptions*. Edited by James M. Scott. JSJSup 56. Leiden: Brill, 1997.

———. *Textual and Historical Studies in the Book of Jubilees*. HSM 14. Missoula, Mont: Scholars Press for Harvard Semitic Museum, 1977.

VanDrunen, David. "Israel's Recapitulation of Adam's Probation under the Law of Moses." *WTJ* 73 (2011): 303–24.

VanGemeren, Willem, ed. *New International Dictionary of Old Testament Theology & Exegesis*. 3 vols. Grand Rapids: Zondervan, 1997.

Versteeg, J. P. *Is Adam a "Teaching Model" in the New Testament?: An Examination of One of the Central Points in the Views of H. M. Kuitert and Others*. Translated by Richard B. Gaffin Jr. Nutley, NJ: P&R, 1977.

Viard, A. "Expectatio Creaturae (Rom 8:19-22)." *RB* 59 (1952): 337–54.

Vos, Geerhardus. *Biblical Theology: Old and New Testaments*. Grand Rapids: Banner of Truth, 1975.

———. *The Eschatology of the Old Testament*. Edited by James T. Dennison. Phillipsburg, NJ: P&R, 2001.

———. *Redemptive History and Biblical Interpretation: The Shorter Writings of Geerhardus Vos*. Edited by Richard B. Gaffin. Phillipsburg, NJ: P&R, 2001.

Wagner, J. Ross. *Heralds of the Good News: Isaiah and Paul "in Concert" in the Letter to the Romans*. NovTSup 101. Leiden: Brill, 2002.

———. "Moses and Isaiah in Concert: Paul's Reading of Isaiah and Deuteronomy in the Letter to the Romans." Pages 87–105 in *"As Those Who Are Taught": The*

*Interpretation of Isaiah from the LXX to the SBL*. Atlanta: Society of Biblical Literature, 2006.

Watson, Francis. *Paul, Judaism, and the Gentiles: Beyond the New Perspective*. Grand Rapids: Eerdmans, 2007.

Watts, John D. W. *Isaiah 1-33*. Rev. ed. WBC 24. Nashville, TN: Thomas Nelson, 1985.

———. *Isaiah 34-66*. WBC 25. Waco, TX: Thomas Nelson, 2000.

Watts, Rikki E. "Consolation or Confrontation: Isaiah 40-55 and the Delay of the New Exodus." *TynBul* 41 (1990): 31–59.

———. *Isaiah's New Exodus and Mark*. WUNT 2/88. Tübingen: Mohr Siebeck, 1997.

———. "Messianic Servant or the End of Israel's Exilic Curses?: Isaiah 53.4 in Matthew 8.17." *JSNT* 38 (2015): 81–95.

Wedderburn, A. J. M. "Theological Structure of Romans 5:12." *NTS* 19 (1973): 339–54.

———. "Adam in Paul's Letter to the Romans." Pages 413–30 in *Studia Biblica 1978: Papers on Paul and Other New Testament Authors*. Vol. 3. Sheffield: JSOT, 1980.

Weitzman, Steven. "Allusion, Artifice, and Exile in the Hymn of Tobit." *JBL* 115 (1996): 49–61.

Wenham, Gordon J. *The Book of Leviticus*. NICOT. Grand Rapids: Eerdmans, 1979.

———. *Story as Torah: Reading the Old Testament Ethically*. Edinburgh: T&T Clark, 2000.

Westermann, Claus. *Genesis 1-11: A Continental Commentary*. Translated by John J. Scullion. Minneapolis: Fortress, 1994.

Wilckens, Ulrich. *Der Brief an Die Römer*. 3 vols. EKKNT 6. Zürich: Benziger; Neukirchen-Vluyn: Neukirchener Verlag, 1978, 1980, 1982.

Wilk, Florian. *Die Bedeutung des Jesajabuches für Paulus*. FRLANT 179. Göttingen: Vandenhoeck & Ruprecht, 1998.

Williamson, H. G. M. "Deuteronomy and Isaiah." Pages 251–68 in *For Our Good Always: Studies on the Message and Influence of Deuteronomy in Honor of Daniel I. Block*. Winona Lake, IN: Eisenbrauns, 2013.

Wise, Michael O. "4QFlorilegium and the Temple of Adam." *RevQ* 15 (1991): 103–32.

Wolff, Hans Walter. "Das Kerygma Des Deuteronomistischen Geschichtswerks." *ZAW* 73 (1961): 171–86.

Wolter, Michael. *Rechtfertigung und zukünftiges Heil: Untersuchungen zu Röm 5, 1-11*. BZNW 43. Berlin: de Gruyter, 1978.

———. *Der Brief an Die Römer: Teilband 1: Rom 1–8*. Vol. 1 of *EKKNT* VI. Vandenhoeck & Ruprecht, 2014.

Wong, Ka Leung. *The Idea of Retribution in the Book of Ezekiel*. VTSup 87. Leiden: Brill, 2001.

———. "The Masoretic and Septuagint Texts of Ezekiel 39,21-29." *ETL* 78 (2002): 130–47.

Wright, N. T. “Adam in Pauline Christology.” Pages 359–89 in *Society of Biblical Literature 1983 Seminar Papers*. SBLSP 22. Atlanta: Society of Biblical Literature, 1983.

———. *The Climax of the Covenant: Christ and the Law in Pauline Theology*. Edinburgh: T&T Clark, 1991.

———. *The New Testament and the People of God*. COQG 1. Minneapolis: Fortress, 1992.

———. *Jesus and the Victory of God*. COQG 2. Minneapolis: Fortress, 1996.

———. “The New Inheritance According to Paul: The Letter to the Romans Re-Enacts for All Peoples the Israelite Exodus from Egypt to the Promised Land-from Slavery to Freedom.” *BR (Washington, D.C.)* 14 (1998): 16, 47.

———. “In Grateful Dialogue: A Response.” Pages 244–77 in *Jesus & the Restoration of Israel: A Critical Assessment of N.T. Wright’s Jesus and the Victory of God*. Edited by Carey Newman and Craig A. Evans. Downers Grove, IL: InverVarsity, 1999.

———. “New Exodus, New Inheritance: The Narrative Substructure of Romans 3-8.” Pages 26–35 in *Romans and the People of God: Essays in Honor of Gordon D. Fee on the Occasion of His 65th Birthday*. Edited by Sven K. Soderlund and N. T. Wright. Grand Rapids: Eerdmans, 1999.

———. “Romans.” *The New Interpreter’s Bible: Acts - First Corinthians*. By Robert W. Wall and J. Paul Sampley. NIBC. Nashville: Abingdon Press, 2002.

———. *Paul and the Faithfulness of God*. 2 vols. COQG 4. Minneapolis: Fortress, 2013.

Yates, John. *The Spirit and Creation in Paul*. WUNT 2/251. Tübingen: Mohr Siebeck, 2008.

Yonge, C. D., trans. *The Works of Philo: Complete and Unabridged*. Hendrickson Publishers, 1993.

Zimmerli, Walther. *Ezekiel 1: A Commentary on the Book of the Prophet Ezekiel, Chapters 1-24*. Edited by Frank Moore Cross and Klaus Baltzer. Translated by Ronald E. Clements. Hermeneia. Philadelphia: Fortress, 1979.

———. *Ezekiel 2: A Commentary on the Book of the Prophet Ezekiel, Chapters 25-48*. Edited by Paul D. Hanson. Translated by James D. Martin. Hermeneia. Philadelphia: Fortress, 1979.

Zimmermann, Frank. *The Book of Tobit: An English Translation with Introduction and Commentary*. JAL. New York: Harper, 1958.

# Index

# Index of Biblical References

# Index of Ancient Sources

# About the Author

**Rev. Dr. David Barry** (PhD, Westminster Theological Seminary) is an associate pastor at Midway Presbyterian Church in Powder Springs, Georgia, and a visiting lecturer in New Testament for Reformed Theological Seminary, Atlanta.